WORKBOOK 1:
WRITING AND ANALYSIS WORKBOOK TO ACCOMPANY

The
COMPLETE MUSICIAN

AN INTEGRATED APPROACH TO THEORY,
ANALYSIS, AND LISTENING

Fifth Edition

Steven G. Laitz
The Juilliard School

Michael R. Callahan
Michigan State University

OXFORD
UNIVERSITY PRESS

OXFORD
UNIVERSITY PRESS

Oxford University Press is a department of the University of Oxford.
It furthers the University's objective of excellence in research, scholarship,
and education by publishing worldwide. Oxford is a registered trade mark
of Oxford University Press in the UK and in certain other countries.

Published in the United States of America by Oxford University Press
198 Madison Avenue, New York, NY 10016, United States of America.

ISBN 9780190924546

Printed by Marquis, Canada

CONTENTS

PREFACE

The workbooks accompanying the fifth edition of *The Complete Musician* maintain the same organization as in the fourth edition, which was designed specifically for greater flexibility. *Workbook 1* contains all written and analytical activities, while *Workbook 2* is devoted to musicianship skills. Each workbook chapter aligns with the corresponding chapter in the text. The materials are organized into discrete assignments. Exercises are carefully graduated, ranging from basic, introductory tasks (such as identification, spelling, and keyboard illustrations) to more open-ended analytical and compositional activities.

Recordings to accompany these exercises—from solo piano to full orchestra—are available on the book's Oxford Learning Link website, www.oup.com/he/laitz-callahan5e. All passages of music are performed on the instruments designated by the composers. Between the two workbooks, there are over 3,900 recorded analytical and dictation examples, and more than 15 hours of recorded music, all of which are in high-quality mp3 format. Additional supplementary material is available on Oxford Learning Link.

Musical Space: Pitches, Scales, and Keys

ASSIGNMENT 1A.1

EXERCISE 1A–A *Identifying Pitches and Locating Octaves and Half Steps*

Label each pitch with both a letter name and an octave number. For exercise numbers 1–8, draw on the staff the pitches *one octave higher* and *one diatonic half step lower*. For numbers 9–16, draw on the staff the pitches *one octave lower* and *one chromatic half step higher*. Label the additional pitches that you draw. A sample is provided.

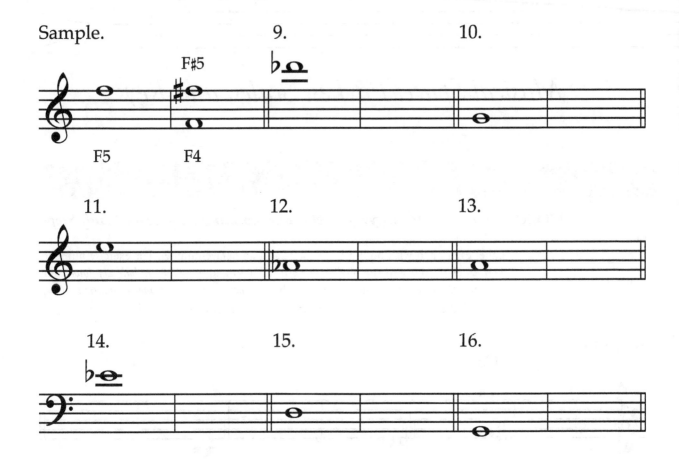

EXERCISE 1A–B *Identifying Enharmonic Equivalents*

Label each pitch with both a letter name and an octave number. For exercise numbers 1–7, draw *one* pitch that is enharmonically equivalent to the given one. For numbers 8–10, draw *two* different pitches that are enharmonically equivalent to the given one. Label the pitch(es) that you draw. A sample is provided.

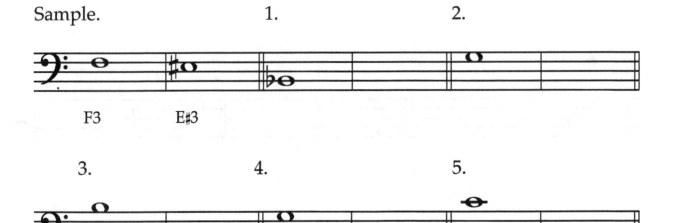

EXERCISE 1A–C   *Building Whole Steps and Half Steps*

Complete the table below following the sample. Make sure that whole steps are spelled with adjacent letter names (such as B♭-C, rather than A♯-C).

	Whole Step Below	Diatonic Half Step Below	Chromatic Half Step Below	**Pitch**	Chromatic Half Step Above	Diatonic Half Step Above	Whole Step Above
Sample.	C⁵	C♯⁵	D♭⁵	D⁵	D♯⁵	E♭⁵	E⁵
1.				A²			
2.				F⁶			
3.				B³			
4.			F⁴				
5.					A²		
6.		B⁴					
7.							F♯⁴

EXERCISE 1A–D   *Grouping Members of the Same Pitch Class*

First, label each pitch with a letter name and an octave number. Then, within each row, draw a circle around each pitch that belongs to the same pitch class as the circled pitch.

ASSIGNMENT 1A.2

EXERCISE 1A–E   *Writing Key Signatures and Tonics*

1. Write each key signature on both staves of the grand staff. Then, write the tonic of the given key on both staves.

Sample.   1.   2.   3.

A major   E♭ major   D minor   B major

4.   5.   6.

G minor   F♯ minor   B♭ minor

2. The key signatures notated below are incorrect. Mark the error(s) in each of them. Then, on the staff that has no key signature, notate the correct key signature from scratch.

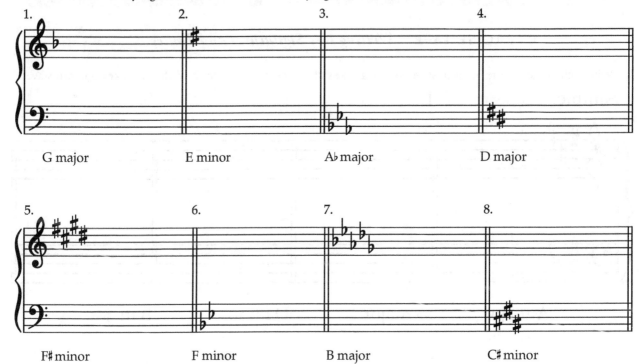

1.	2.	3.	4.
G major	E minor	A♭ major	D major

5.	6.	7.	8.
F♯ minor	F minor	B major	C♯ minor

EXERCISE 1A–F   *Writing Key Signatures and Identifying Relative Keys*

For each given key, name its relative key below the grand staff. Next, on both staves, draw the key signature that the two relative keys share. Finally, write the tonic pitch of the *given* key on the treble-clef staff and the tonic pitch of its *relative* key on the bass-clef staff. A sample is provided for you.

Sample.	1.	2.	3.
E♭ major	A♭ major	B major	F major

Relative keys:

C minor   _____   _____   _____

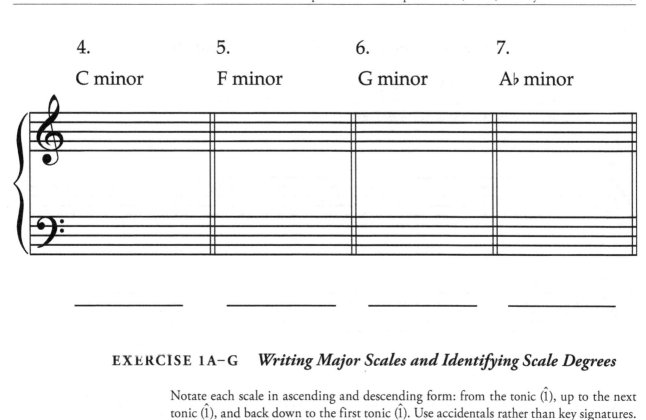

4.   5.   6.   7.
C minor   F minor   G minor   A♭ minor

EXERCISE 1A–G   *Writing Major Scales and Identifying Scale Degrees*

Notate each scale in ascending and descending form: from the tonic (1̂), up to the next tonic (1̂), and back down to the first tonic (1̂). Use accidentals rather than key signatures. Circle all instances of the parenthesized scale degree.

1. B♭ major (5̂)

2. E major (7̂)

3. A♭ major (2̂)

4. D major (6̂)

EXERCISE 1A–H   *Writing Minor Scales and Identifying Scale Degrees*

Notate each scale in ascending and descending form: from the tonic ($\hat{1}$), up to the next tonic ($\hat{1}$), and back down to the first tonic ($\hat{1}$). Use key signatures plus any necessary accidentals. Circle all instances of the parenthesized scale degree.

1. E harmonic minor ($\hat{3}$)

2. C natural minor ($\hat{7}$)

3. C♯ melodic minor ($\hat{4}$)

4. F harmonic minor ($\hat{6}$)

ASSIGNMENT 1A.3

EXERCISE 1A–I *Correcting Misspelled Scales*

The scales below are misspelled. Correct the errors by adding, changing, and/or crossing off accidentals.

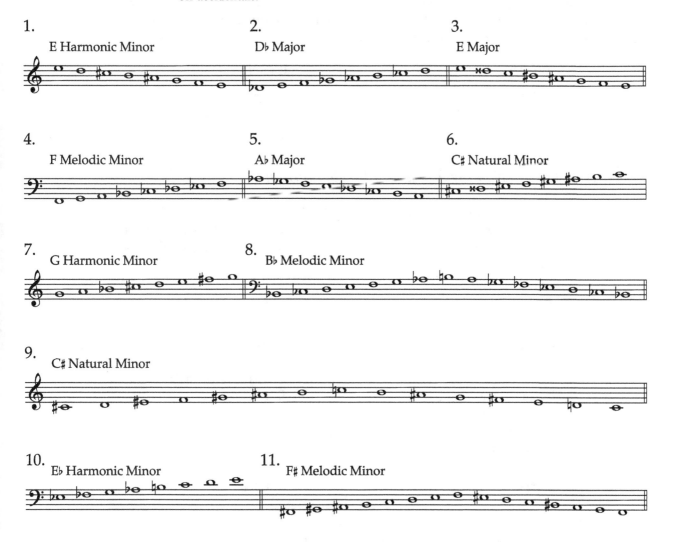

1. E Harmonic Minor
2. D♭ Major
3. E Major
4. F Melodic Minor
5. A♭ Major
6. C♯ Natural Minor
7. G Harmonic Minor
8. B♭ Melodic Minor
9. C♯ Natural Minor
10. E♭ Harmonic Minor
11. F♯ Melodic Minor

EXERCISE 1A–J *Contextualizing Fragments of Major Scales*

Name all of the major scales that contain each pair of tones listed below. The number of scales is in parentheses. In addition, list the scale-degree numbers of the two tones in each scale. A sample is provided.

Sample. A♯-B (2)   B Major ($\hat{7}$-$\hat{1}$), F♯ Major ($\hat{3}$-$\hat{4}$)

1. D-E (5)
2. A-B (5)
3. C-D♭ (2)
4. B♭-D (3)

5. G-C (6)
6. E-G♯ (3)
7. F♯-A♯ (3)
8. D♭-G (1)

EXERCISE 1A–K   *Contextualizing Fragments of Minor Scales*

Name all of the minor scales that contain each pair of tones listed below. The number of different tonics is in parentheses. In addition, list the scale-degree numbers of the two tones in each scale. Specify the forms of minor for each tonic. A sample is provided.

Sample. D-E (7)

D natural, harmonic, and melodic minor ($\hat{1}$-$\hat{2}$), E natural and descending melodic minor ($\hat{7}$-$\hat{1}$), B natural, harmonic, and melodic minor ($\hat{3}$-$\hat{4}$), A natural, harmonic, and melodic minor ($\hat{4}$-$\hat{5}$), G ascending melodic minor ($\hat{5}$-$\hat{6}$), F♯ natural and descending melodic minor ($\hat{6}$-$\hat{7}$), F ascending melodic minor ($\hat{6}$-$\hat{7}$)

1. A♭-C (3)

2. A♭-B (1)

3. F♯-G (3)

4. B-F (2)

5. F-A (4)

6. C♯-F (1)

EXERCISE 1A–L   *Naming Scales and Key Signatures*

1. Name the sharps and flats that belong to the key signature of:
    a. the parallel minor of A major
    b. the parallel major of B minor
    c. the parallel minor of F♯ major
    d. the parallel major of E♭ minor
2. Name the major scale in which:
    a. G♯ is $\hat{3}$
    b. C is $\hat{4}$
    c. G♯ is $\hat{6}$
    d. C♯ is $\hat{6}$
    e. B♭ is $\hat{2}$
    f. B♭ is $\hat{4}$
    g. B♭ is $\hat{7}$
    h. E♯ is $\hat{3}$
3. Name the major scale in which:
    a. A is the supertonic
    b. D is the mediant
    c. F is the submediant
    d. B is the dominant
    e. E is the supertonic
    f. E is the subdominant
    g. E is the leading tone
    h. B♭ is the tonic
4. Name the harmonic minor scale in which:
    a. A is $\hat{3}$
    b. C♯ is $\hat{7}$
    c. E is $\hat{5}$
    d. E is $\hat{6}$

EXERCISE 1A–M   *Contextualizing Longer Scale Fragments*

Each group of three tones can be found in some number of major scales and minor scales. Name all of those scales along with the scale degrees that the three tones would be in each scale. Specify the forms of minor. A sample is provided for you.

Sample. C♯-D-E

A major ($\hat{3}$-$\hat{4}$-$\hat{5}$); D major ($\hat{7}$-$\hat{1}$-$\hat{2}$); B minor (all three forms, $\hat{2}$-$\hat{3}$-$\hat{4}$); F♯ natural and descending melodic minor ($\hat{5}$-$\hat{6}$-$\hat{7}$)

1. E♭-F-G

2. F♯-G♯-A

3. B-C-D

ASSIGNMENT 1A.4

EXERCISE 1A–N   *Identifying the Keys of Major-Mode Melodies*

Each melody below is in a major key, but it is notated without a key signature. The melodies may begin on any scale degree. Label each melody's key and label each pitch with a scale-degree number in that key.

4. Germaine Tailleferre, *Berceuse* for Violin and Piano (1913)

5. Henry Thacker Burleigh, *Southland Sketches* (1916), iii, *Allegretto grazioso*

EXERCISE 1A–O *Identifying the Keys of Minor-Mode Melodies*

Each melody below is in a minor key, but it is notated without a key signature. The melodies may begin on any scale degree. Label each melody's key and label each pitch with a scale-degree number in that key. Keep in mind that minor-mode melodies often include a leading tone that is not present in the key signature.

1. Akiana Molina, Sonatina, op. 5 (2007), i, *Allegro molto*

2. Robert Schumann, "Hör ich das Liedchen klingen" ("When I Hear the Little Song") from *Dichterliebe*, op. 48 (1840)

3. Samuel Coleridge-Taylor, *Hiawathan Sketches*, op. 16 (1896), ii

4. Robert Schumann, "Wilder Reiter" from *Album für die Jugend*, op. 68 (1848), no. 8

5. W. A. Mozart, Symphony no. 40 in G minor, K. 550 (1788), *Allegro molto*

ASSIGNMENT 1A.5

EXERCISE 1A–P   *Identifying Forms of Minor Scales*

Each passage below is in a minor key. First, label the key. Next, find each occurrence of scale degrees 6 and 7 and label each with a specific form: ↑6̂, ↓6̂, ↑7̂, or ↓7̂.

1. Pedro Ximénez Abril Tirado (1784–1856), Symphony no. 15, i, *Adagio-Allegro*

2. Ludwig van Beethoven, String Quartet in F minor, op. 95 (1810), *Allegro con brio*

3. César Cortinas, Violin Sonata (1909), ii, *Adagio ma non troppo*

4. J. S. Bach, "Herr Jesu Christ, du höchstes Gut," BWV 113 (1724)

Lord   Je – sus   Christ,   my   on – ly   Stay,
My   grief   Thou   know – est,   canst   al – lay;

5. Franz Joseph Haydn, Piano Sonata in D major, Hob. XVI:33 (1773), *Adagio*

EXERCISE 1A–Q   *Unscrambling Major and Minor Scales*

Rearrange each set of scrambled pitches to form a major scale and a natural minor scale that share those pitches. Notate the two scales in an interlocking, ascending form as shown in the sample.

Sample.

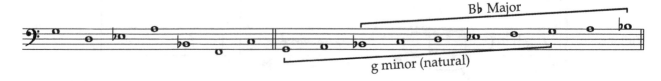

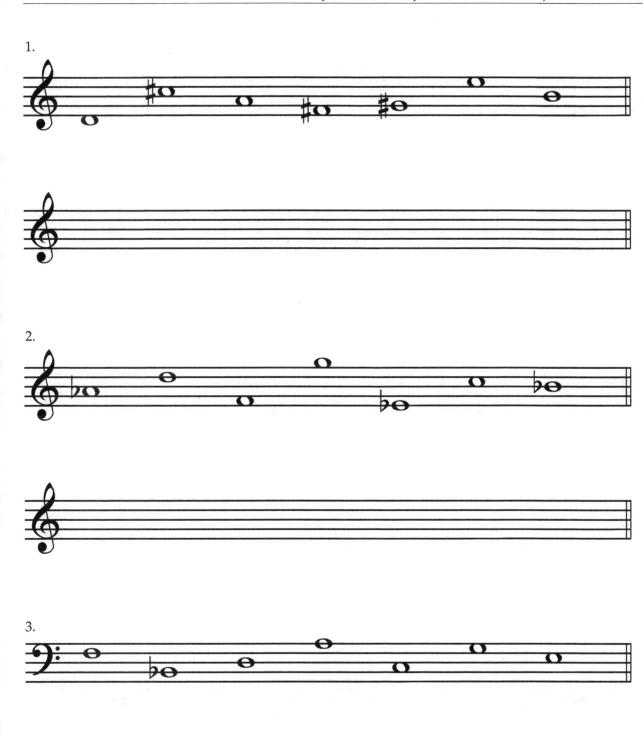

4.

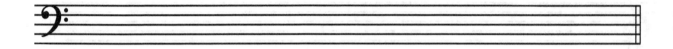

5.

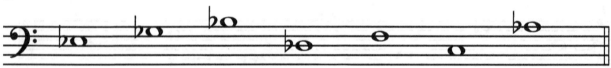

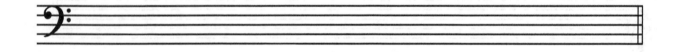

6.

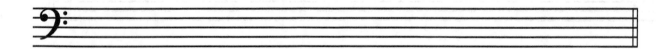

ASSIGNMENT 1A.6

EXERCISE 1A–R   *Analyzing Keys and Renotating in Parallel and Relative Keys*

First, label the key of each melodic excerpt and label the scale degree number of each pitch. Then, renotate the melody as follows: If the original is in the *major* mode, renotate it in the *parallel minor*. If the original is in the *minor* mode, renotate it in the *relative major*. Add the necessary key signatures.

1. Emma Louise Ashford, *Lead Kindly Light* (1901)

2. W. A. Mozart, Violin Sonata in F major, K. 377 (1781), ii

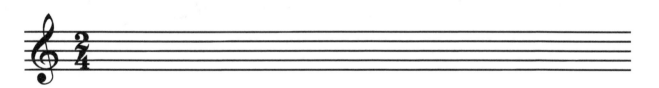

3. Henry Thacker Burleigh (1866–1949), "Just Because"

4. W. A. Mozart, Violin Concerto no. 3 in G major, K. 216 (1775), *Rondeau*

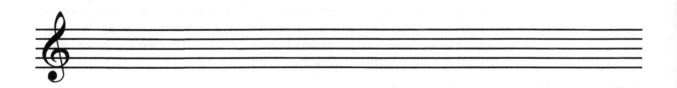

EXERCISE 1A–S   *Comparing Tonal Relationships*

Each pair of excerpts comes from the same piece, but they are in two different keys. First, identify the two keys by name. Then, identify the *relationship* between the two keys as either relative (one major and one minor key that share a key signature), parallel (one major and one minor key that share the same tonic), or dominant (two major or two minor keys where the second key's tonic is scale-degree 5 in the first key).

1. Ludwig van Beethoven, Piano Sonata in G major, op. 31, no. 1 (1802)
   A.

   B.

2. Hélène de Montgeroult, Piano Sonata, op. 5, no. 2 (1811), iii, *Allegro agitato con fuoco*

A.

B.

3. Franz Joseph Haydn, Piano Sonata in F major, Hob. XVI:47 (1767)

A.

B.

ASSIGNMENT 1A.7

EXERCISE 1A–T   *Comparing Tonal Relationships*

Each pair of excerpts comes from the same piece, but they are in two different keys. First, identify the two keys by name. Then, identify the *relationship* between the two keys as either relative (one major and one minor key that share a key signature), parallel (one major and one minor key that share the same tonic), or dominant (two major or two minor keys where the second key's tonic is scale-degree 5 in the first key).

1. Joseph Bologne, Violin Sonata, op. 1a, no. 1 (ca. 1770), i, *Allegro*

A.

B.

2. Franz Joseph Haydn, Piano Sonata in F major, Hob. XVI:47 (1767)

A.   B.

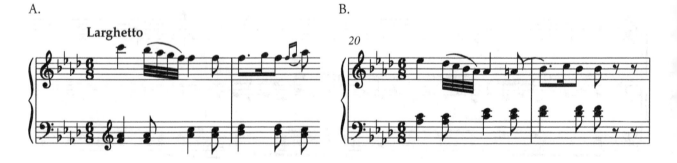

3. Scott Joplin, "The Sacred Tree" from *Treemonisha* (1911)

A.

One Au-tumn night in   bed I was ly - ing,

B.

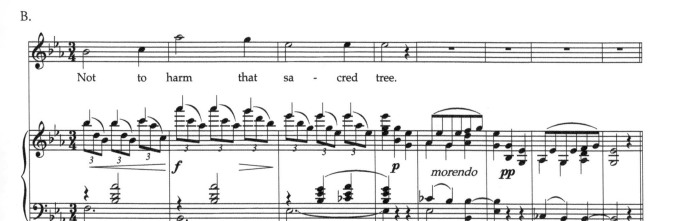

Not   to   harm   that   sa -   cred   tree.

4. Franz Schubert, *Moment Musicale* in C♯ minor, D. 780 (1823). *Hint: An enharmonically respelled tonic still counts as the same tonic!*

A.

B.

Musical Time: Meter and Rhythm

ASSIGNMENT 1B.1

EXERCISE 1B-A   *Matching Equivalent Rhythmic Durations*

Match each rhythm in column X (numbers 1 through 9) with a rhythm in column Y (letters A through I) that has the same total duration. Use each rhythm exactly once. The first example in column X is matched for you.

EXERCISE 1B–B   *Adding Up Separate Rhythmic Durations*

Write a *single* rhythmic value that is equivalent in length to each group of notes and/or rests. *Hint: One answer requires the use of a double dot.*

Sample.   ♪ ♪ ♪   =   ♩.

1. ♫♫ =

2. ♫ =

3. ♫♫ =

4. ♫♫ =

5. ♪♩ ♩.♫ ♩ =

6. ♫. ‧ =

7. ‧♫♫♫ =

8. ♫♫ =

9. ‧♫♫ ‧♫♫ ‧ =

10. ♪♩ ♫♫ ♪ =

EXERCISE 1B–C   *Distinguishing Ties from Phrasing Slurs*

In the passage from Johannes Brahms's Intermezzo in F minor, op. 118, no. 4 (1893), label each tie with a "T" and each phrasing slur with an "S."

Allegretto un poco agitato

EXERCISE 1B–D   *Determining Equivalent Rhythms*

First, perform each rhythm. Then, determine how many of each rhythmic duration you would need in order to achieve the same total length as the given rhythm.

Sample solution: ♫ ♩ ♫. ♩ ♩ = __6__ ♩ = __3__ ♩ = __4__ ♩.

1. ♫ ♩ ♪ ♩ ♪ = ___ ♩ = ___ 𝅝 = ___ ♩

2. ♫♫ ♪. ♩ ♪ ♪ = ___ ♪ = ___ ♩. = ___ ♩.

3. ♩ ♪ ♩ ♩. ♫ = ___ ♩ = ___ ♩ = ___ ♩.

4. ♫ ♫. ♪ ♪ = ___ ♪ = ___ ♩ = ___ ♪

5. ♩ ♩ ♪ ♫ = ___ 𝅝 = ___ ♪ = ___ ♩

EXERCISE 1B–E *Correcting Rhythms*

The first measure of each example contains the correct number of beats, but all other measures contain an *incorrect* number of beats. First, use the first measure to write a time signature at the beginning of each passage. Then, shorten or lengthen each duration marked with an arrow so that the number of beats in each measure is correct. Write either a note (N) or a rest (R) as indicated.

Sample solution:

ASSIGNMENT 1B.2

EXERCISE 1B–F   *Adding Time Signatures*

Add a time signature to each of the following examples. Consider both the number of beats in each measure and their beaming patterns.

1. ♩ 𝅗𝅥   ♩ | ♫♫ 𝅗𝅥.   ‖   5. 𝅗𝅥 ♩♩♩ | 𝅝   𝅗𝅥 ‖

2. ♩ ♪ ♫♫ | 𝅗𝅥.   ‖   6. ♫♫ | ♫♫ ‖

3. ♫ ♩. ♪ | ♫♫ 𝅗𝅥   ‖   7. ♩ ♬♬♪♩. | ♪♩ ♪♫ ♬♬ ‖

4. ♩. ♫♫ ♩. | 𝅗𝅥. ♫.♫ ‖

EXERCISE 1B–G   *Adding Time Signatures, Beams, and Ties*

Each rhythm below fills one measure of music. Examples 2, 4, 6, 7, 8, and 9 are in simple meters, and examples 1, 3, 5, and 10 are in compound meters. First, perform each rhythm. Then, write an appropriate time signature. Finally, if any beaming changes or ties are necessary, rewrite the rhythm in the space underneath.

1. ♩ ♫ ♩ ♩ ♫ ♩ ‖   6. 𝄾 ♩ 𝄾 ♩ ‖

2. 𝅗𝅥 ♩ ♩ ♩ ♩ ♫ ‖   7. ♩. ♪ ♪ ♫ ‖

3. ♪ ♪ ♪ ♩ ♪ ♩. ‖   8. 𝅗𝅥. ♩ ♩ ♩ ‖

4. ♪ ♫ ♪ ♪ ♪. ♪ ♫ ‖   9. ♫ ♫ ♬♬ ‖

5. ♩ ♩ ♩ ♩ ‖   10. ♩ ♫ ♪. ♪ ♪ ♪ ♫ ♩ ♩ ‖

EXERCISE 1B–H *Determining Meter in Context*

First, draw a three-level dot diagram (division, beat, and beat grouping) under the score of each passage. Then, add the most logical time signature for each passage. Finally, support your answer in a sentence or two.

1. Robert Nathaniel Dett, "Barcarolle of Tears" from *Eight Bible Vignettes* (1941)

Tempo primo

2. Ludwig van Beethoven, Piano Sonata in E♭ major, op. 7 (1797), *Adagio*

3. Franz Joseph Haydn, String Quartet in G minor, op. 74, no. 3 (1793), *Allegro*

4. Josquin Des Prez, Credo from *Missa Pange Lingua* (c. 1514)

Translation: And he was crucified.

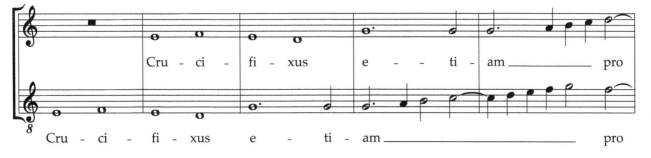

5. Isak Roux (b. 1959), *Township Guitar*

ASSIGNMENT 1B.3

EXERCISE 1B–I   *Completing Incomplete Measures*

Some measures in the examples that follow do not contain enough beats. Add a *single note* to each measure that has too few beats. In addition, in a rewritten version beneath the original, add ties and add or remove beams whenever necessary to clarify the meter visually.

1.

2.

3.

4.

5.

6.

EXERCISE 1B-J   *Matching Rhythms of Equal Duration*

Match each rhythm in column X with a rhythm in column Y that has the same total duration. Use each rhythm exactly once. The first example in column X is matched for you.

EXERCISE 1B–K   *Correcting Rhythmic Durations*

First, circle each measure that contains an incorrect number of beats. Then, in the space below the rhythm, rewrite the circled measures so that they have the correct number of beats. When there are too many beats, it is your choice whether to shorten a value or delete a value; when there are too few beats, it is your choice whether to lengthen a value or insert a value.

ASSIGNMENT 1B.4

EXERCISE 1B–L   *Renotating Rhythms to Match the Time Signature*

Each measure below contains the correct number of beats, but rhythmic values are not notated in a way that clearly conveys the meter. First, perform each rhythm. Then, renotate each example in the space provided. You will need to do the following: (1) add beams, (2) separate beamed rhythms, (3) split a rhythmic value into smaller rhythms tied together, (4) combine tied rhythms into a single rhythmic value, and (5) combine multiple rests into a single longer rest. Double-check your work by performing your renotated rhythm while conducting.

1.

2.

3.

4. 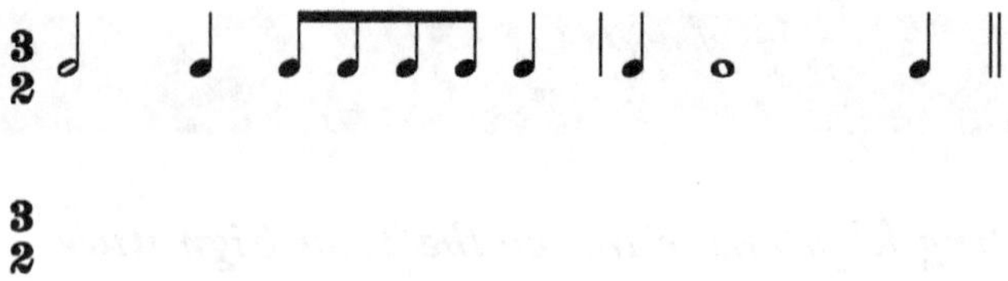

5. 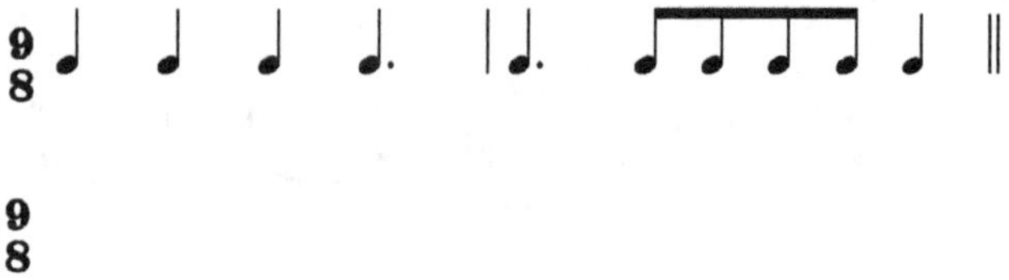

6. 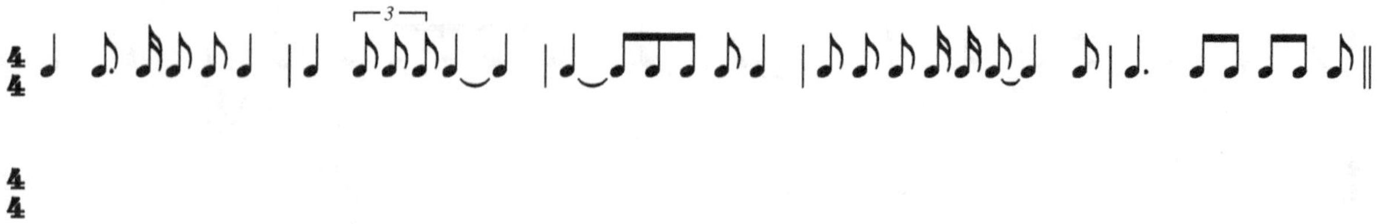

7. 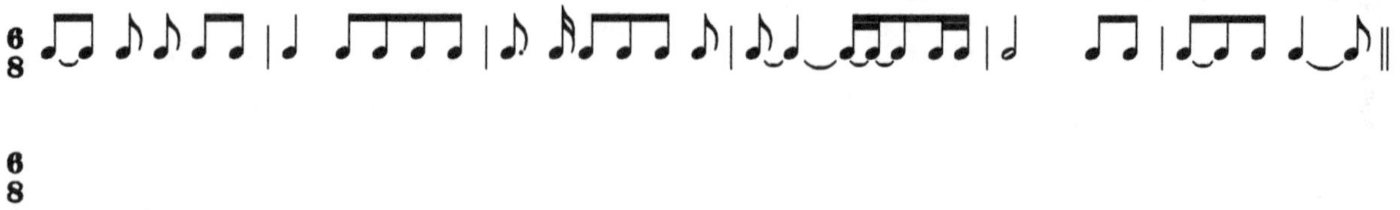

EXERCISE 1B–M   *Adding Bar Lines*

First, add bar lines to each rhythm below so that each measure contains the correct number of beats. If a bar line falls in the middle of a rhythmic value, split the rhythm with a tie across the bar line. Then, renotate any measures where the rhythmic values do not make the meter visually clear. You may need to split larger values into smaller tied values, combine tied values into a single larger one, and/or add beams. Finally, write the entire, correct rhythm in the provided space. Double-check your work by performing the rhythms while conducting.

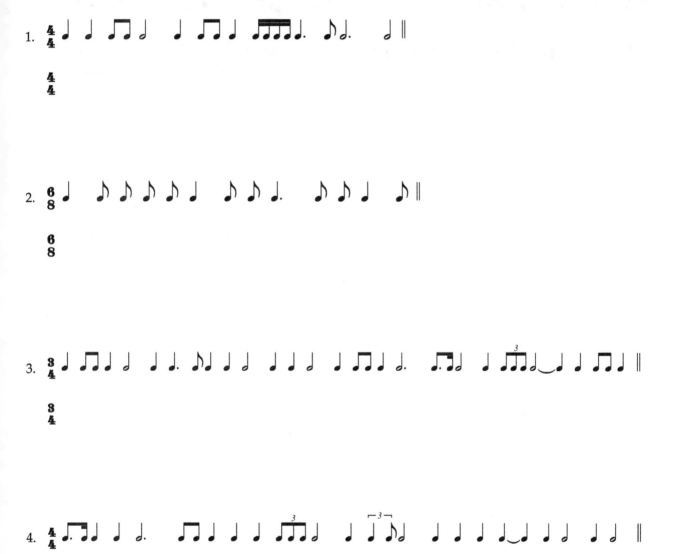

EXERCISE 1B–N   *Determining Meter and Adding Bar Lines*

First, draw a three-layer dot diagram (division, beat, and beat grouping) underneath and aligned with the passage from J. S. Bach's Prelude in D minor from the *Klavierbüchlein für Wilhelm Friedemann Bach*, BWV 926 (1720). Then, add a time signature and bar lines. Finally, write one to two sentences explaining why you interpreted the meter as you did.

ASSIGNMENT 1B.5

EXERCISE 1B-O   *Adding Bar Lines*

First, add bar lines so that each measure contains the correct number of beats. If a bar line falls in the middle of a rhythmic value, split the rhythm with a tie across the bar line. Then, renotate any measures where the rhythmic values do not make the meter visually clear. You may need to split larger values into smaller tied values, combine tied values into a single larger one, and/or add beams. Finally, write the entire, correct rhythm in the provided space. Double-check your work by performing the rhythms while conducting.

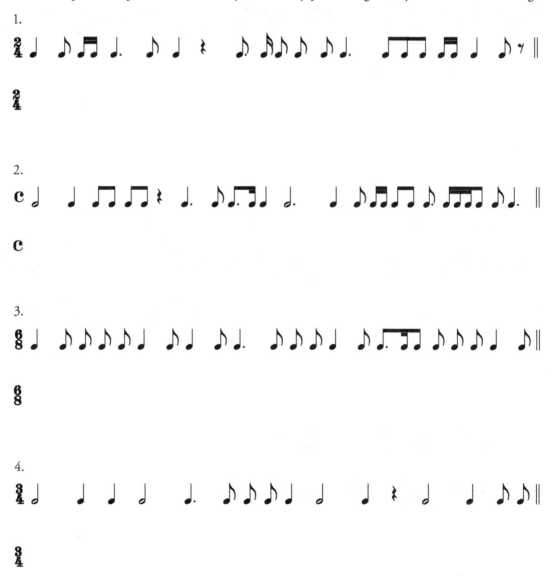

EXERCISE 1B–P   *Determining Meter and Adding Bar Lines*

First, draw a three-layer dot diagram (division, beat, and beat grouping) underneath and aligned with each score. Then, add a time signature and bar lines. Finally, write one to two sentences explaining why you interpreted the meter as you did.

1. Florence B. Price, "Silk Hat and Walking Cane" from *Dances in the Canebrakes* (1953)

2. J. S. Bach, Prelude no. 4 in A minor from *Sechs kleine Präludien*, BWV 942 (c. 1717)

3. Edvard Grieg, *Lyriske stykker* (*Lyric Pieces*), op. 12, no. 1 (1867). This is the first of Edvard Grieg's sixty-six *Lyric Pieces*. The excerpt in exercise 4, "Remembrances," was written several decades later and is the last *Lyric Piece*. Do you hear any similarities?

4. Edvard Grieg, "Efterklang" ("Remembrances") from *Lyriske stykker X (Lyric Pieces X)*, op. 71, no. 7 (1901)

ASSIGNMENT 1B.6

EXERCISE 1B-Q   *Determining Meter and Adding Bar Lines*

Each melody below is shown without a time signature or bar lines. First, sing or play through the tune, trying to determine the most logical time signature. Keep in mind that long notes often coincide with metrical accents. Next, renotate the melody with bar lines and a time signature on the provided blank staff. As you renotate, you may need to add or remove ties and beams, as shown in the sample.

Sample solution:

Given

Renotated

1.

EXERCISE 1B–R *Determining Meter and Adding Bar Lines*

First, draw a three-layer dot diagram (division, beat, and beat grouping) underneath and aligned with each score. Then, add a time signature and bar lines. Finally, write one to two sentences explaining why you interpreted the meter as you did.

1. Estelle D. Ricketts, *Rippling Spring Waltz* (1893)

2. Ignacio Álvarez (1837–1888), *El canto de la tarde*

EXERCISE 1B–S   *Completing Single Measures*

Add either a single rest (R) or a single note (N) to each measure where shown in order to achieve the correct number of beats in the measure.

Sample solution:

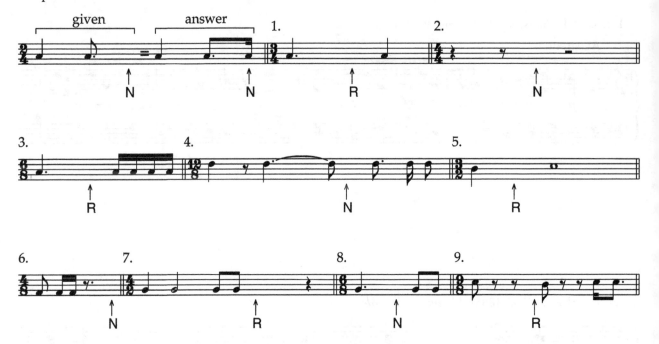

ASSIGNMENT 1B.7

EXERCISE 1B–T   *Identifying Syncopation and Hemiola*

First, draw a three-layer dot diagram (division, beat, and beat grouping) underneath and aligned with each passage. Next, circle or bracket all instances where the meter is challenged by one or more types of accent that do not align with it. Label each instance as either syncopation (S) or hemiola (H) and identify the type(s) of accent.

1. H. Leslie Adams (b. 1932), Etude in C♯ Minor from *12 Etudes for Piano*

2. Johannes Brahms, "Wenn du nur zuweilen lächelst," op. 57, no. 2 (1871)

Translation: If you only sometimes smile, only sometimes fan chilliness.

3. W. A. Mozart, Symphony no. 40 in G minor, K. 550 (1788), *Menuetto*

Allegretto

4. Isak Roux (b. 1959), *Township Guitar*

EXERCISE 1B–U   *Converting Simple Meter to Compound Meter (and vice versa)*

It is often possible to notate a rhythm in either simple triple meter *or* compound meter and have it sound the same. In the space provided, rewrite each melody below using the requested time signature. The renotated melody will last the number of measures provided. Sing both versions of each melody while conducting to ensure that they sound alike.

Sample solution ($\frac{6}{8}$):

Given

simple triple

Renotated

compound duple

1.

2.

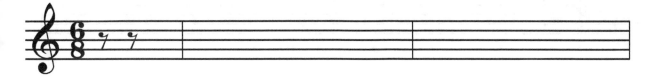

3.

ASSIGNMENT 1B.8

EXERCISE 1B–V   *Identifying Syncopation and Hemiola*

First, draw a three-layer dot diagram (division, beat, and beat grouping) underneath and aligned with each passage. Next, circle or bracket all instances where the meter is challenged by one or more types of accent that do not align with it. Label each instance as either syncopation (S) or hemiola (H) and identify the type(s) of accent.

1.

2. Adolphus Hailstork, *Fantasy, Elegy, and Caprice for Cello and Piano* (2018)

3. Johannes Brahms, Violin Concerto, op. 77 (1879), *Allegro non troppo*

1 Viol.

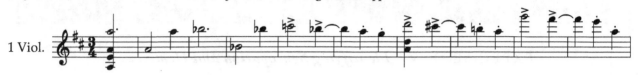

4. Ludwig van Beethoven, Piano Sonata in E♭ major, op. 31, no. 3 (1802), *Trio*

5. Samuel Coleridge-Taylor, Clarinet Quintet, op. 10 (1906), i

6. Amy Beach, Mazurka from *Three Compositions for Violin and Piano*, op. 40 (1898)

7. Florence B. Price, "Silk Hat and Walking Cane" from *Dances in the Canebrakes* (1953)

ASSIGNMENT 1B.9

EXERCISE 1B-W   *Identifying Syncopation and Hemiola*

First, draw a three-layer dot diagram (division, beat, and beat grouping) underneath and aligned with each passage. Next, circle or bracket all instances where the meter is challenged by one or more types of accent that do not align with it. Label each instance as either syncopation (S) or hemiola (H) and identify the type(s) of accent.

1. Ludwig van Beethoven, Piano Sonata in A♭ major, op. 110 (1821), *Allegro molto*

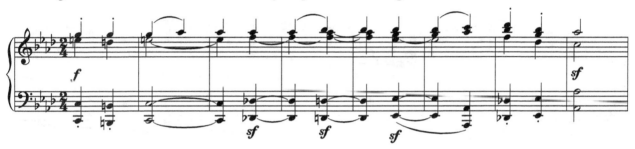

2. Joseph Hanson Kwabene Nketia, "Volta Fantasy" from *Twelve Pedagogical Pieces* (1961)

3. Scott Joplin, *The Cascades* (1904)

4. Arcangelo Corelli, Chamber Sonata in E minor, op. 2, no. 4 (1685)

5. Pyotr Ilyich Tchaikovsky, from *Sleeping Beauty* (1890)

6. Johannes Brahms, Variation 7 from *Variations on a Theme by Haydn*, op. 56b (1873)

Musical Distance: Intervals

EXERCISE 1C–A *Locating Generic Intervals Above and Below a Letter Name*

Write the pitch letter names (no accidentals or octave numbers) located the requested generic interval above and below each given letter name. A sample is provided.

	Letter Name, Interval	Above	Below		Letter Name, Interval	Above	Below
Sample.	C, 5th	G	F	5.	E, 6th		
1.	D, 3rd			6.	D, octave		
2.	B, 4th			7.	G, 10th		
3.	F, 7th			8.	C, 9th		
4.	G, 2nd			9.	A, 12th		

EXERCISE 1C–B *Identifying Generic Intervals*

Fill in three pieces of information for each circled interval, as in the sample: (1) its generic size as a number, (2) whether it is a melodic (mel) or harmonic (har) interval, and (3) whether it is simple (s) or compound (c).

1.

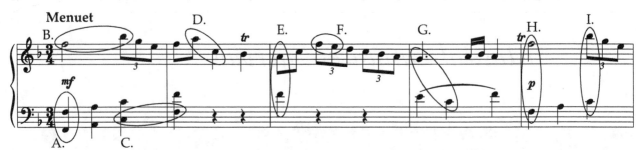

A. 1. <u>8</u>	2. <u>har</u>	3. <u>s</u>	F. 1. _____	2. _____	3. _____
B. 1. _____	2. _____	3. _____	G. 1. _____	2. _____	3. _____
C. 1. _____	2. _____	3. _____	H. 1. _____	2. _____	3. _____
D. 1. _____	2. _____	3. _____	I. 1. _____	2. _____	3. _____
E. 1. _____	2. _____	3. _____			

2. Betty Jackson King, "Spring Intermezzo" from *Four Seasonal Sketches* (1955)

A. 1. _____	2. _____	3. _____	F. 1. _____	2. _____	3. _____
B. 1. _____	2. _____	3. _____	G. 1. _____	2. _____	3. _____
C. 1. _____	2. _____	3. _____	H. 1. _____	2. _____	3. _____
D. 1. _____	2. _____	3. _____	I. 1. _____	2. _____	3. _____
E. 1. _____	2. _____	3. _____			

EXERCISE 1C-C   *Identifying Specific Intervals*

Label both the numeric size and the specific quality of each harmonic interval. In addition, label each interval as either a perfect consonance (PC), an imperfect consonance (IC), or a dissonance (Diss). A sample is provided.

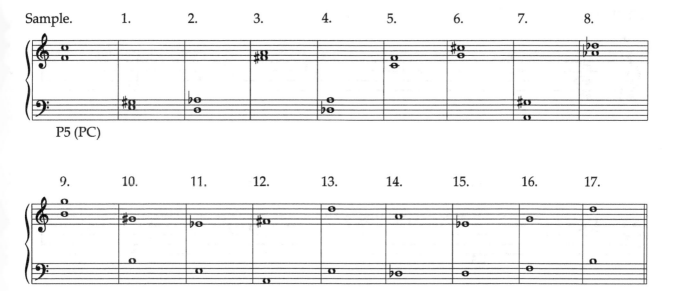

P5 (PC)

EXERCISE 1C-D   *Generating Perfect Fifths Above and Below a Given Pitch*

In closed noteheads, notate the pitches that lie a perfect fifth higher and a perfect fifth lower than the provided one. Be sure to use any necessary accidentals. A sample is provided.

EXERCISE 1C–E *Generating Perfect Fourths Above and Below a Given Pitch*

In closed noteheads, notate the pitches that lie a perfect fourth higher and a perfect fourth lower than the provided one. Be sure to use any necessary accidentals. A sample is provided.

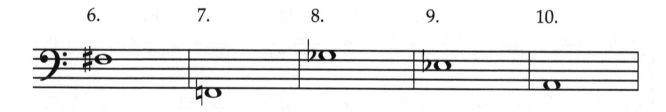

ASSIGNMENT 1C.2

EXERCISE 1C–F   *Generating Major Thirds Above and Below a Given Pitch*

In closed noteheads, notate the pitches that lie a major third higher and a major third lower than the provided one. Be sure to use any necessary accidentals. A sample is provided.

EXERCISE 1C–G   *Generating Minor Thirds Above and Below a Given Pitch*

In closed noteheads, notate the pitches that lie a minor third higher and a minor third lower than the provided one. Be sure to use any necessary accidentals. A sample is provided.

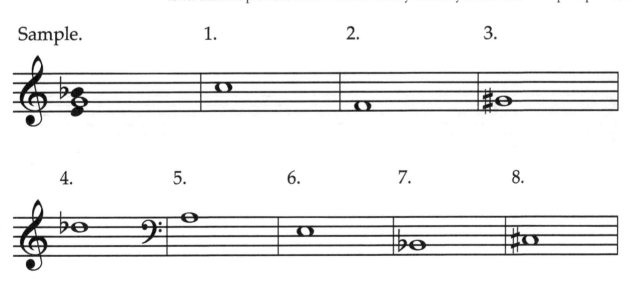

EXERCISE 1C–H   *Generating Major Sixths Above and Below a Given Pitch*

In closed noteheads, notate the pitches that lie a major sixth higher and a major sixth lower than the provided one. Be sure to use any necessary accidentals. A sample is provided.

EXERCISE 1C–I   *Generating Minor Sixths Above and Below a Given Pitch*

In closed noteheads, notate the pitches that lie a minor sixth higher and a minor sixth lower than the provided one. Be sure to use any necessary accidentals. A sample is provided.

EXERCISE 1C-J   *Generating a Mix of Intervals Above a Given Pitch*

Locate the pitch that lies the requested interval *above* the given pitch. Write the new pitch on the same staff as the given pitch. In addition, label each interval as either a perfect consonance (PC), an imperfect consonance (IC), or a dissonance (Diss).

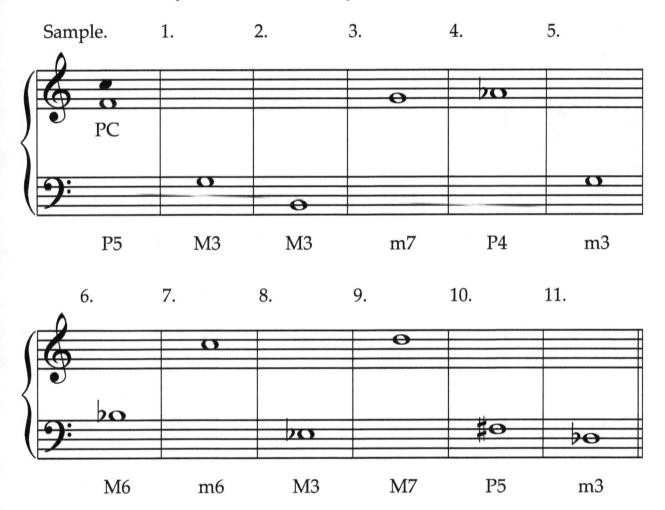

EXERCISE 1C-K *Generating a Mix of Intervals Below a Given Pitch*

Locate the pitch that lies the requested interval *below* the given pitch. Write the new pitch on the same staff as the given pitch. In addition, label each interval as either a perfect consonance (PC), an imperfect consonance (IC), or a dissonance (Diss).

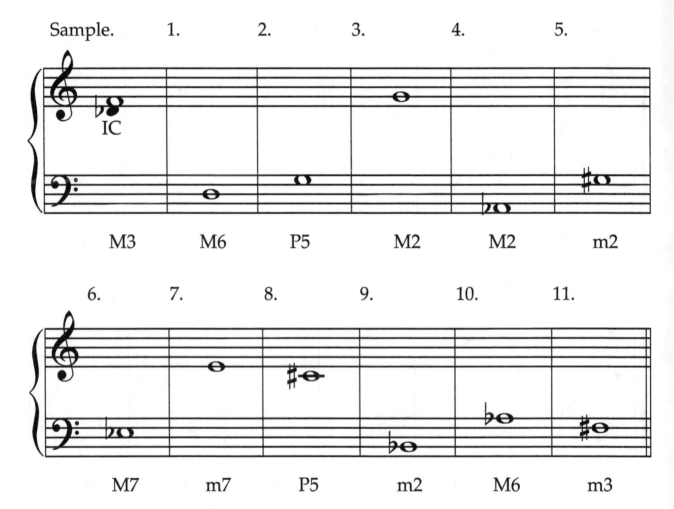

EXERCISE 1C-L *Identifying Descending Melodic Intervals*

Label each descending melodic interval with both a numeric size and a specific quality. In addition, label each interval as either a perfect consonance (PC), an imperfect consonance (IC), or a dissonance (Diss). A sample is provided.

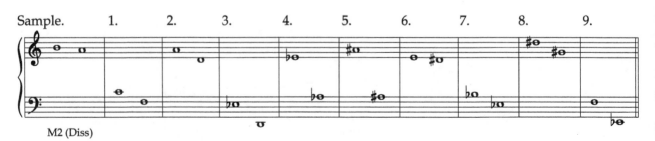

EXERCISE 1C-M   *Adjusting Interval Qualities*

1. Without changing the numeric size, write the specific interval that is one half step *larger*.

   Sample. P5: A5   a. m3:   b. M2:   c. M7:   d. d3:   e. d8:

2. Without changing the numeric size, write the specific interval that is one half step *smaller*.

   Sample. m6: d6   a. M3:   b. P4:   c. A6:   d. P5:   e. m3:

ASSIGNMENT 1C.3

EXERCISE 1C–N   *Creating Intervals*

1. Fill in the pitches that are located each interval *above* A^3, C^2, and $E\flat^5$. A sample is provided.

	A^3	C^2	$E\flat^5$
Sample. P4	D^4	F^2	$A\flat^5$
a. m3			
b. M7			
c. d8			
d. m2			
e. A5			
f. P5			

2. Fill in the pitches that are located each interval *below* D^4, $B\flat^3$, and F^6. A sample is provided.

	D^4	$B\flat^3$	F^6
Sample. M2	C^4	$A\flat^3$	$E\flat^6$
a. P5			
b. m3			
c. d5			
d. M7			
e. A2			

EXERCISE 1C–O   *Naming Intervals within a Scale*

Name all instances of the requested interval that can be found within the given scale. The parenthesized number shows you how many to find.

1. In the F major scale, name all possible major seconds (4).

2. In the B♭ major scale, name all possible minor seconds (2).

3. In the C harmonic minor scale, name all possible major thirds (3).

4. In the F♯ major scale, name all possible minor sixths (3).

EXERCISE 1C–P   *Transposing Melodic Fragments*

On the provided blank staff, transpose each melodic fragment by the requested interval. Play the original and the transposed version back to back to proofread your work aurally.

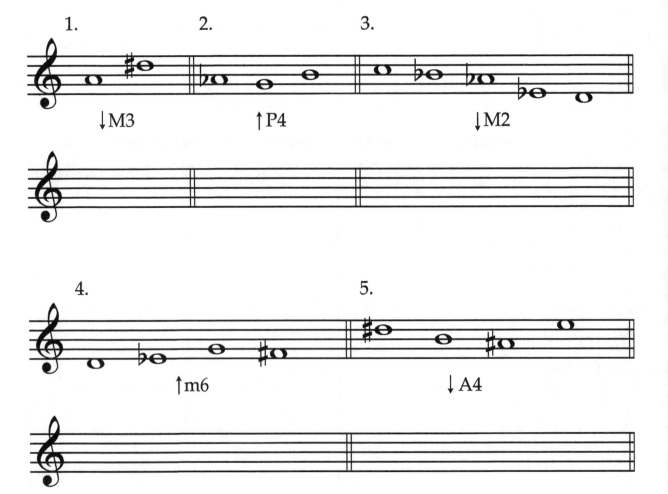

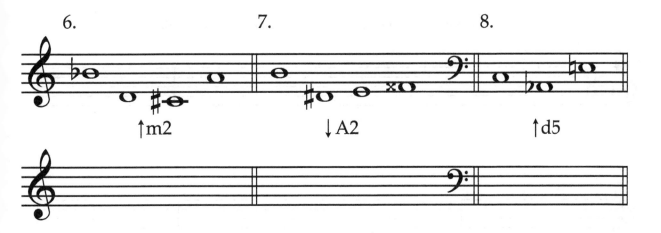

EXERCISE 1C–Q   *Creating Parts for Transposing Instruments*

Let's imagine that you would like to perform Louise Farrenc's Piano Trio in E minor, op. 45, which was originally composed in 1857 for flute, cello, and piano. Your trio includes B♭ clarinet, baritone saxophone, and piano instead. You will need to create parts for the two wind players to read.

- Create the B♭ clarinet part by transposing the flute part up by a major second. Write in treble clef. *Hint: Begin by thinking about what the key signature will be.*
- Create the E♭ baritone saxophone part by transposing the cello part up by a major sixth plus an octave. Write in treble clef. *Hint: Begin by thinking about what the key signature will be.*

B♭ Clarinet Part (transpose the upper staff above up by a major second):

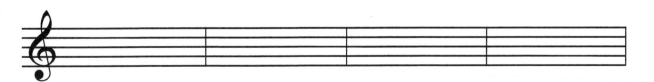

Eb Baritone Saxophone Part (transpose the lower staff above up by a major sixth plus an octave):

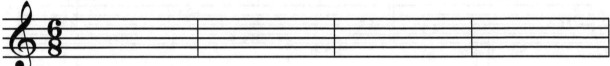

ASSIGNMENT 1C.4

EXERCISE 1C–R   *Creating Parts for Transposing Instruments*

Let's imagine that you would like to perform Florence B. Price's String Quartet no. 2, which was originally composed in 1935 for two violins, viola, and cello. Your chamber ensemble consists of soprano saxophone, alto saxophone, F horn, and bassoon. The bassoonist can read from the cello part untransposed, but you will need to create parts for the upper three instruments as follows:

- Create the B♭ soprano saxophone part by transposing the Violin 1 part up by a major second.
- Create the E♭ alto saxophone part by transposing the Violin 2 part up by a major sixth.
- Create the F Horn part by transposing the Viola part up by a perfect fifth. Write it in treble clef.

Bb Soprano Saxophone Part (transpose the Violin 1 part above up by a major second):

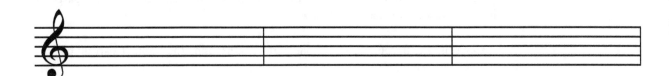

Eb Alto Saxophone Part (transpose the Violin 2 part above up by a major sixth):

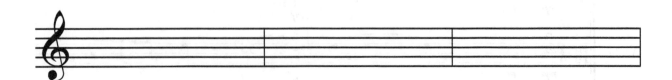

F Horn Part (transpose the Viola part above up by a perfect fifth):

EXERCISE 1C–S *Identifying Intervals*

For each boxed pair of pitches in the passage from Ludwig van Beethoven's String Quartet no. 14 in C# minor, op. 131 (1826), label the following: (1) the specific interval, (2) whether it is a perfect consonance (PC), an imperfect consonance (IC), or a dissonance (DISS), and (3) the interval's inversion. A sample is provided.

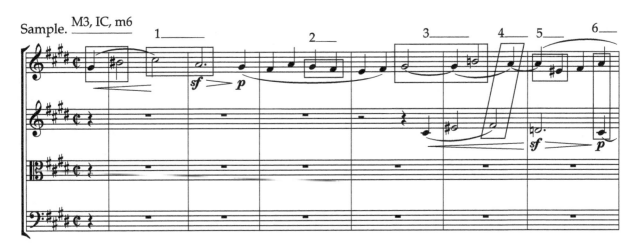

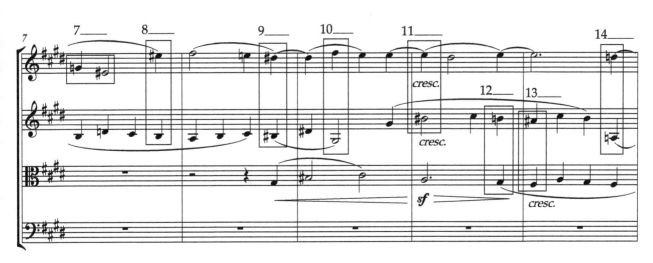

CHAPTER 2

Pitch and Meter Combine: Melody and Counterpoint

EXERCISE 2–A   *Analyzing Melodies*

First, play or sing each melody. Then, in one paragraph per melody, answer the following questions:

- What are the overall shape, range, and tessitura? Is there a climax?
- How is the tonic triad emphasized?
- What is the primary type of melodic motion (conjunct or disjunct)? By which interval(s) does the melody leap? Are those leaps recovered?

1. Zenobia Powell Perry, "Homage" from *Piano Potpourri* (1990)

2. W. A. Mozart, "Zum Leiden bin ich auserkoren" from *Die Zauberflöte* (*The Magic Flute*), K. 620 (1791), Act 1

3. Gaetano Donizetti, "Regnava nel silenzio" from *Lucia di Lammermoor* (1819), Act 1

Translation: The high and dark night reigned in silence.

Re - gna-va nel___ si - len - zi - o   al - ta la not - te e   bru - na

4. Undine Smith Moore (text by Sappho), "Love Let the Wind Cry . . . How I Adore Thee" (1961)

With passion – pressing forward

Love,_____   let   the   wind   cry   on   the   dark

moun - tain,___   Bend-ing   the   ash   trees___   and the   tall   hem - locks   with

5. Robert Schumann, "Träumerei" from *Kinderszenen* (Scenes from Childhood), op. 15 (1838), no. 7

Moderato

6. Frédéric Chopin, Prelude in D♭ major ("Raindrop"), op. 28 (1839)

EXERCISE 2–B   *Completing a Melodic Contour*

Insert one pitch at each arrow in order to create a more stepwise line. Sing your completed melody.

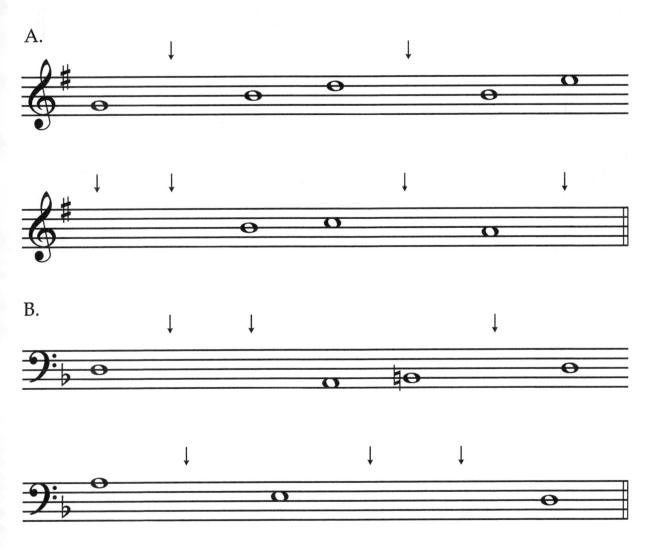

EXERCISE 2–C *Composing Melodic Contours*

Below are the starting pitches, climaxes, and contour sketches of two 12- to 16-note melodic contours. Compose the two melodic contours using these shapes as guidelines.

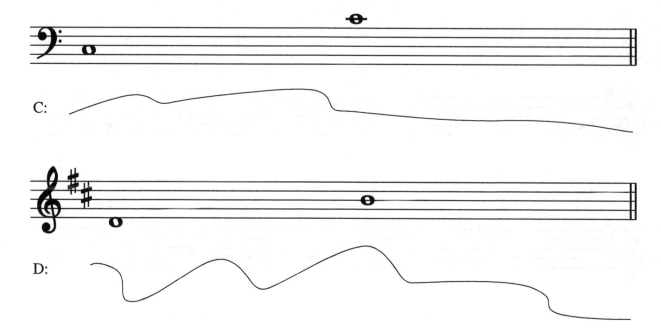

ASSIGNMENT 2.2

EXERCISE 2-D *Adding Multiple Counterpoints to Fragments of a Cantus Firmus*

Following the sample, compose four different first-species counterpoints *above* each three-note cantus firmus fragment and four different ones *below* it. Each fragment comes from the middle of a longer cantus firmus, so you do not need to treat it as a beginning or an ending. Label each harmonic interval, drawing a box around each perfect consonance.

Sample.

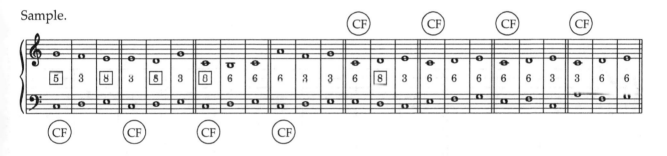

1.

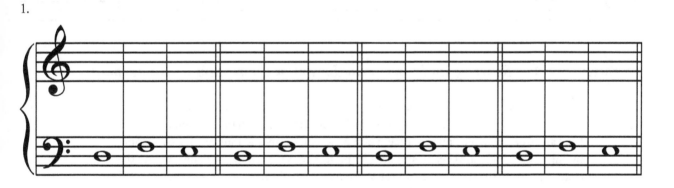

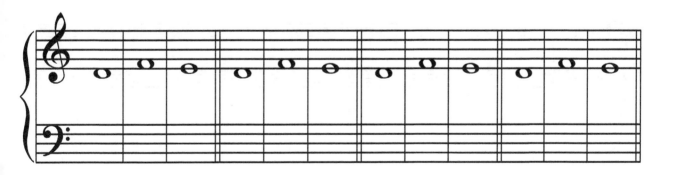

2.

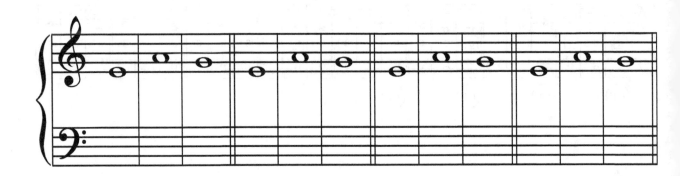

EXERCISE 2-E   *Spotting and Correcting Errors in First-Species Counterpoint*

First, play the first-species counterpoint below. Next, label each harmonic interval, drawing a box around the interval number of each perfect consonance. Then, locate and label all errors, which belong to three types: dissonant harmonic intervals (Diss), leaping by augmented interval (+Leap), and parallel perfect consonances (//). Finally, rewrite the counterpoint line without errors in the space provided, aiming for contrary motion and parallel imperfect consonances. Use mostly stepwise motion and recover each leap of a fourth or larger.

Counterpoint

intervals:

CF
key:

Counterpoint

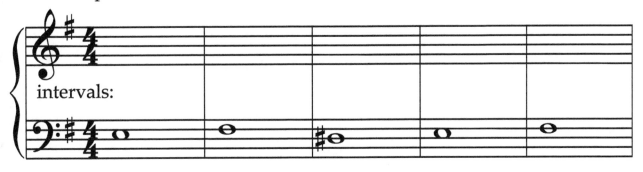

CF

ASSIGNMENT 2.3

EXERCISE 2–F *Composing First-Species Counterpoint*

Write a first-species counterpoint line on each of the blank staves below. Some are above the cantus firmus, and others are below. Label each harmonic interval, and draw a box around any perfect consonances. *Hint: If you avoid fifths between the counterpoint and the cantus firmus, the same melodic line will work above and below the same cantus firmus.*

1.

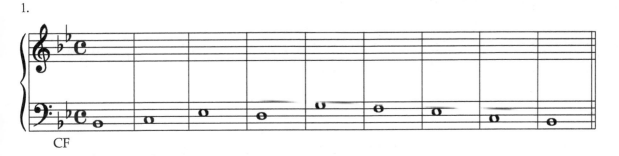

2.

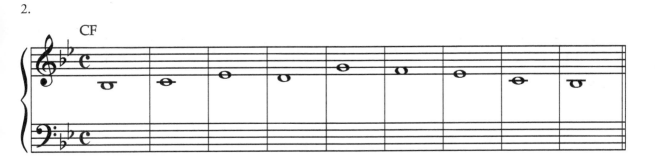

3.

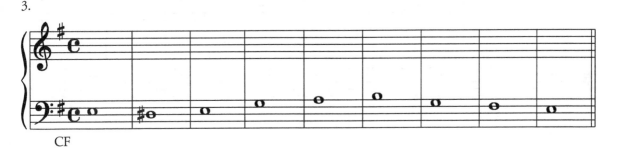

4.

EXERCISE 2–G   *Composing First-Species Counterpoint*

Write a first-species counterpoint line on each of the blank staves below. Some are above
the cantus firmus, and others are below. Label each harmonic interval, and draw a box
around any perfect consonances. *Hint: If you avoid fifths between the counterpoint and
the cantus firmus, the same melodic line will work above and below the same cantus firmus.*

1.

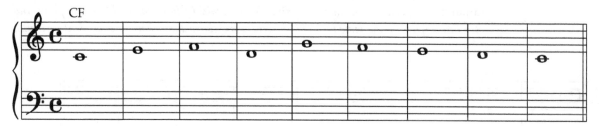

2.

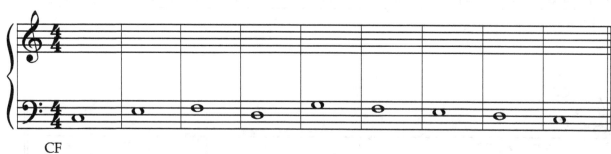

3.

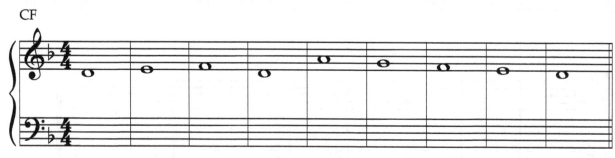

4.

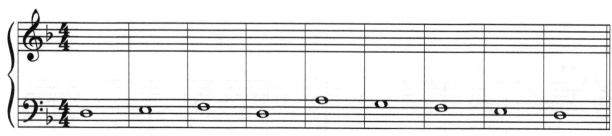

ASSIGNMENT 2.4

EXERCISE 2–H *Analyzing Types of Contrapuntal Motion in Outer Voices*

First, listen to each passage and locate its two outer voices. Next, under the bass, label all harmonic intervals between the outer voices. Then, using brackets above the staff, label at least two different types of contrapuntal motions in each passage: parallel (P), similar (S), oblique (O), and contrary (C).

1. César Cortinas, *Ave Maria III* (1917)

Translation: And blessed is the fruit of your womb, Jesus

2. Henry Thacker Burleigh (text by Laurence Hope), "Kashmiri Song" from *Five Songs of Laurence Hope* (1915)

3. Franz Joseph Haydn, String Quartet in G major, op. 20, no. 4 (1772), *Allegretto alla zingarese*

EXERCISE 2–I   *Spotting Errors in Second-Species Counterpoint*

First, play the second-species counterpoints below on keyboard. Next, label each harmonic interval, boxing each perfect consonance and circling each dissonance. Then, locate and label all errors, which belong to five types: dissonant downbeat (DD), non-passing dissonance on the weak beat (NPD), parallel perfect consonances (//), unrecovered leap (UL), and missing leading tone (LT).

1.

2.

EXERCISE 2–J   *Completing a Compositional Etude*

Just as an etude rehearses a particular performance skill, this exercise rehearses a particular compositional skill. Compose a second-species counterpoint on each blank staff, but *use consonances only* (no passing tones). Use a mix of steps, skips, and a few recovered leaps. Label all harmonic intervals, boxing perfect consonances.

1.

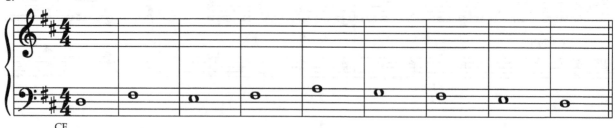

CF

2.

CF

ASSIGNMENT 2.5

EXERCISE 2–K   *Adding Multiple Counterpoints to Fragments of a Cantus Firmus*

Following the sample, compose three different second-species counterpoints *above* each three-note cantus firmus fragment and two different ones *below* it. Each fragment comes from the middle of a longer cantus firmus, so you do not need to treat it as a beginning or an ending. Use a whole note in the final measure of each pattern. Label each harmonic interval, drawing a box around each perfect consonance and circling each dissonance.

Sample solution: F–D–E

Sample.

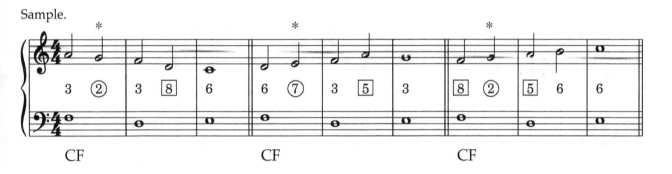

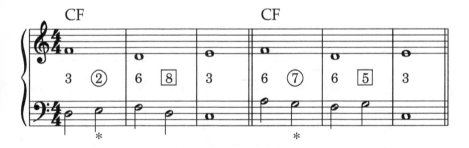

1.

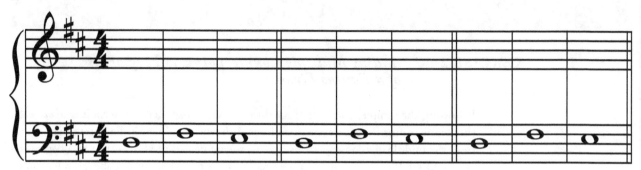

2.

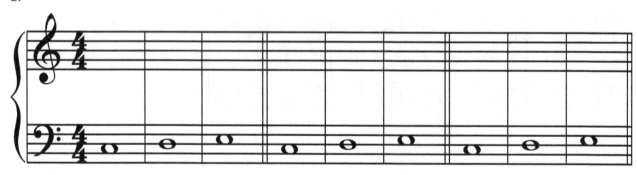

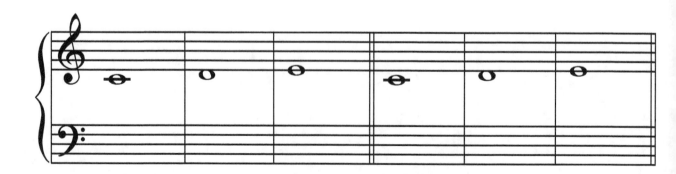

3.

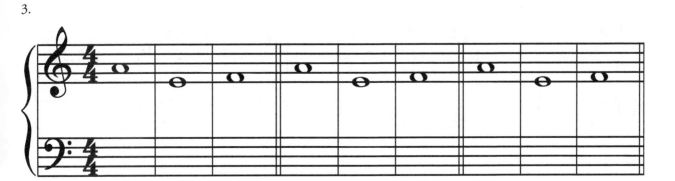

EXERCISE 2-L   *Composing Second-Species Counterpoint*

Compose a second-species counterpoint line on each blank staff. Remember that down-beats must be consonant with the cantus firmus, and that unaccented half notes may be either passing tones or consonances. Label all harmonic intervals, boxing perfect consonances and circling dissonances.

1.

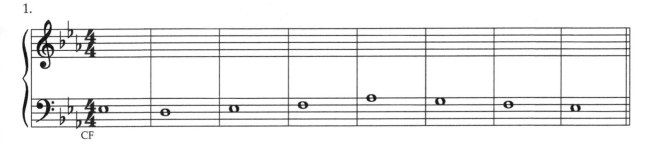

2.

EXERCISE 2–M   *Analyzing Outer-Voice Counterpoint*

The passage below, from Fanny Hensel's Piano Trio, op. 11 (1850), is held together by the first-species counterpoint between the outer voices. Notice that you can locate the bass voice on two different staves (doubled in octaves), and the soprano voice on two different staves as well (also doubled in octaves). Label the harmonic intervals between the outer voices, boxing perfect consonances and circling dissonances. *Hint: A few outer-voice intervals in this passage are dissonant, which differs from the strict first-species writing that you have been doing.*

ASSIGNMENT 2.6

EXERCISE 2–N   *Analyzing Outer-Voice Counterpoint*

The examples that follow are held together by outer-voice counterpoint. Circle the structural outer-voice pitches that create this counterpoint and label each harmonic interval between the circled tones, boxing any perfect consonances and circling any dissonances.

1. Robert Schumann, Grosse Sonata in F♯ minor, op. 11 (1835)

2. José White, *Zamacueca*, op. 30 (1897). *Hint: The outer voices do not actually sound simultaneously; the bass always comes before the soprano.*

3. J. S. Bach, Chorale from Cantata no. 5, BWV 5 (1724)

4. Robert Schumann, "Humming Song" from *Album für die Jugend*, op. 68 (1848), no. 3. *Hint: Only every other pitch on the lower staff acts as a bass note, so find four of them per measure, not eight.*

Nicht schnell

5. Ludwig van Beethoven, Violin Sonata no. 10 in G major, op. 96 (1812), *Adagio espressivo*

6. Maria Szymanowska, *Six Menuets*, no. 2 (1819). *Hint: For each bass note on the lower staff, decide which one pitch on the upper staff pairs with it as the soprano voice.*

7. Ludwig van Beethoven, Violin Sonata no. 9 in A major ("Kreutzer"), op. 47 (1804), *Andante con Variazioni. Hint: The parenthesized pitches do not participate in the structural outer voices. The pitches that come after them do.*

CHAPTER 3

Triads, Seventh Chords, and Texture

ASSIGNMENT 3.1

EXERCISE 3-A *Writing Triads*

Notate each requested root-position triad in close position using any necessary accidentals.

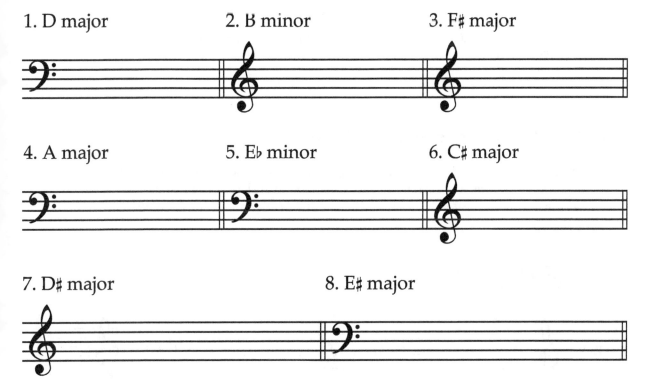

1. D major   2. B minor   3. F♯ major

4. A major   5. E♭ minor   6. C♯ major

7. D♯ major   8. E♯ major

EXERCISE 3–B   *Determining the Root of a Triad from its Third or Fifth*

Write the root of each triad in the provided blank.

1. C is the third of a(n) _____ major triad and the fifth of a(n) _____ minor triad.

2. A♭ is the third of a(n) _____ major triad and the fifth of a(n) _____ diminished triad.

3. E is the third of a(n) _____ minor triad and the fifth of a(n) _____ major triad.

4. G is the third of a(n) _____ diminished triad and the fifth of a(n) _____ diminished triad.

EXERCISE 3–C   *Correcting Misspelled Triads*

Each root-position triad below is misspelled using the enharmonic equivalent of one of the correct triad members. First, notate the corrected triad in close position on the provided staff, ensuring that it can stack in thirds. Next, label the triad's root and quality.

Sample solution:

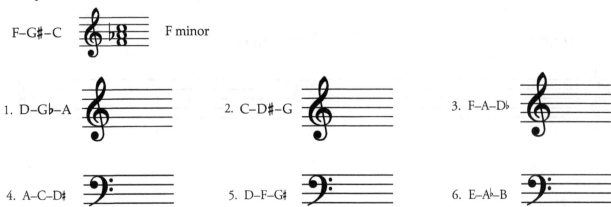

EXERCISE 3-D *Writing Triads on a Single Staff*

Write each requested triad in root position in the requested spacing. A sample is provided.

Sample: AM (open)   1. BM (close)   2. DM (open)   3. FM (open)   4. F♯M (close)

5. cm (open)   6. bm (close)   7. gm (open)   8. e♭m (open)   9. b♭m (close)

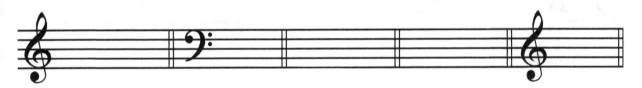

10. d° (open)   11. e° (close)   12. b♭° (open)   13. f♯° (open)   14. b° (close)

EXERCISE 3–E   *Writing Triads on a Grand Staff*

Realize each requested triad in root position in two ways: (1) in close position on a single staff, and (2) in open position spread out on the two staves of the grand staff. A sample is provided.

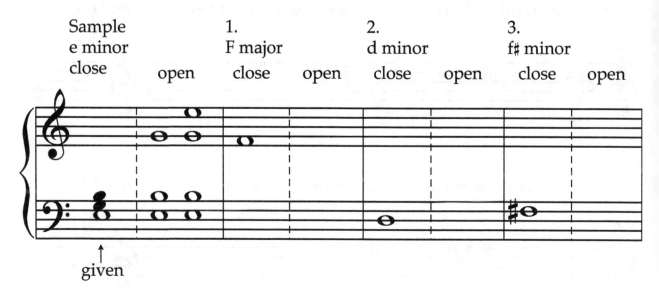

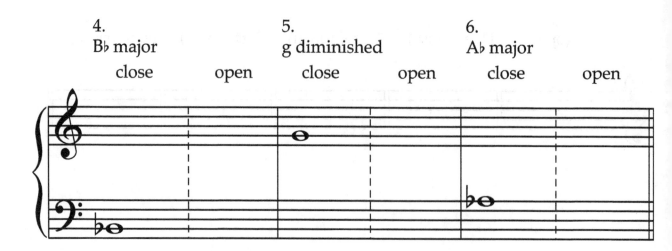

ASSIGNMENT 3.2

EXERCISE 3–F   *Writing Inverted Triads in Close Position*

Each given pitch is the bass note of an inverted triad. Realize the specified triad quality and inversion by adding two pitches above the given one. Label each triad with a chord symbol using slash notation.

1. First-inversion major triads:

2. Second-inversion major triads:

3. First-inversion minor triads:

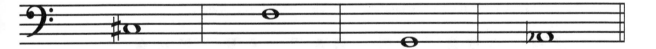

4. Second-inversion minor triads:

5. First-inversion diminished triads:

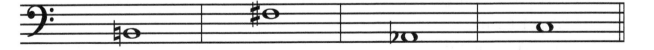

EXERCISE 3–G *Building Triads from a Single Chord Member*

Each given pitch belongs to three major triads (the root of one, the third of another, and the fifth of another), three minor triads, and three diminished triads. Write the chord symbols of all nine triads. A sample is provided.

	Pitch	Root	Third	Fifth
Sample.	D	DM, Dm, D°	B♭M, Bm, B°	GM, Gm, G♯°
1.	C			
2.	F			
3.	B♭			
4.	C♯			
5.	F♯			
6.	E♭			

EXERCISE 3–H *Finding Triadic Shapes at the Keyboard*

Each triad forms a visual shape at the keyboard that consists of some combination of black keys (B) and/or white keys (W). For example, a D major triad is W-B-W: a white root (D), a black third (F♯), and a white fifth (A). Next to each triad quality and keyboard shape, write the chord symbols for the specified number of triads. A sample is provided.

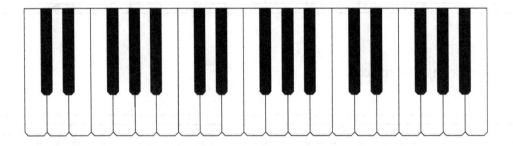

Sample. Major, W-W-W (3): CM, FM, GM

1. Major, B-W-B (3):

2. Minor, W-B-W (3):

3. Diminished, W-W-B (3):

4. Major, B-B-B (1):

5. Diminished, B-B-W (2):

6. Minor, B-W-B (3):

EXERCISE 3-I *Completing Triads*

Each column of the diagram below represents a triad of the quality shown at the bottom. Fill in the blanks in order to create complete triads. A sample is provided for you: Given A as the fifth of a major triad, the two missing members are D (root) and F# (third).

fifth	A	___	___	___	D♯	___	___	___	___	G♯	B
third	(F♯)	A	G♭	___	___	___	F♯	C♯	___	___	___
root	(D)	___	___	B	___	C♭	___	___	F	___	___
quality	M	M	m	d	m	M	d	M	d	m	M

EXERCISE 3-J *Identifying Triads in a Repertoire Passage*

The following passage from Jeraldine Saunders Herbison's *Saltarello* for Cello and Piano, op. 30, no. 2 (2000) features many triads that sound one note at a time. In each blank below the score, write the chord symbol of the triad that sounds during that span of time.

EXERCISE 3-K   *Solving a Brain Twister*

Each pair of pitches belongs to multiple triads. The number of triads is shown in parentheses. Using chord symbols, list all of the major, minor, diminished, and/or augmented triads that include each pair. A sample is provided.

Sample. G and B (4) (GM, G+, Em, E♭+)

1. A and C (4)   2. D and F♯ (4)   3. B♭ and D♭ (4)

4. F and C (2)   5. C and A♭ (4)   6. C♯ and E (4)

ASSIGNMENT 3.3

EXERCISE 3–L *Analyzing Triads in Repertoire*

First, label the key of each passage. Then, analyze each boxed triad by adding a roman numeral and any necessary figured bass.

1. W. A. Mozart, "Drei Knäbchen" from *The Magic Flute* (1791)

2. W. A. Mozart, "Wie? Wie? Wie?" from *The Magic Flute* (1791)

3. W. A. Mozart, String Quartet in B♭ major, K. 458 (1784), *Allegro vivace assai*

EXERCISE 3-M   *Completing Triads*

Add a third pitch to each given pair of pitches in order to form the specified triad quality. Then, label each triad with a chord symbol in the space provided. Do *not* alter any of the given pitches. For example, the sample provides D and A and requests a minor triad; F is the missing pitch and Dm is the chord symbol.

EXERCISE 3-N   *Realizing Figured Basses*

Realize each figured bass by adding two more pitches above the given one. Then, label each triad with a chord symbol. Use close position. Play your solutions.

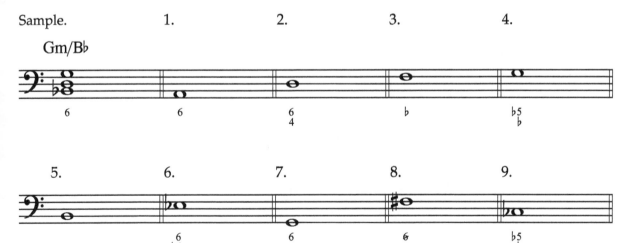

ASSIGNMENT 3.4

EXERCISE 3-O   *Notating Triads in Root Position and Inversion Within a Key*

Notate each triad in two ways as shown in the sample solution:

(1) in three voices, in close position, on the bass-clef staff

(2) in four voices with the root doubled, in open position, spread out on the two staves

Use accidentals rather than key signatures.

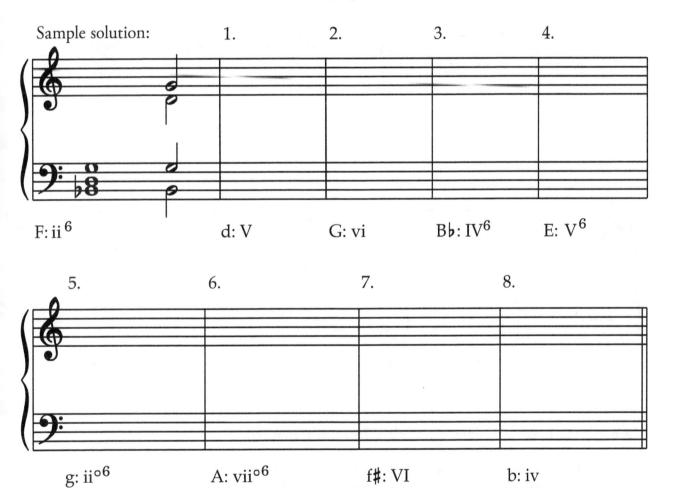

Sample solution: 1.   2.   3.   4.

F: ii^6 d: V   G: vi   B♭: IV^6 E: V^6

5.   6.   7.   8.

g: ii$^{\circ 6}$ A: vii$^{\circ 6}$ f♯: VI   b: iv

EXERCISE 3-P *Realizing Figured Basses*

Realize each figured bass note by adding two pitches to the upper staff. Include any necessary accidentals. Analyze each chord with a chord symbol. Play each chord at the keyboard.

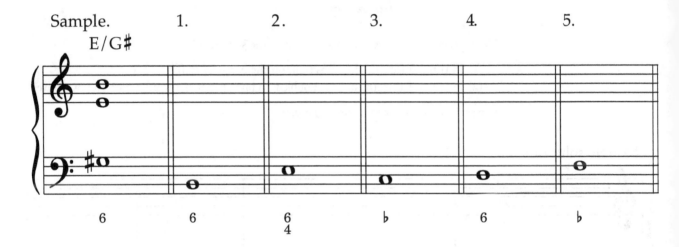

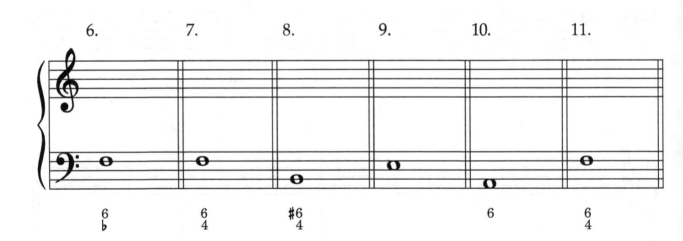

EXERCISE 3-Q *Analyzing Triads Within Major Keys*

All key signatures below represent *major* keys. First, label each key. Next, label each chord with a roman numeral and any necessary figured bass.

EXERCISE 3-R   *Analyzing Triads in Various Spacings*

First, play each triad at the keyboard. Next, label the root and quality of the triad. Then, indicate whether the root (R), third (3), or fifth (5) of the chord is in the bass, and whether the root (R), third (3), or fifth (5) of the chord is doubled. Finally, provide two kinds of shorthand for the triad: (1) the figured bass without any abbreviations (keeping in mind that there is no key signature), and (2) the chord symbol.

	Sample.	1.	2.	3.	4.	5.	6.	7.	8.	9.	10.	11.
root	Ab											
chord quality	M											
chord member in bass	R											
doubled chord member	R											
figured bass	b5 3											
chord symbol	AbM											

EXERCISE 3-S   *Notating Triads in Various Spacings*

Using the given key and roman numeral, notate each triad with two voices on each staff. Follow the specified spacing. Use accidentals rather than a key signature, and double the root of each triad.

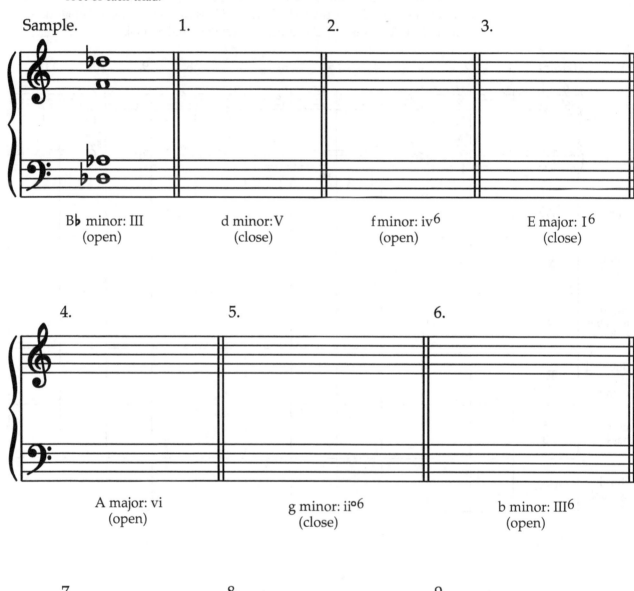

Sample.   1.   2.   3.

Bb minor: III   d minor: V   f minor: iv^6 E major: I^6
(open)   (close)   (open)   (close)

4.   5.   6.

A major: vi   g minor: ii^{o6} b minor: III^6
(open)   (close)   (open)

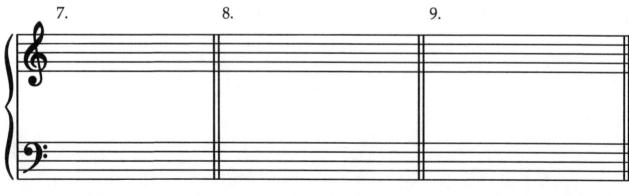

7.   8.   9.

Eb major: ii$^6_4$ C# minor: V^6 f# minor: vii^{o6}
(close)   (close)   (close)

ASSIGNMENT 3.5

EXERCISE 3-T   *Writing Triads in a Key*

First, notate the key signature for the specified key on both staves. Next, write each triad as instructed. Finally, analyze your work with roman numerals.

1. In D minor, write the following four chords in root position: i, III, V, VI. Write in four-voice keyboard style with the root doubled: the bass note on the lower staff, and three voices in close position on the upper staff.

2. In B♭ major, write the following four chords in root position: ii, IV, vi, vii°. Write in four-voice chorale style, in open spacing, with the root doubled: two voices on each staff.

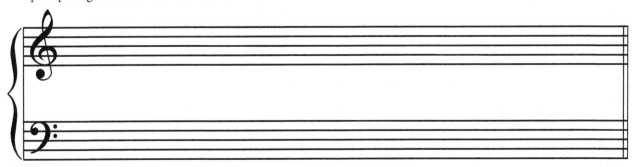

3. In C minor, write the following eight chords, some of which are inverted: i⁶, ii°, III, iv⁶, V, V⁶, VI, vii°⁶. Write in four voices, doubling the root. Write in keyboard style: the bass note on the lower staff, and three voices in close position on the upper staff.

EXERCISE 3-U *Analyzing Triads in Various Spacings*

First, play each triad at the keyboard. Next, label the root and quality of the triad. Then, indicate whether the root (R), third (3), or fifth (5) of the chord is in the soprano and in the bass, and whether the root (R), third (3), or fifth (5) of the chord is doubled. Finally, provide two kinds of shorthand for the triad: (1) the figured bass without any abbreviations (keeping in mind that there is no key signature), and (2) the chord symbol.

	Sample.	1.	2.	3.	4.	5.	6.	7.	8.	9.
root	D									
chord quality	m									
soprano chord member	5th									
chord member in bass	3rd									
doubled chord member	R									
figured bass	6 3									
chord symbol	Dm/F									

EXERCISE 3–V   *Realizing Figured Basses*

First, identify each key. Next, realize each figured bass note by adding two higher voices in close position. Finally, label the root and quality of each chord.

Sample solution:

Key: __DM__ D major 6   6   6   5 — 6   Key: _____   6   6   6   5 — 6 ♯

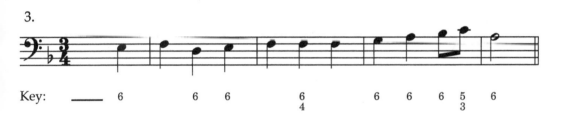

Key: _____ 6   6   6   6   6   6   6 5   6
                                             4   3

ASSIGNMENT 3.6

EXERCISE 3-W   *Generating Triads from Various Scale Degrees*

Each given pitch is the root of a triad within the specified key. First, add the third and fifth of each triad in close spacing above the root. Next, add all necessary accidentals so that all pitches belong to the key. Finally, label each triad with a roman numeral. *Hint: You can check your work by remembering which roman numerals are major, minor, and diminished in major keys and in minor keys.*

1. Given the key of D major and the following scale degrees:

2. Given the key of B major and the following scale degrees:

3. Given the key of G minor and the following scale degrees:

EXERCISE 3-X   *Analyzing Triads in Context*

First, listen to the passage from W. A. Mozart's Violin Sonata in B♭, K. 379 (1781). Next, identify the key of the passage. Then, identify the root, quality, and inversion of each bracketed triad, remembering that the pitches of each harmony sound successively rather than all at once. Finally, analyze each triad with a roman numeral and any necessary figured bass. A sample is provided. Parenthesized pitches are not part of chords.

Key: _____

Chord symbols: Gm⁵₃ ___ ___ ___ ___ ___ ___ ___ ___

Roman numerals: ___ ___ ___ ___ ___ ___ ___ ___

EXERCISE 3–Y   *Analyzing Phrases with Roman Numerals*

First, label the key of each passage. Then, analyze each triad with a roman numeral and any necessary figured bass.

1.

Key:

2.

Key:

EXERCISE 3–Z   *Solving a Brain Twister*

For each triad listed, name the major keys and the minor keys in which it appears, along with the roman numeral that the triad has in each key. A sample is provided.

	Major Keys	**Minor Keys**
Sample. D major:	I in D, IV in A, V in G	III in b, VI in f♯, VII in e
1. A minor:		
2. F major:		
3. B♭ major:		
4. E minor:		
5. D diminished:		

ASSIGNMENT 3.7

EXERCISE 3-AA   *Identifying and Transposing Root-Position Seventh Chords*

First, play each seventh chord at the keyboard. Next, identify its quality (MM, Mm, mm, dm, or dd). Finally, on the blank staff, write the same quality of seventh chord with a root a whole step higher than the original. (Choose whichever register fits comfortably on the staff.)

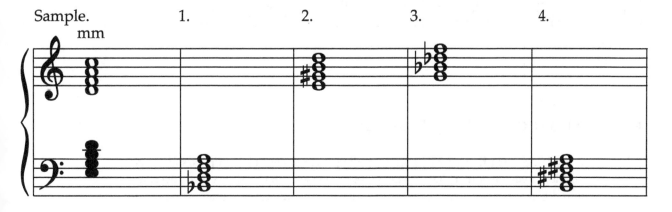

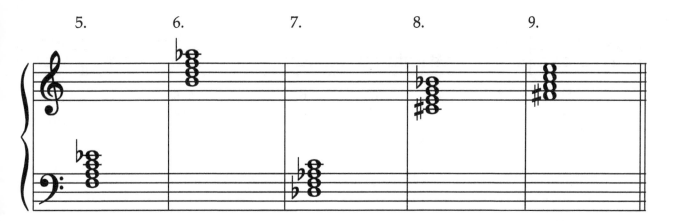

EXERCISE 3-BB   *Adding Figured-Bass Symbols*

First, play each seventh chord at the keyboard. Next, label its quality (MM, Mm, mm, dm, or dd) and its basic figured bass (^{7}, $^6_5$, $^4_3$, or $^4_2$). Finally, write its full figured bass (without abbreviations), including any necessary accidentals. A sample is provided.

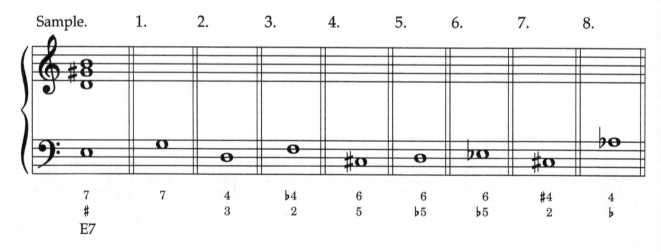

EXERCISE 3-CC   *Realizing Figured Basses*

First, realize each figured bass note by adding three pitches to the upper staff in close position. Remember that there are no doublings for seventh chords because they contain four different pitches. Then, label each chord with a chord symbol. A sample is provided.

EXERCISE 3–DD   *Constructing Seventh Chords from a Recipe of Intervals*

Starting with the given pitch, follow the recipe of intervals in order to cook the rest of a seventh chord. Once you generate all four members of the chord, label the the root, quality, and inversion as shown in the sample.

Sample solution:

1.   2.

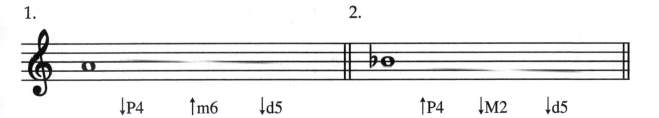

3.   4.

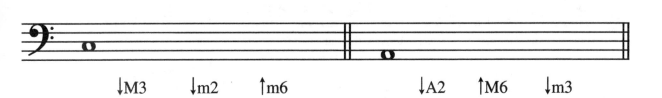

5.   6.

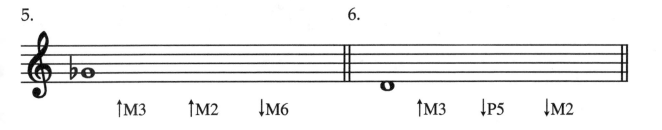

EXERCISE 3–EE   *Analyzing Triads and Seventh Chords in Context*

First, listen to the passage from Lena McLin's "The Little Baby" (1971) and label its
key. Next, write a chord symbol in each blank to label the chord that sounds during
that span. The notes in parentheses are embellishments that are not part of the chords.
Expect to encounter both triads and seventh chords. The first chord is done as a sample.

Key: GM

ASSIGNMENT 3.8

EXERCISE 3–FF   *Analyzing with Roman Numerals and Figured Bass*

First, play or listen to each short phrase. Then, label the key and analyze each chord by adding a roman numeral and any necessary figured bass. Finally, circle the chordal seventh of each seventh chord. A head start is provided for the first phrase.

1.

G: I

2. Vincenzo Bellini, "Ah! Si, fa core, abbraciami" from *Norma* (1831), Act 1

3.

4.

EXERCISE 3–GG   *Analyzing Seventh Chords in a Variety of Inversions and Spacings*

Following the sample, analyze each chord by labeling the following: (1) the full figured bass, (2) the quality of seventh chord (MM, Mm, mm, dm, or dd), (3) the member of the chord that is circled, (4) the member of the chord that is in the bass, (5) the scale degree of the bass note in the key of D minor, and (6) the chord symbol. *Note that the key signature carries through the entire exercise.*

	Sample.	1.	2.	3.	4.	5.	6.	7.	8.	9.
full figured bass d:	6 5 3									
quality of 7th chord	Mm									
member of chord that is circled	7th									
member of chord in the bass	3rd									
scale degree in the bass	↑$\hat{7}$									
chord symbol	A7/C♯									

EXERCISE 3-HH *Writing Seventh Chords in a Key*

Fill in all blanks below so that each seventh chord has all four of its members notated on the staff (with the correct tone in the bass) and has both its key and its roman numeral in that key labeled.

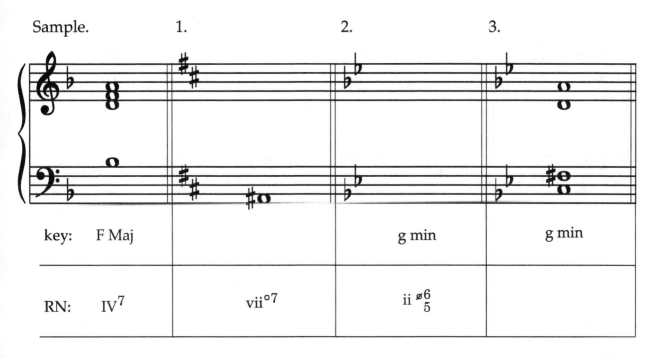

	Sample.	1.	2.	3.
key:	F Maj		g min	g min
RN:	IV^7	vii$^{\circ 7}$	ii$^{\o 6}_{5}$	

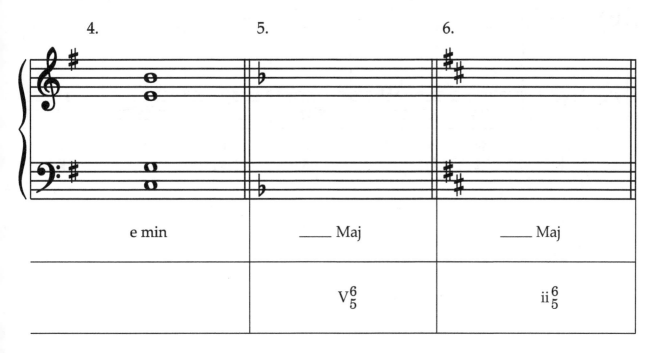

	4.	5.	6.
key:	e min	___ Maj	___ Maj
RN:		V$^6_5$	ii$^6_5$

EXERCISE 3-11 *Realizing Figured Basses*

Realize each figured bass note by adding three pitches to the upper staff, including any
necessary accidentals. Double the root of each triad. Seventh chords will have no doubled
tones. Finally, analyze with chord symbols.

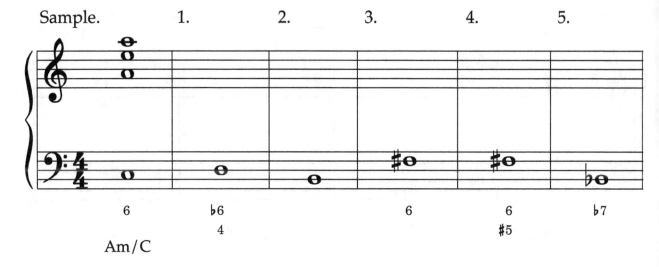

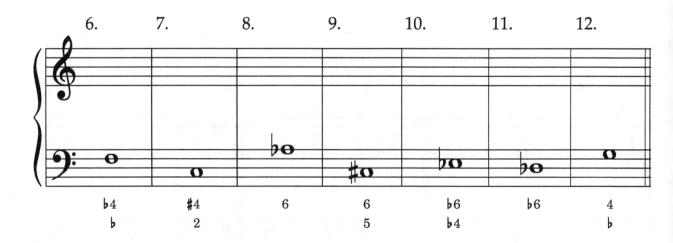

ASSIGNMENT 3.9

EXERCISE 3–JJ *Solving Brain Twisters*

1. Write the name of the chord root that answers each question.

   a. F is:
   - the third of which Mm seventh chord?
   - the fifth of which Mm seventh chord?
   - the seventh of which Mm seventh chord?
   - the seventh of which dd seventh chord?

   b. D is:
   - the third of which dd seventh chord?
   - the fifth of which mm seventh chord?
   - the seventh of which MM seventh chord?
   - the seventh of which dm seventh chord?

   c. B♭ is:
   - the third of which mm seventh chord?
   - the fifth of which Mm seventh chord?
   - the seventh of which MM seventh chord?
   - the seventh of which Mm seventh chord?

   d. E is:
   - the root of which dd seventh chord?
   - the fifth of which mm seventh chord?
   - the seventh of which Mm seventh chord?
   - the seventh of which MM seventh chord?

2. Spell the requested chords by writing the letter names of their four members.

   a. two Mm seventh chords that contain both F and D:

   b. two MM seventh chords that contain both A♭ and C:

   c. two mm seventh chords that contain both G♯ and B:

   d. two dm seventh chords that contain both C and E♭:

3. Spell the requested chords by writing the letter names of their four members.

a. the MM^7 chord with C as its bass note:

b. the mm$^6_5$ chord with C as its bass note:

c. the dd^7 chord with C as its bass note:

d. the Mm$^4_2$ chord with C as its bass note:

e. the Mm$^6_5$ chord with F as its bass note:

f. the MM$^4_3$ chord with F as its bass note:

g. the mm$^4_3$ chord with F as its bass note:

EXERCISE 3–KK   *Analyzing Triads and Seventh Chords in Context*

First, listen to each passage. Next, analyze each circled chord by labeling its root, quality, and inversion. If the circle includes more than one bass note, consider the *lowest* bass pitch as the functioning bass. A sample is provided.

1. Florence B. Price, Fantasy for Violin and Piano in F♯ minor (1940)

2. Samuel Coleridge-Taylor, *The Bamboula*, op. 59, no. 8 (1905)

3. Robert Schumann, "Anfangs wollt' ich fast verzagen" ("At First I Almost Despaired") from *Liederkreis*, op. 24 (1840). The chords are not circled in this passage, but label each quarter-note beat.

    Translation: At first, I almost felt like giving up, and I thought I never cheated.

ASSIGNMENT 3.10

EXERCISE 3-LL   *Analyzing Triads and Seventh Chords in Context*

First, listen to each passage. Next, analyze each chord with a chord symbol. Parenthesized pitches are embellishments that are not part of the sounding harmonies. You need to determine how often the harmony changes. A head start is provided.

1. Lena McLin (b. 1928), text by Robert Browning, "The Year's at the Spring"

2. W. A. Mozart, Violin Sonata in D minor, K. 421 (1783)

3. J. S. Bach, "Christ ist erstanden" from Cantata no. 66, *Erfreut euch, ihr Herzen*, BWV 66 (1724)

4. Florence B. Price (text by Louise C. Wallace), "Night" (1946). As a head start, an arrow marks the beginning of each harmony. When a harmony includes more than one bass note, consider the *lowest* bass pitch to be the functioning bass.

ASSIGNMENT 3.11

EXERCISE 3-MM   *Analyzing Triads and Seventh Chords in Context*

First, listen to each passage. Next, analyze each chord with a chord symbol. Parenthesized pitches are embellishments that are not part of the sounding harmonies. You need to determine how often the harmony changes.

1. Florence B. Price (arranger), "Go Down, Moses" (1942). As a head start, an arrow marks the beginning of each harmony.

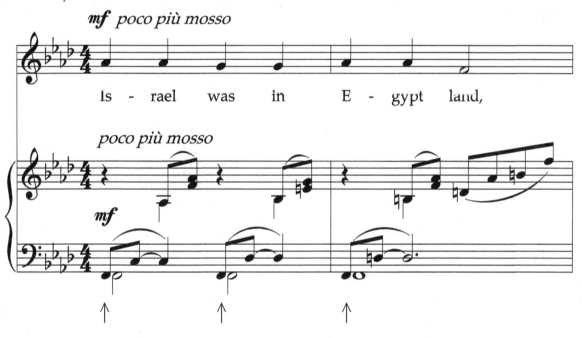

2. Pyotr Ilyich Tchaikovsky, "Morning Prayer" from *Children's Album*, op. 39 (1878), no. 1

3. Arcangelo Corelli, Concerto Grosso no. 9 in F major, op. 6 (c. 1685), *Adagio*

4. Johannes Brahms, "Ich stund an einem Morgen" ("One Morning I Stood") from *Deutsche Volkslieder*, WoO 32 (1858), no. 9. *Note: The very first chord of this passage has no third. Imagine that it has a major third.*

Translation (first stanza only): One morning, I stood secretly in a place where I would have hidden myself. I heard pitiful words.

5. Florence B. Price (1887–1953) (text by Mary Rolofson Gamble), "Love-in-a-mist." Horizontal lines underneath the score show how long each harmony lasts.

6. Franz Joseph Haydn, String Quartet, op. 20, no. 5 (1772), *Adagio.* Include a roman-numeral analysis.

ASSIGNMENT 3.12

EXERCISE 3–NN   *Reducing and Analyzing Figurated Textures*

Each passage below includes broken chords. In order to analyze the harmonies, you need to imagine them aligned so that chord members sound simultaneously rather than successively. Complete the following tasks:

1. Renotate the passage *as a reduction in block chords* on the provided blank staves. Preserve the same pitches that sound in the original, but realign them. Make sure that you use rhythmic values that correspond to the time signature.
2. Under the reduction, analyze each chord with a chord symbol.
3. Write one to two sentences describing the harmonic rhythm of the passage. In which rhythmic value(s) does it typically change? Is it regular, or is it faster in some places and slower in others?

1. W. A. Mozart, Sonata for Piano and Violin in F major, K. 377 (1781), *Tema*

Include just the pitches of the keyboard part (the two lowest staves) in your reduction:

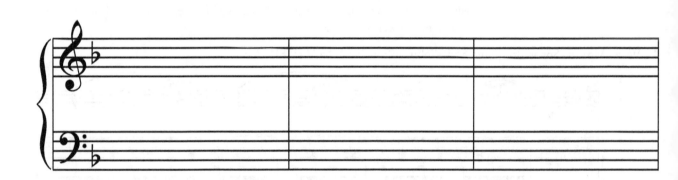

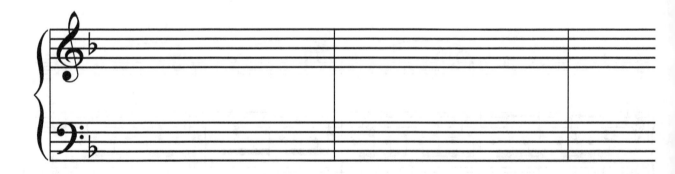

2. Arcangelo Corelli, Concerto Grosso no. 2 in F major (c. 1712), *Allegro*

27

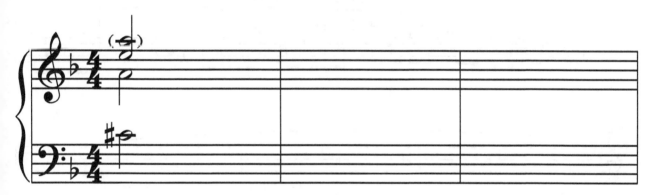

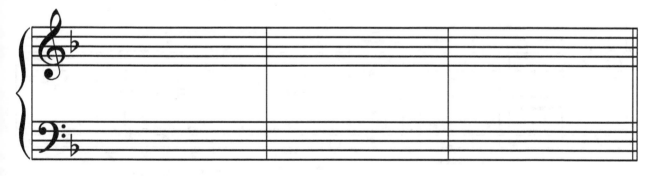

3. Ludwig van Beethoven, Piano Trio in E♭, op. 1, no. 1 (1793), *Finale*

4. J. S. Bach, Prelude in C major, BWV 846, from *Well-Tempered Clavier*, Book 1 (1722)

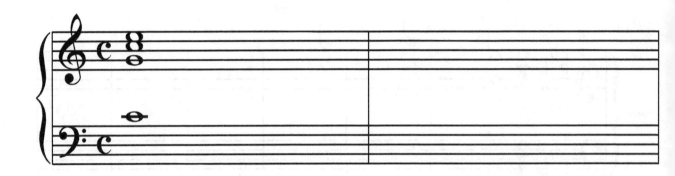

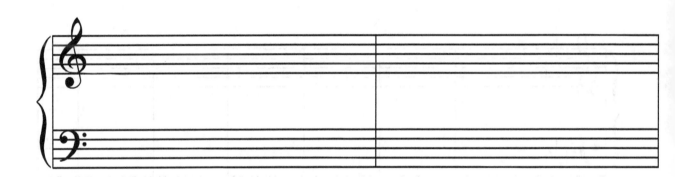

The Role of Context: Embellishing Tones and Melodic Shape

ASSIGNMENT 4.1

EXERCISE 4–A *Analyzing Chords and Melodic Embellishments*

Analyze the passages below by marking each of the following on the score. Do not analyze with roman numerals.

- Root, quality, and inversion of each chord
- Each consonant passing tone (CPT), dissonant passing tone (DPT), upper neighboring tone (UN), lower neighboring tone (LN), chordal leap (CL), and arpeggiation (ARP)

1. Marianne Martines, Keyboard Sonata No. 3 in E major (1762), *Allegro*

2. W. A. Mozart, Variations on "Ah! vous dirais-je, Maman," K. 265 (1785), Variation 6. *Hint: The embellishing tones appear on the lower staff, so you will need to consider the right-hand chords in order to distinguish between chord tones and nonchord tones in the left hand. Ignore parenthesized pitches.*

3. Ludwig van Beethoven, Violin Sonata no. 3 in E♭ major, op. 12, no. 3 (1798), *Rondo*

4. Francesca Lebrun (1756–1791), Sonata No. 1 in B♭ major, *Rondo*. Beginning at m. 9, how does the violin part (uppermost staff) relate to the upper staff of the piano part? Answer in one sentence.

ASSIGNMENT 4.2

EXERCISE 4–B   *Realigning and Analyzing Broken-Chord Figurations*

The examples that follow include broken-chord figurations. First, rewrite each example on the provided staves by realigning the broken chords into block chords that sound simultaneously. Second, analyze each harmony by labeling its root, quality, and inversion. Do not use roman numerals unless it is requested.

1. Josephine Lang (1815–1880), Arabesque in F major from *Drei Klavierstücke*. What factors contribute to the sense of acceleration or intensification in the second half of this passage? Answer in one sentence.

2. Robert Schumann, "Wiegenliedchen" from *Kinderszenen*, op. 124 (1838), no. 6. Analyze mm.
   1–6 using roman numerals. *Hint: The parenthesized B near the end of the passage is an escape tone,
   not a chord tone.*

3. Jesús Castillo (1877–1946), *Fiesta de Pájaros*. This passage includes some upper neighboring tones (both complete and incomplete) on its upper staff. Do not include them in your reduction.

4. Ludwig van Beethoven, Piano Sonata in C major, op. 2, no. 3 (1796), *Trio*. Ignore the parenthesized pitch.

ASSIGNMENT 4.3

EXERCISE 4–C *Analyzing Chords and Melodic Embellishments*

Analyze the passages below by marking each of the following on the score. Do not analyze with roman numerals.

- Root, quality, and inversion of each chord
- Each consonant passing tone (CPT), dissonant passing tone (DPT), upper neighboring tone (UN), lower neighboring tone (LN), chordal leap (CL), and arpeggiation (ARP)

1. Franz Schubert, Waltz in A♭ major from *36 Originaltänze*, op. 9a, D. 365 (1821). Ignore the parenthesized pitches. *Hint: As is typical in a waltz, the downbeat pitches of the lower staff act as the bass notes throughout the measure, even though they do not actually sustain. Horizontal lines show the duration of each chord.*

2. Franz Joseph Haydn, String Quartet in C major, op. 20, no. 2 (1772), *Adagio*

3. Basile Barès (1845–1902), *La Creole*, op. 10

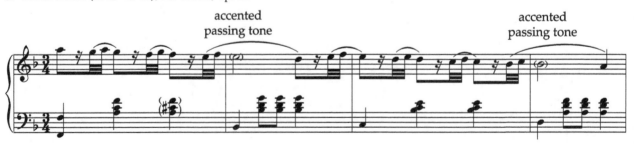

4. Robert Schumann, "Ich will meine Seele tauchen" from *Dichterliebe* (1840). To give you a head start, each embellishing tone in the melody is marked with an arrow.

Translation: I want to immerse my soul in the lily's cup. The lily shall whisper a song of my beloved.

ASSIGNMENT 4.4

EXERCISE 4-D   *Analyzing Melodic Fluency in a Harmonic Context*

First, fill in each blank beneath the staff with one roman numeral and any necessary figured bass. Next, stem and beam the slowly moving stepwise line within each passage's florid upper-voice melody. The first pitch of this line is stemmed for you. Make sure that each stemmed pitch is a chord tone.

1. Juan Bautista Alberdi (1810–1884), *La candorosa*

2. Franz Joseph Haydn, String Quartet in F minor, op. 20, no. 5 (1772), *Allegro moderato*

3. W. A. Mozart, String Quartet in E♭ major, K. 171 (1773), *Adagio. Ignore the parenthesized pitches.*

EXERCISE 4-E   *Analyzing Instances of Gap-Fill*

Each melody below consists of one or more gaps (i.e., leaps) that are subsequently filled in by step, either immediately or over a longer span of music. Mark each gap with the symbol —//—, and then add an extra-long upward stem to each subsequent pitch that participates in the stepwise filling-in of the gap. Add an asterisk (*) above the tone that completes that filling-in process.

1. Alejandro Monestel Zamora, *Contemplación* (1914)

2. Fanny Hensel, Piano Trio in D minor, op. 11 (1846), ii

3. Samuel Coleridge-Taylor, *Three Silhouettes*, op. 38 (1904), no. 3

4. Basile Barès (1845–1902), *Regina Waltz*, op. 29

5. Francesca Lebrun, Violin Sonata in A major, op. 2, no. 5 (1780), *Rondo Allegro*

6. Harold Arlen, "Over the Rainbow" (1939)

ASSIGNMENT 4.5

EXERCISE 4-F   *Analyzing Melodically Fluent Melodies*

First, sing or play each melody. Next, locate a slow-moving stepwise line that spans across all or most of the passage. The line may continue in a single direction throughout the excerpt, or it may change direction just once, but it should not waver up and down multiple times. Stem and beam the pitches of this melodically fluent line.

1. Ludwig van Beethoven, Symphony no. 6 in F major (1808), *Allegretto*

2. Frederick Loewe, "I Could Have Danced All Night" from *My Fair Lady* (1956)

3. Antonio Barbieri (1892–1979), *Ave Maria*

Translation: Blessed are you among women and blessed is the fruit of your womb, Jesus.

4. Ludwig van Beethoven, *German Dance* (1797)

5. Giuseppe Verdi, "La donna è mobile" from *Rigoletto* (1851), Act 3

6. W. A. Mozart, "Notte e giorno faticar" from *Don Giovanni*, K. 527 (1787), Act 1, Scene 1

Leporello. (wrapped in a dark mantle, impatiently pacing to and fro before the steps to the palace)

7. Tomaso Albinoni, Sonata in C for Oboe and Basso Continuo (c. 1720), *Menuet*. In addition to stemming and beaming the melodically fluent line, add one roman numeral and any necessary figured bass in each blank beneath the staff. Finally, label the type of embellishing tone marked by each arrow.

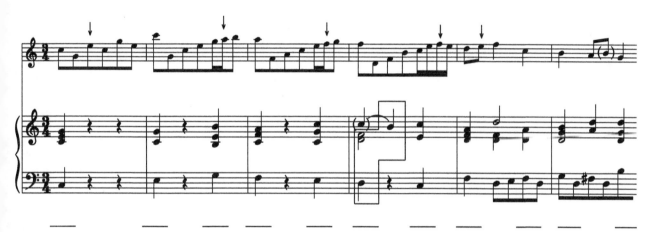

ASSIGNMENT 4.6

EXERCISE 4–G   *Analyzing Melodic Fluency in a Harmonic Context*

First, fill in each blank beneath the staff with one roman numeral and any necessary figured bass. Next, stem and beam the slowly moving stepwise line within the florid upper-voice melody. The first pitch of this line is stemmed for you. Make sure that each stemmed pitch is a chord tone. The passage is from W. A. Mozart's "Porgi, amor, qualche ristoro" from *Le Nozze di Figaro (The Marriage of Figaro)*, K. 492 (1786).

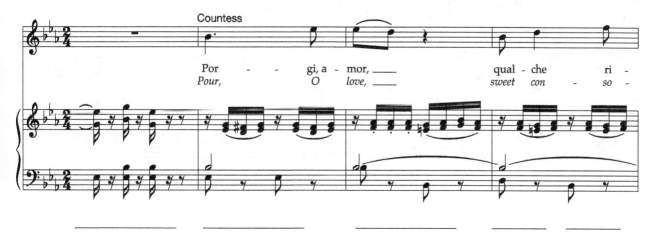

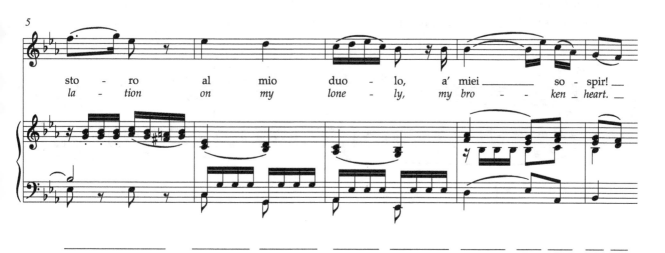

EXERCISE 4–H *Analyzing Melodic Fluency, Gap-Fill, and Harmony*

Analyze each passage as specified.

1. Christian Alejandro Almada, *Ave Regina Caelorum* (2017). Annotate each gap (—//—) and stem each subsequent stepwise filling-in within the upper voice. Next, label the root, quality, and inversion (not the roman numeral) of each chord marked with a line beneath the score. Finally, circle and label each embellishing tone.

Translation: Hail, Queen of the Heavens. Hail, Lady of Angels.

2. Robert Schumann, "Winterzeit II" from *Album für die Jugend*, op. 68, no. 39 (1848). Stem and beam the upper-voice pitches that participate in a melodically fluent (i.e., stepwise) ascent and then descent.

3. Amancio Jacinto Alcorta (1805–1862), *Nocturno* for Flute and Piano. Fill in each blank beneath the staff with a root, quality, and inversion (not a roman numeral). Then, stem and beam a melodically fluent line beginning with the initial F#[5] of the flute part. (It's okay for the line to change direction once.)

4. Herman Bemberg Ocampo, "Viens à moi" (1891). Annotate each gap (—//—) and stem each
   subsequent stepwise filling-in within the upper voice. In addition, add a roman numeral and any
   necessary figured bass to each blank underneath the score.

CHAPTER 5

Tonic, Dominant, and Voice Leading

ASSIGNMENT 5.1

EXERCISE 5–A *Spelling Tonic and Dominant Triads*

Spell the tonic triad (either I or i) and the dominant triad (V) in each key.

	D major	E minor	A major	G minor	B minor	A♭ minor	F♯ minor
I or i	D-F♯-A						
V							

EXERCISE 5–B *Playing and Transposing a Phrase in Keyboard Style*

1. Play the two given outer voices in F major.
2. Using close position, add two inner voices to the treble staff to create a keyboard-style realization. Use only I and V chords in root position. The first chord is provided as a head start.
3. Transpose the entire phrase to D major using the provided hints.
4. Play your realizations on keyboard.

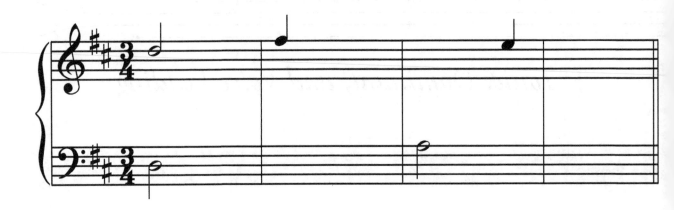

EXERCISE 5–C   *Analyzing Tonic and Dominant Chords*

Analyze each harmony with a roman numeral. Circle and label each embellishing tone.

1. Miriam Kekāuluohi Keahelapalapa Kapili, *Lei Ohaoha* (1907)

Na - ni - wa - le au e i - ke ne - i   I ke ka e - la ku i - ke a - lo pa - li
How I love to gaze on thy dwell - ing, Thy far off hut in the tall   hills

2. Ludwig van Beethoven, Violin Sonata in G major, op. 30, no. 3 (1802), *Allegro assai.* Hint:
   During the sixteenth notes in m. 1 and m. 5, only the Gs act as bass tones.

EXERCISE 5-D   *Filling in Missing Voices*

One voice is missing from each of the phrases below. Label the key, cadence, and roman numerals. Each chord is either a tonic triad or a dominant triad. Then, fill in the missing voice on the treble clef to create a four-voice texture.

1. *Keyboard style.* The tenor voice is missing.

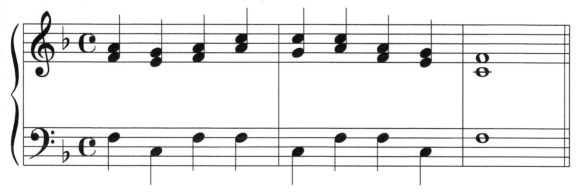

2. *Chorale style.* Use the stems to determine which voice is missing.

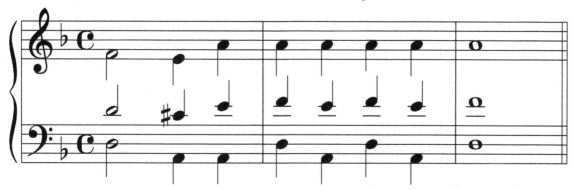

ASSIGNMENT 5.2

EXERCISE 5–E *Analyzing and Transcribing Chords*

For each chord in the following phrases, label:

- The roman numeral (I, i, or V)
- Whether the chord is in close position (C) or open position (O)
- Which note is doubled—circle it and indicate whether it is the root, third, or fifth (R, 3, 5)

Then, transcribe each phrase in the space provided. Preserve the exact register of each voice.

1. Chorale style:

Transcribe the phrase above for string quartet in open score.

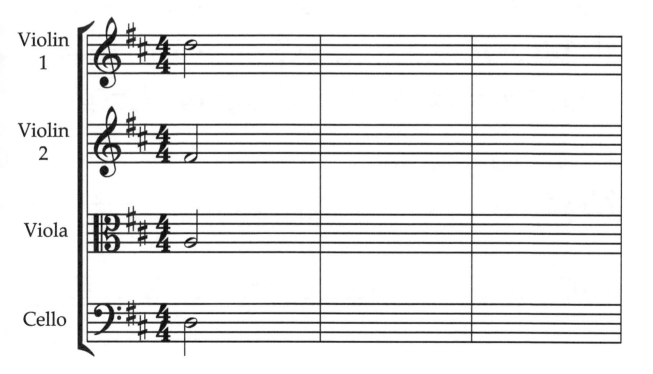

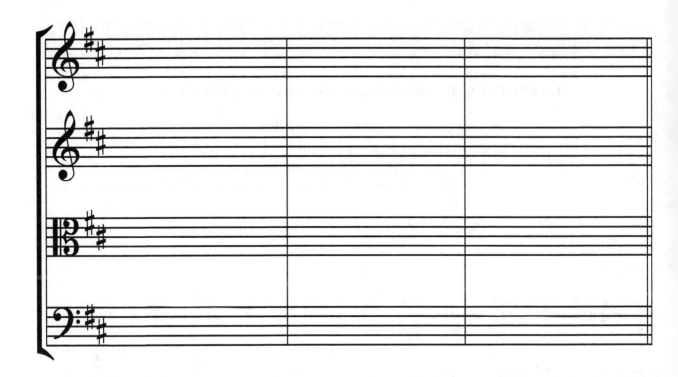

2. String quartet in open score:

Transcribe the phrase above in chorale style.

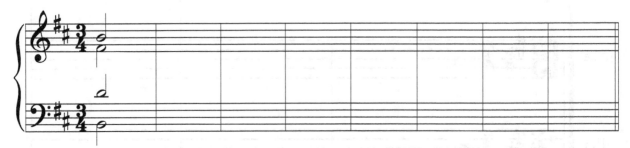

EXERCISE 5-F   *Writing Cadences*

Using only tonic and dominant triads in root position, write each cadence. Follow these four steps:

- Add the appropriate key signature.
- Write the two roman numerals.
- Write the two outer voices.
- Add the two inner voices.

A model of each texture is provided. Use that same texture in your realizations.

1. Write in keyboard style. Play what you write.

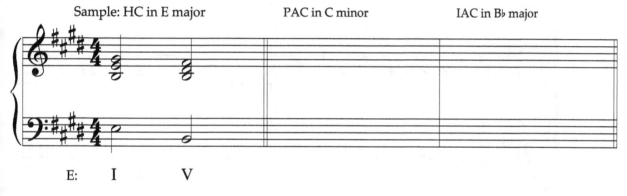

2. Write in chorale style. Play what you write.

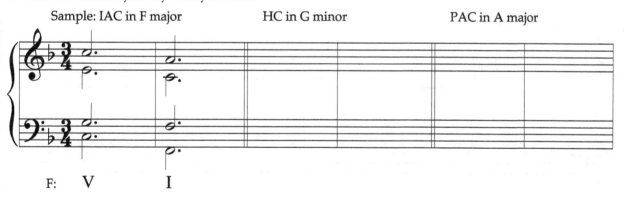

3. Write in the figurated texture modeled in the sample (for string quartet).

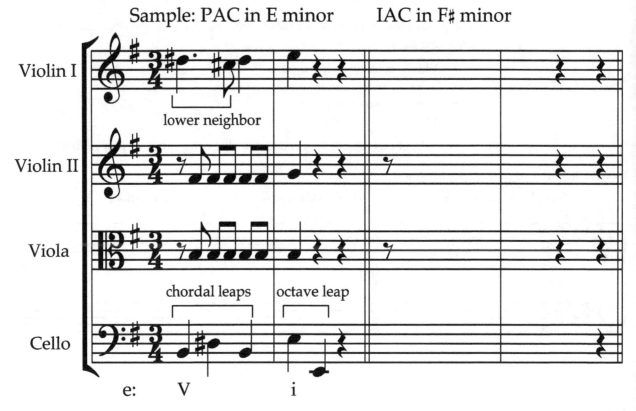

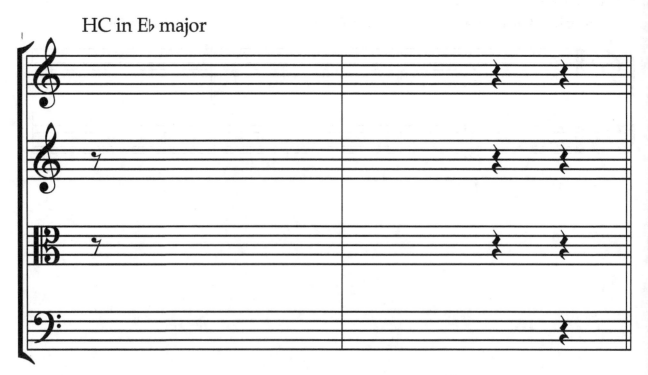

ASSIGNMENT 5.3

EXERCISE 5–G   *Analyzing Tonic and Dominant Chords*

In this passage by Charles Ignatius Sancho, from *Minuets for the Violin, Mandolin, German Flute, and Harpsichord*, Book 2 (1769), label the key, any cadences, and the roman numeral for each chord.

EXERCISE 5–H   *Detecting and Correcting Errors*

Each authentic or half cadence that follows contains either one or two errors. Do the following:

- Label the key, the roman numerals, and the cadence type (PAC, IAC, or HC).
- Play the cadence to check aurally for errors. There are two types of errors:

Chord Construction	Voice Leading
missing member of the chord	parallel perfect consonances
incorrect spacing	unresolved leading tone in an outer voice
doubling of a tone other than the root	direct fifth or octave between outer voices
	voice overlap

- Mark each error and rewrite a corrected version in the space provided. Change only what is necessary to correct the error.
- Play the corrected version to double-check your work aurally.

Keyboard style:

Chorale style:

EXERCISE 5-1   *Filling in Missing Voices*

The root-position tonic and dominant triads below are missing voices. Label the key and roman numerals. Then, fill in the missing voices to complete the four-voice texture.

1. *SATB choir in open score.* Note that the tenor voice sounds an octave lower than where it appears
   in treble clef.

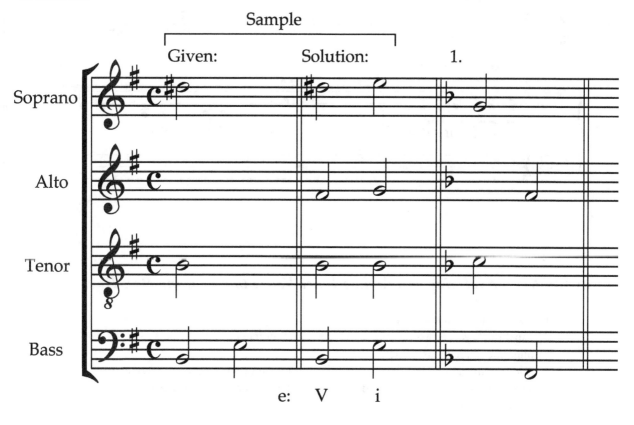

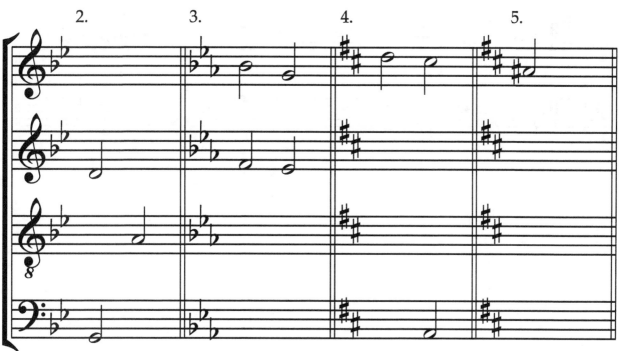

2. *Voice with piano accompaniment:*

EXERCISE 5-J   *Analyzing and Adding Inner Voices to a Soprano-Bass Duet*

1. Play the given duet on keyboard.
2. Label the key, the two cadences, and the roman numerals. Use the bass to determine the implied harmonies.
3. Add two inner voices to the right hand to create a four-voice version in keyboard style. The first chord is provided as a sample. Do not harmonize the parenthesized passing tones.

ASSIGNMENT 5.4

EXERCISE 5–K   *Detecting and Correcting Errors*

- Label the key of each incorrectly written authentic cadence.
- Play each cadence on keyboard to notice spelling and doubling errors aurally. Each chord should be in root position, complete, and with a doubled root.
- Label each error as shown in the model.
- Rewrite a corrected version in the space provided. Change only what is necessary to correct the error.
- Play the corrected version to double-check your work aurally.

Model:

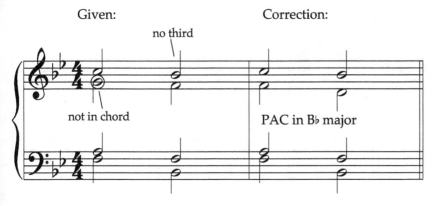

Keyboard style:

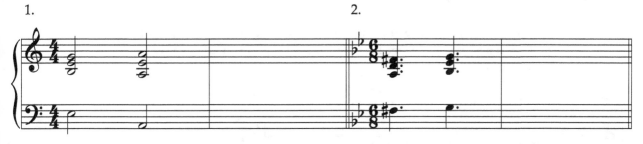

Chorale style:

Figurated textures (begin by locating each of the four voices):

5.

6.

EXERCISE 5-L   *Realizing Figured Basses*

Label the key and roman numerals. Then, realize each figured bass in keyboard style. When the bass note repeats, change the right-hand voicing. Use mostly stepwise motion in the soprano voice.

EXERCISE 5–M   *Accompanying a Given Melody*

- Label the key and harmonize the melody by adding a roman numeral (either I, i, or V) for each melody note.
- Realize your harmonization as a four-voice accompaniment that continues the given pattern. *Hint: The highest voice of your accompaniment will consist of the same pitches as the given melody.*
- Play your accompaniment on keyboard while singing the given melody.

EXERCISE 5–N   *Analyzing Tonic and Dominant Chords*

Use a roman numeral to label each chord in the *Thema* of Josepha Barbara Auernhammer's (1758–1820) *Ten Variations*, op. 63.

ASSIGNMENT 5.5

EXERCISE 5-O   *Detecting and Correcting Errors in a Longer Passage*

When writing in four voices, common errors fall into two categories: (1) errors in how chords are constructed, and (2) errors in how chords are connected to each other.

Chord Construction Errors	Chord Connection (or Voice Leading) Errors
• incomplete chord (IC) • $\hat{7}$ not raised in minor (LT) • voice crossing (VC) • doubled leading tone (DLT) • misspelled chord (MS) • incorrect doubling (ID) • spacing error (SP)	• parallel perfect octaves (//8) or perfect fifths (//5) • contrary (or "antiparallel") octaves (C8) or perfect fifths (C5) • leap of a diminished, augmented, or large interval (L) • unresolved leading tone in an outer voice (ULT)

Here is a sample. Play through it and see whether you can notice each of the errors that are marked.

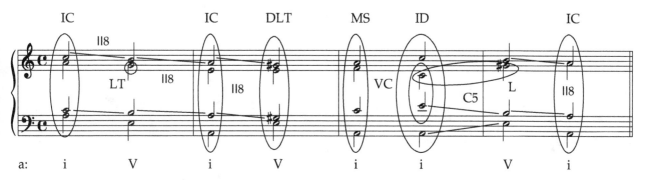

Play the following passage on keyboard, grabbing the three upper voices with your right hand except in the last two chords. Then, label the key, analyze with roman numerals, and mark all instances of the errors listed above.

Next, write a corrected version. Preserve the entire bass voice and all soprano pitches except the last one. A starting point for your revision is provided below. Play your correction.

EXERCISE 5-P   *Analyzing and Reducing Passages*

1. Arcangelo Corelli, Concerto Grosso in G minor ("Christmas"), op. 6, no. 8 (c. 1690), *Vivace*

   a. Label the key and the roman numerals. *Hint: Do not trust the key signatures.*
   b. For each measure, circle one primary tone in the soprano line and one primary tone in the bass line. Your chosen soprano pitches must form a stepwise line (repeated pitches are okay) and must form strong counterpoint with the bass.
   c. Create a keyboard reduction of the passage using the circled tones as your outer voices. Fill in alto and tenor voices in keyboard style in the right hand. The first measure is done for you.

Passage:

Keyboard reduction (follow the given rhythm):

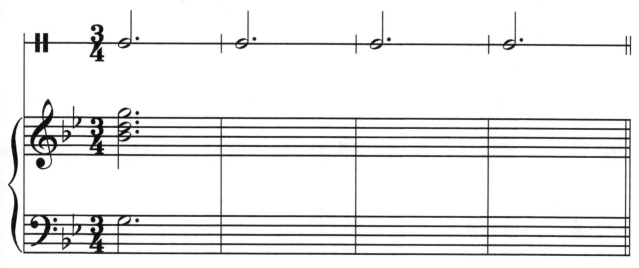

2. Arcangelo Corelli, Sonata, op. 1, no. 9 (1681), *Allegro*. Label the key, the roman numerals, and any cadences.

EXERCISE 5-Q   *Writing in Keyboard Style*

Write a four-voice progression in keyboard style using each of the prompts below. Use only root-position tonic (I/i) and dominant (V) triads. Label keys, cadence types, and roman numerals.

1. Write a passing soprano line.

2. Harmonize a neighboring soprano line.

3. Add upper voices to a bass.

4. Realize a progression of roman numerals.

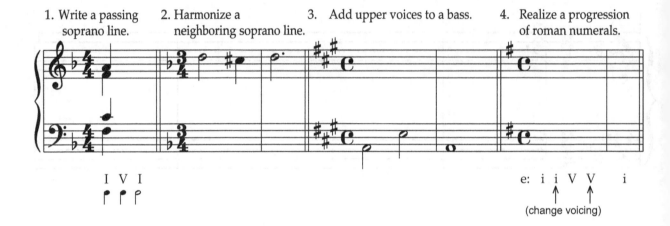

ASSIGNMENT 5.6

EXERCISE 5-R   *Writing in Chorale Style*

Write a four-voice progression in chorale style using each of the prompts below. Use only root-position tonic (I/i) and dominant (V) triads. Label keys, cadence types, and roman numerals. Add the necessary key signature for Part 2.

1. Add upper voices to a bass.   2.   Realize a progression of roman numerals.

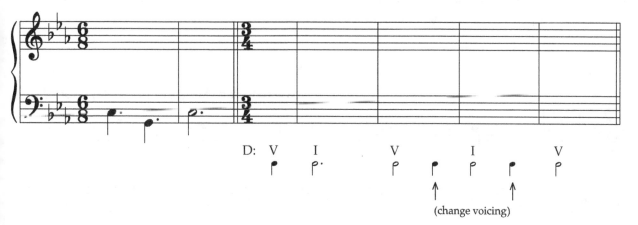

EXERCISE 5-S   *Harmonizing Short Melodies*

At a keyboard, harmonize each soprano melody using only I/i and V in root position. Follow the texture given in the model: a sustained bass in the left hand, and three-note broken chords in the right hand. Work in this order:

- Label the key and cadence type.
- Add a bass and roman numerals.
- Add inner voices.
- Sing the melody while playing your harmonization.

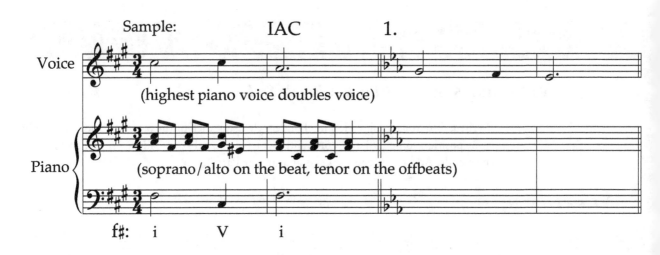

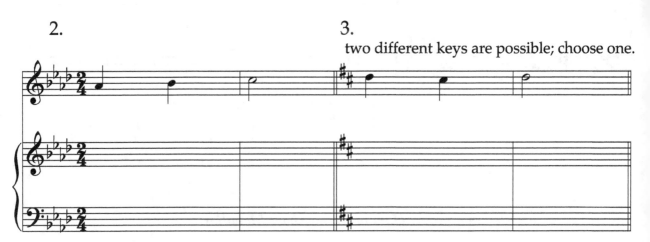

EXERCISE 5-T *Harmonizing Melodies in a Variety of Keyboard Textures*

Below, the same melody is harmonized in keyboard style and then in three different figurated textures.

Model: harmonize $\hat{5}$–$\hat{5}$–$\hat{3}$–$\hat{2}$–$\hat{3}$ (IAC) in A major

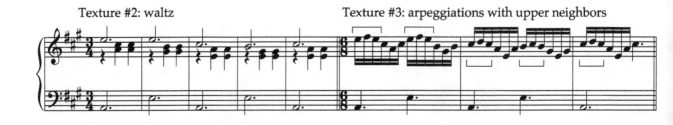

- Determine a suitable bass line and roman numerals for each melody. Use only tonic (I/i) and dominant (V) triads in root position.
- Add inner voices.
- Realize each harmonization in keyboard style and then in the specified texture.
- Play the result.

1. Harmonize 3̂–2̂–1̂–7̂–1̂ (PAC) in D minor, in keyboard style and then in texture #1 (arpeggiations).

2. Harmonize 1̂–7̂–1̂–2̂–3̂ (IAC) in E major, in keyboard style and then in texture #2 (waltz).

3. Harmonize $\hat{1}$–$\hat{2}$–$\hat{3}$–$\hat{2}$ (HC) in E minor, in keyboard style and then in texture #3 (arpeggiation with neighbors).

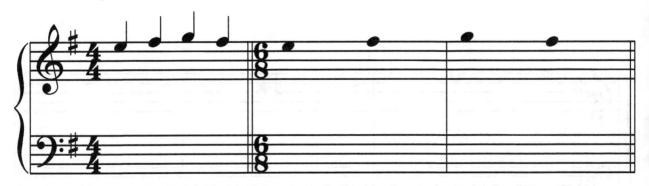

CHAPTER 6

V^7 and Two-Level Analysis

ASSIGNMENT 6.1

EXERCISE 6–A *Playing Chordal Sevenths and Their Resolutions*

1. In **two** voices, play and write the resolution of the chordal seventh in the upper voice. Analyze, using the key signature to determine whether the key is major or minor.

2. In **four** voices, play and write the resolution of each V^7 chord to its tonic triad (I or i). Resolve the chordal seventh *downward* by step in the same voice. Resolve the leading tone *upward* by step when it is in the soprano. Analyze.

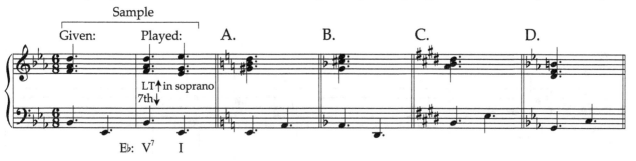

EXERCISE 6–B *Detecting and Correcting Errors*

First, label the key and add roman numerals. Next, mark the error(s) in each progression. Observe the treatment of chordal sevenths and leading tones. Finally, rewrite a corrected version in the space provided.

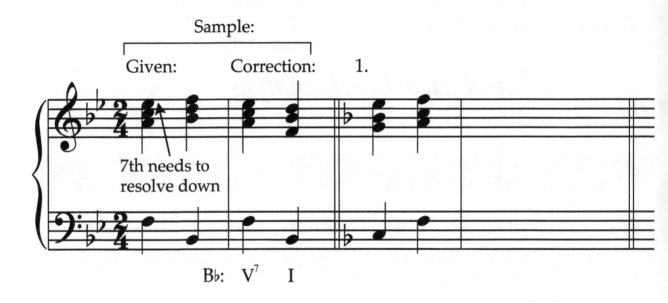

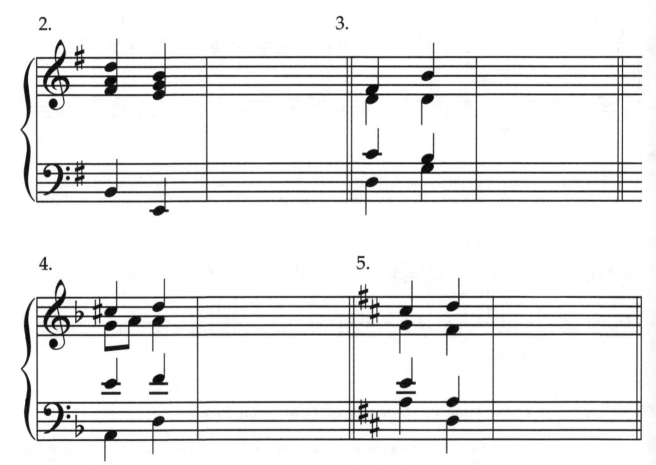

EXERCISE 6-C   *Analyzing V⁷ Chords in Context*

Label the key and add roman numerals. Make sure that you distinguish between V and V⁷.

1. George Frideric Handel, Violin Sonata in F major, no. 3, HWV 370 (1730), *Allegro*

After you analyze, write a harmonic reduction in half notes in keyboard style:

- The boxed pitches in the score above will be the outer voices.
- Follow the rhythm shown above the grand staff.
- Play your reduction on keyboard and sing along with the slow, stepwise ascent in the soprano.

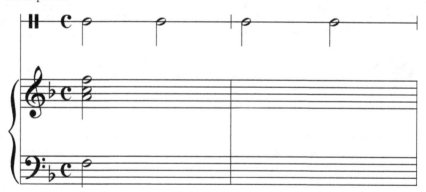

2. Franz Schubert, "Wiegenlied," op. 98, no. 2, D. 498 (1816)

Translation: Sleep, sleep, lovely, sweet boy. You are gently rocked by your mother's hand.

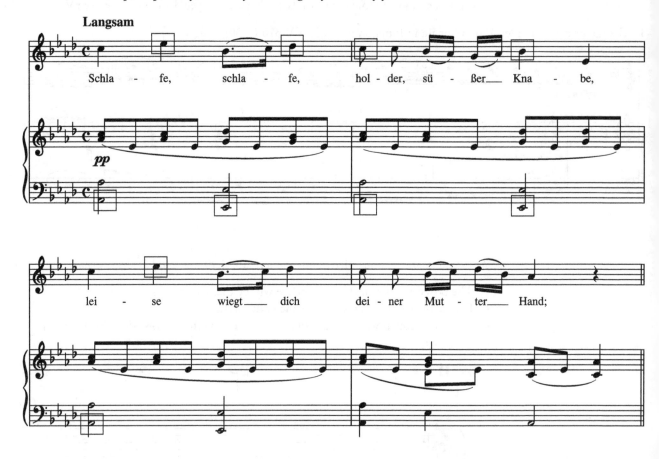

On the score above, add boxes to the remaining outer voices (in mm. 3–4). The upper voice will descend by step all the way to 1̂. Write your keyboard-style reduction following the template below, and play it.

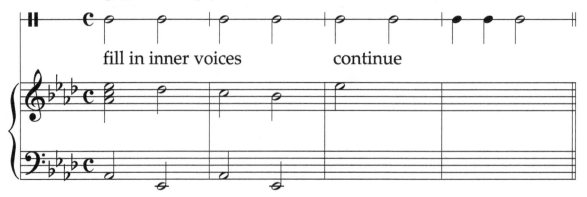

ASSIGNMENT 6.2

EXERCISE 6–D   *Playing and Resolving V^7 in Three Voices*

1. Label the key and roman numerals. Each progression consists of V^7 resolving to a tonic triad.
2. Add the missing voice(s) to create a V^7 chord in three voices. The stem direction will tell you which voice (if any) is given on the upper staff.
3. Resolve each V^7 to its tonic triad. It may be necessary to omit the fifth of either the V^7 chord or the tonic chord, replacing it with an additional root.
4. Play the progression to check for errors aurally.

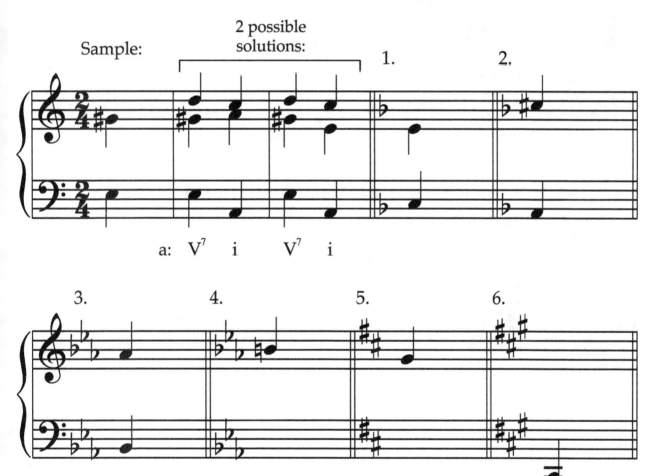

EXERCISE 6-E *Harmonizing Melodic Fragments*

First, harmonize each melody by writing a bass voice and roman numerals. Use I/i, V, and V^7 only. Then, following the sample texture, add the remaining voices.

1. The three upper voices will be in a broken-chord figuration. Your highest voice will double the given melody.

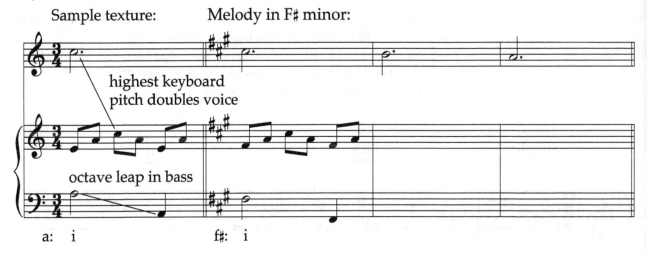

2. You will add the alto, tenor, and bass voices in the block-chord figuration shown in the sample.

EXERCISE 6–F   *Analyzing V^7 Chords in Context*

For each passage from the literature, label the key and cadence(s), and add roman numerals.

1. Josepha Barbara Auernhammer, Eight Variations for Harpsichord or Piano (1794)

2. Joseph W. Postlewaite, *Annie Polka Mazurka* (1854)

3. W. A. Mozart, Serenade in D major ("Posthorn"), K. 320 (1776), *Andante grazioso*

ASSIGNMENT 6.3

EXERCISE 6–G   *Writing Cadences for String Quartet*

First, label the key and roman numerals. Each progression consists of V[7] resolving to a tonic triad. Next, fill in the missing voices, ensuring that tendency tones resolve properly and that spacing and voice leading are strong. It may be necessary to omit the fifth of either the V[7] chord or the tonic chord, replacing it with an additional root. Finally, label each chord as either complete (C) or incomplete (I).

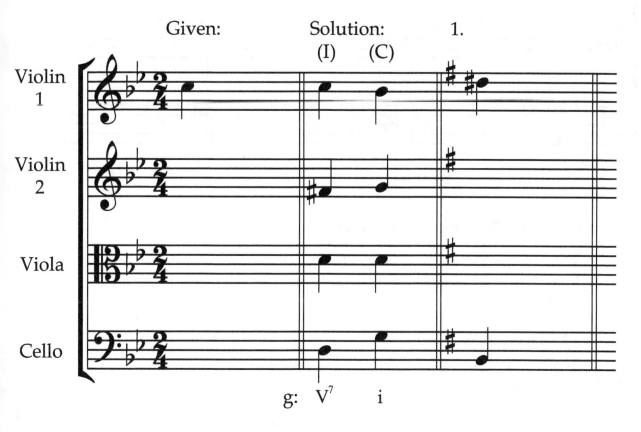

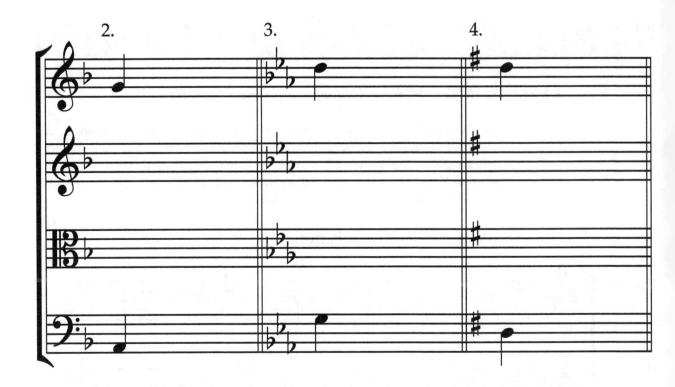

EXERCISE 6–H   *Realizing Figured Basses*

Realize the figured basses in four voices. The soprano should move mostly stepwise, but not become overly repetitive. Sing along with the soprano as you work to ensure the quality of the line. Analyze on two levels.

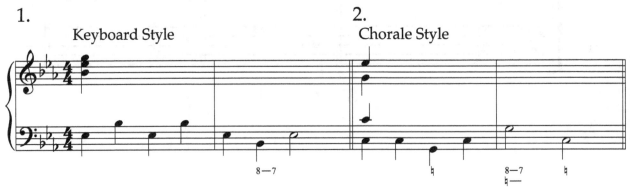

EXERCISE 6-I   *Analyzing Repertoire on Two Levels*

Analyze the passage from Emma Hartmann's (1807–1851) *Klaverstykker*, no. 1 on two levels. Label any cadences.

EXERCISE 6-J   *Writing Short Progressions with V⁷*

Two different figurations for voice and piano are modeled below. Realize the specified chord progressions and soprano motions in the assigned textures. Head starts are provided for you.

Texture A	Texture B
piano: keyboard style, sustained bass notes with repeated chords	*piano:* open spacing, arpeggiations from bass to soprano and back to bass within each chord
voice: structural pitches are embellished with double neighbors	*voice:* structural pitches are embellished with chordal leaps and passing motion
meter: $\frac{4}{4}$	*meter:* $\frac{12}{8}$
harmonic rhythm: two chords per measure	*harmonic rhythm:* one chord per measure

Texture A:

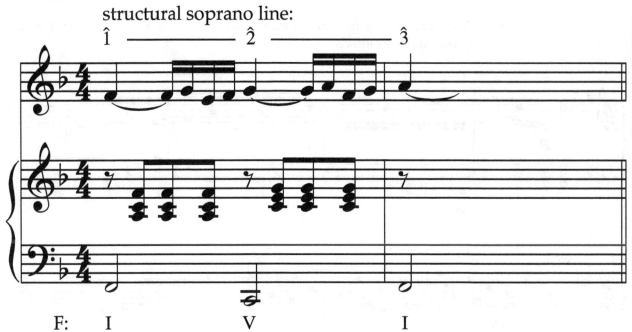

Texture B:

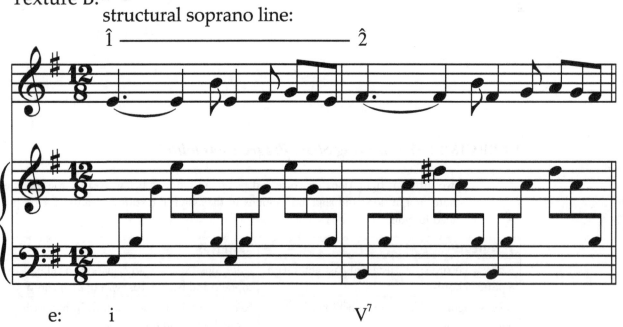

1. Write I–V⁷–I (or i–V⁷–i) with $\hat{3}$–$\hat{2}$–$\hat{1}$ as a structural soprano.

in D major with Texture A

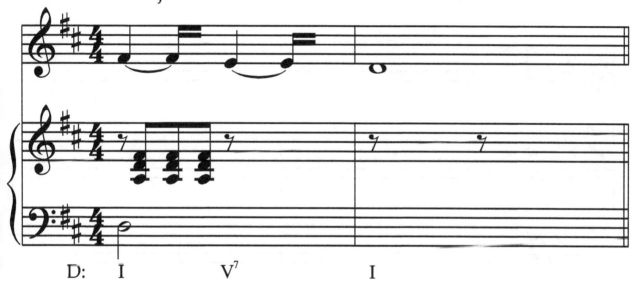

and in G minor with Texture B

2. Write I–V^7–I (or i–V^7–i) with $\hat{3}$–$\hat{4}$–$\hat{3}$ as a structural soprano.

in C minor with Texture A

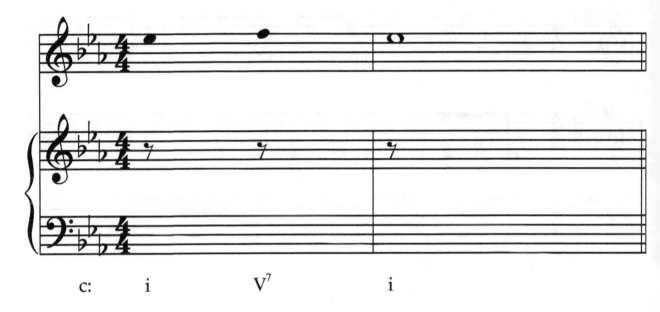

and in E major with Texture B

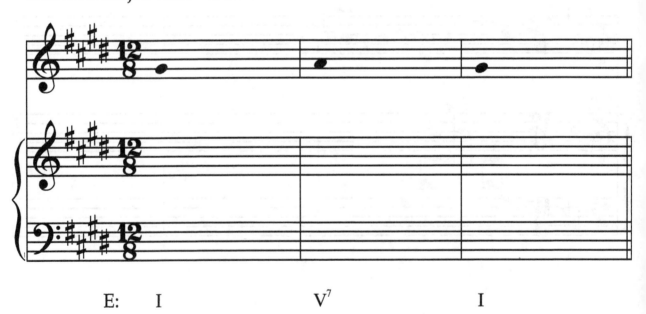

ASSIGNMENT 6.4

EXERCISE 6–K   *Analyzing and Reducing Passages*

Analyze the following passages on two levels. After analyzing passages 1–3, play a three-chord harmonic reduction in keyboard style using the boxed pitches as the outer voices.

1. W. A. Mozart, Symphony no. 22 in C major, K. 162 (1773), *Allegro assai*. Sing the first oboe part while you play your reduction.

2. W. A. Mozart, String Quartet in A major, K. 464 (1785), *Allegro*. Sing the first violin part while you play your reduction.

3. Isaac Hazzard, "Davis Quick Step" (1843). Sing the uppermost voice of the original passage as you play your reduction.

4. Ignacio Álvarez (1837–1888), *El canto de la tarde*. Do not be deceived by the key signature. What key is this passage in?

EXERCISE 6-L   *Detecting and Correcting Errors*

Each short progression contains one or more errors in chord construction (spelling, spacing, doubling) and/or voice leading (resolution of chordal seventh and leading tone, parallel perfect consonances). First, label the key and roman numerals. Next, play the example to detect errors aurally. You may need to play the tenor voice with the right hand. Then, circle and label each error. Finally, rewrite a corrected version in the space provided. Play your revision to check your work.

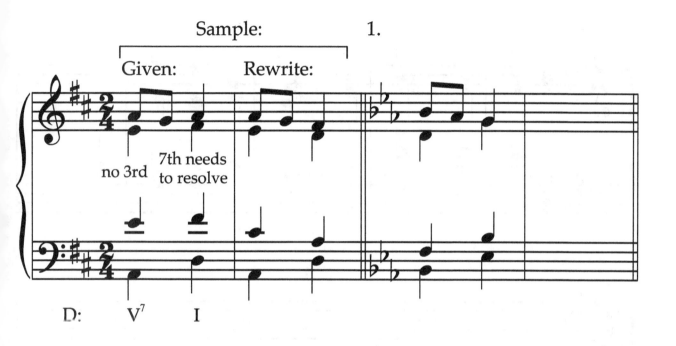

Sample: 1.

Given: Rewrite:

no 3rd   7th needs
          to resolve

D: V⁷   I

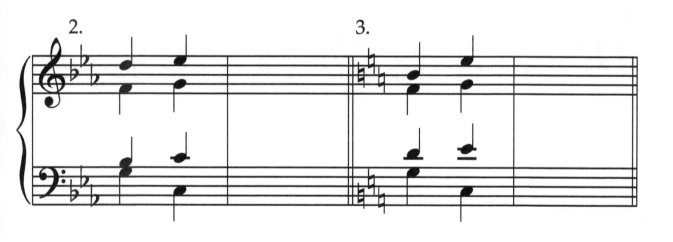

2.   3.

4.   5.

6.

ASSIGNMENT 6.5

EXERCISE 6-M   *Writing Authentic Cadences from Figured Basses*

First, label the key and roman numerals. Next, using the provided head starts, write either a perfect authentic cadence (PAC) or an imperfect authentic cadence (IAC). When 8–7 appears in the figures, keep this passing chordal seventh within a single voice. Finally, label each cadence type.

Write in keyboard style.

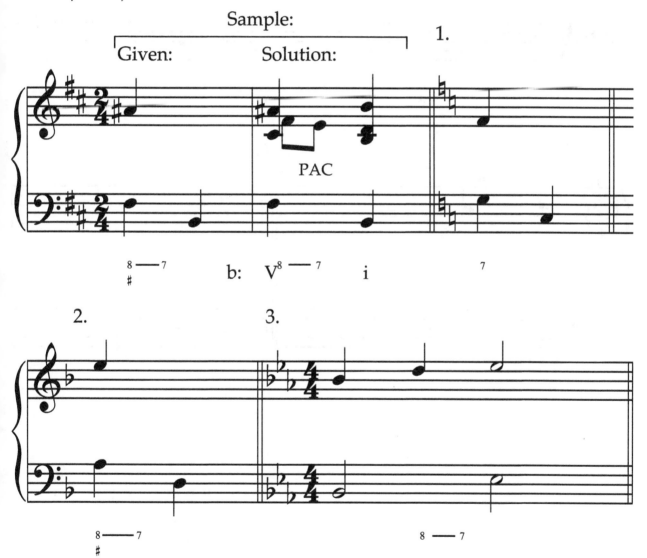

Write in chorale style.

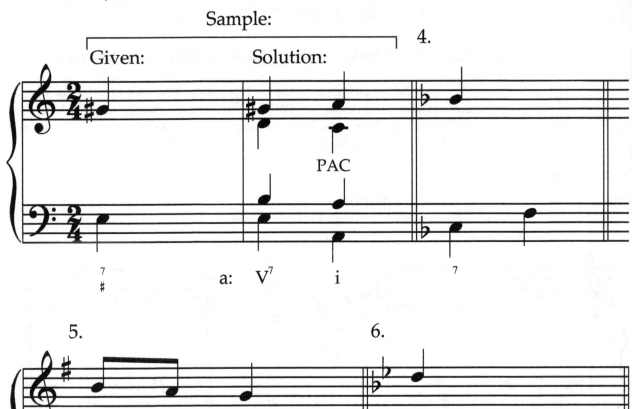

Create a figurated texture for solo keyboard. Following the model, add three upper voices in a broken-chord pattern, including a lower neighbor in the soprano voice.

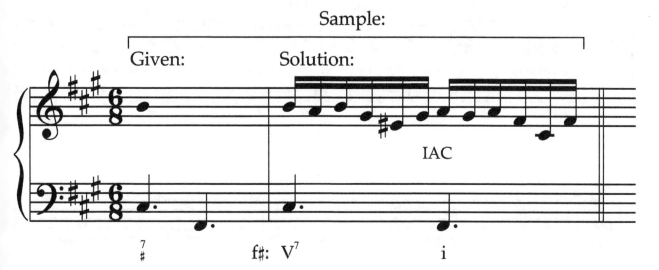

EXERCISE 6–N   *Composing an Accompaniment to a Melody*

Below are two melodies for clarinet, shown in concert pitch. Each melody is florid; embellishing tones (passing and neighboring tones, chordal leaps) have been added to a structural melodic line that moves mostly by step.

- a. Label the key and cadence type of each given melody.
- b. Circle the pitches that constitute the structural line. These will move at a mostly even pace, and mostly by step.
- c. Write roman numerals for a progression that harmonizes this structural line. Use I/i, V, and V⁷ only.
- d. Choose one of the four sample textures and realize your harmonies to create a piano accompaniment. Each texture includes four voices.

Model Keyboard Textures (all in four voices, all with the same voicing of I–V⁷–I in E♭ major):

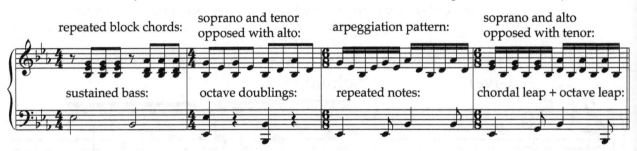

repeated block chords: soprano and tenor opposed with alto: arpeggiation pattern: soprano and alto opposed with tenor:

sustained bass: octave doublings: repeated notes: chordal leap + octave leap:

1.

3

2.

ASSIGNMENT 6.6

EXERCISE 6-O   *Harmonizing Melodic Fragments in Figurated Textures*

- Add a different key signature and time signature for each of the four soprano fragments below.
- Using only I/i, V, and V⁷, decide how to harmonize the given melody.
- Decide how long each harmony will last, add bar lines, and write the roman numerals in the corresponding places beneath the bottom staff.
- Realize your harmonization in a rhythmically active texture, following the guidelines in the sample below.

Sample. $\hat{3}-\hat{4}-\hat{3}$ **in F major**

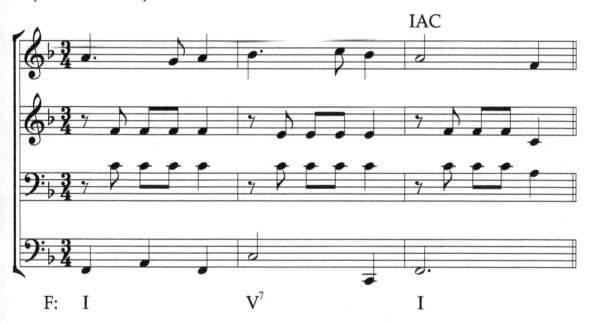

To create a more interesting texture, add embellishments to your realization, such as:

- **In the bass:** chordal leaps between root and third, octave leaps, and/or repeated notes
- **In the melody:** neighboring tones, chordal leaps, and/or passing tones to and from another chord tone
- **In the inner voices:** a combination of repeated notes and rests

Write for SATB choir.

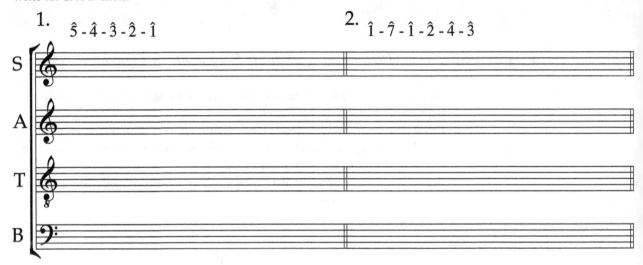

Write for brass quartet. Write all parts in concert pitch.

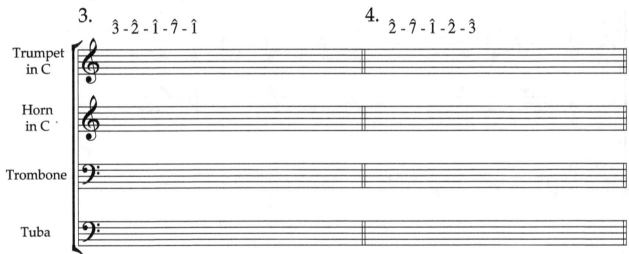

EXERCISE 6-P *Harmonizing Florid Melodies*

- Sing or play each melody to identify the key and any cadence(s). Label them.
- Study the leaps and metrically accented pitches. Leaps among $\hat{1}$, $\hat{3}$, and $\hat{5}$ demand tonic harmony, and leaps among $\hat{5}$, $\hat{7}$, $\hat{2}$, and $\hat{4}$ demand dominant harmony.
- Using only I/i, V, and V^7 in root position, harmonize each melody by adding roman numerals beneath the staff. Each harmony will last at least one measure, or may extend to multiple measures if the melody permits.
- Label each passing tone (PT) and each neighboring tone (NT).
- Play or sing the melody while playing the bass notes of your chosen harmonies on keyboard.

Sample. W. A. Mozart, "Longing for Spring," K. 596 (1796), *Giocoso*

1. Pauline Duchambge (1778–1858), "Le Matelot." The asterisked escape tones are not part of the harmony.

   Translation: The happy heart of a sailor sailing far from shore sang its tender fires.

Un Ma - te - lot   à - bord loin du ri - va - ge   le coeur con -tent chan - tait ses tend-res feux

2. W. A. Mozart, Symphony no. 39, K. 543 (1788), *Allegretto*

3. George Bridgetower, *Henry: A Ballad* (1812). The asterisked embellishing tones that are not part of the harmony.

4. Folk tune, *Andante grazioso*

EXERCISE 6-Q   *Analyzing V⁷ Chords in Context*

Analyze the passage from the Trio of Maria Szymanowska's *Six Menuets Pour le Piano-forte*, no. 5 (1819) on two levels. The beat with the *sforzando* does not introduce a new chord. Is there a melodic way of understanding what happens there? What's going on in the upper voice there? In the bass? Consider context.

CHAPTER 7

Expanding Tonic and Dominant with First-Inversion Triads

EXERCISE 7–A   *Analyzing First-Inversion Triads in Context*

The following passages contain tonic and/or dominant triads in first inversion. Analyze them on two levels.

Sample. Johann Adolph Hasse, Trio Sonata no. 1 in E minor for Two Flutes and Basso Continuo (1735), *Largo*

1. Lucy Broadwood (arranger), "I Will Give You the Keys of Heaven" (1893)

2. Lucy Broadwood (arranger), "The Nottinghamshire Poacher" (1893)

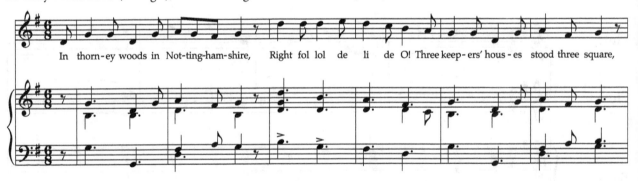

EXERCISE 7–B *Analyzing and Composing with First-Inversion Triads*

Analyze the passage from Fanny Hensel's *Six Melodies for the Piano*, op. 4, no. 3 (1847).
Then, using what you know about the chord in m. 2, compose the next measure of music
(a single chord), continuing the figuration and texture of the first two measures.

Allegro molto quasi Presto

EXERCISE 7-C   *Playing Neutral Position at the Keyboard*

In keyboard style, neutral position is when the right hand has *no chordal third*. It can have either two roots (2R) or two fifths (2F) in either open (O) or close (C) position. Neutral position is common in I⁶, i⁶, and V⁶, but not in vii°⁶.

Step 1: Play each prolongation below while singing along with the soprano voice.

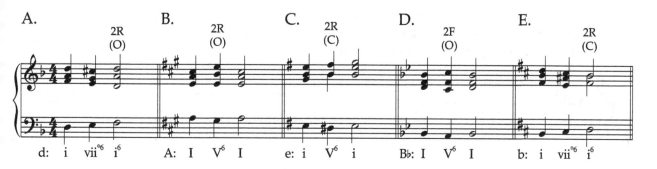

Step 2: For each of the five progressions below, write the letter (A through E) of the progression from Step 1 that has the same outer voices. Then, analyze on two levels and add inner voices modeled after the illustrations in Step 1, using a neutral position at each asterisk (*). Chord choices are I/i, I⁶/i⁶, V, V⁶, and vii°⁶.

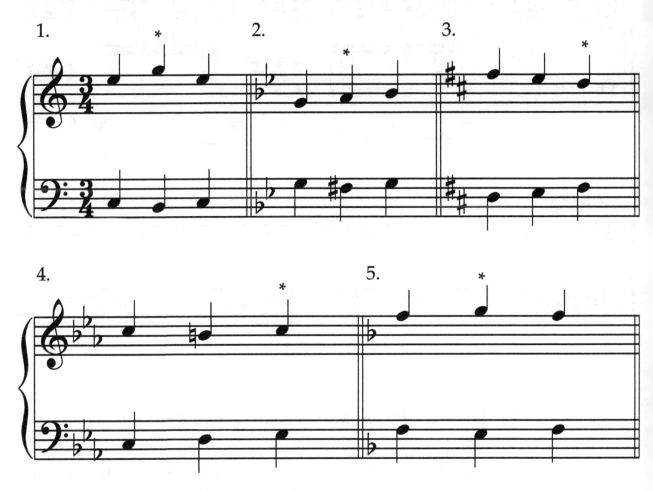

EXERCISE 7-D   *Realizing a Figured Bass in Keyboard Style*

Analyze the figured bass on two levels and realize it in keyboard style. Use neutral position for first-inversion tonic and dominant triads. Aim for a mostly stepwise soprano that creates strong counterpoint with the bass.

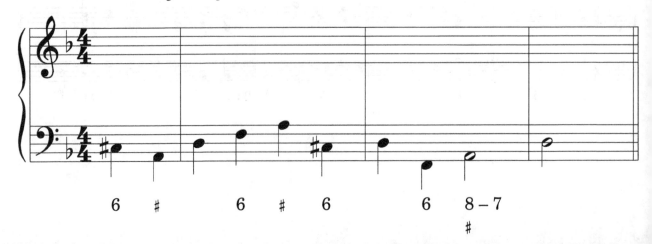

ASSIGNMENT 7.2

EXERCISE 7–E   *Analyzing First-Inversion Triads in Context*

Each passage contains a mix of first-inversion triads. Analyze on two levels.

1. Mary Gossell, Suite no. 1 in E major (2017), *Menuet I*

2. Ludwig van Beethoven, "Freudvoll und leidvoll" ("Joyful and Sorrowful"), op. 84, no. 4 (1810). Perform it yourself: sing the melody while playing the piano part, omitting octave doublings in the bass if you need to.

   Translation: Full of joy, and full of sorrow, full of thoughts.

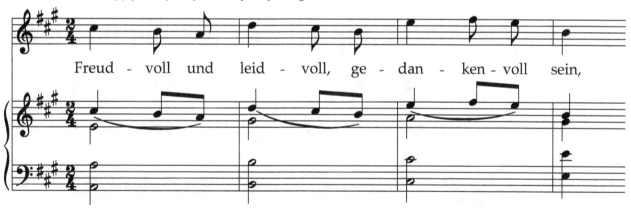

3. Marianna Martines, Piano Sonata in A major (1765), *Adagio*

4. W. A. Mozart, Piano Sonata in F major, K. 280 (1774), *Allegro assai*

EXERCISE 7–F   *Analyzing and Reducing a Passage*

First, listen to this passage and analyze it on two levels. Next, write and play a keyboard-style reduction using the highest staff of the template to guide you as to when to change chords. Keeping melodic fluency in mind, decide which pitch follows the G^5 that begins the piece in the violins.

Antonio Vivaldi (1678–1741), Concerto Grosso in G major, op. 9, no. 10, *Allegro molto*

Reduction (fill in and play):

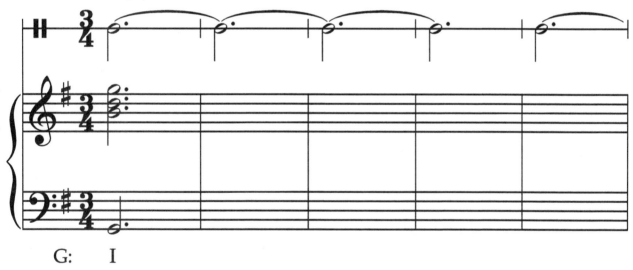

G: I

6

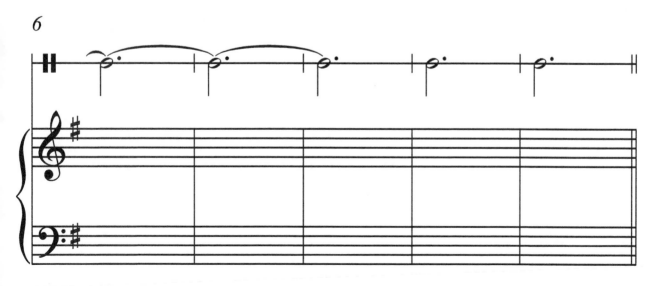

ASSIGNMENT 7.3

EXERCISE 7-G   *Composing with Harmonic Progressions*

Write as instructed and analyze on two levels. Try to play each example, however slowly.

1. In chorale style, set the progression I–vii°⁶–I⁶ three times in D major, each in a different meter and with a different soprano melody. Choose rhythmic values that make the progression last two measures each time.

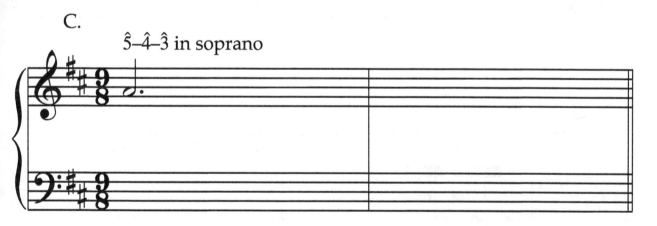

2. Set the progression i–vii°6–i6–V6–i–V7–i in D minor, adding as many bar lines as you need. Maintain the given figuration: octave leaps in the bass, and broken chords in the three upper voices with lower neighbors in soprano.

3. Set the same progression, i–vii°6–i6–V6–i–V7–i, but now in a different meter, key, and figuration, as shown below. There are now two voices per staff, and the alto voice includes lower neighbors.

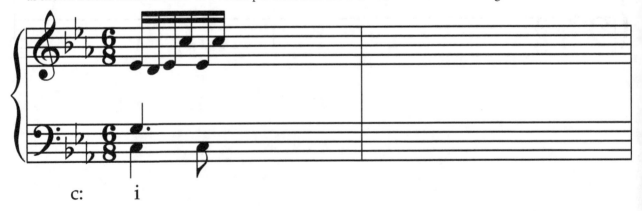

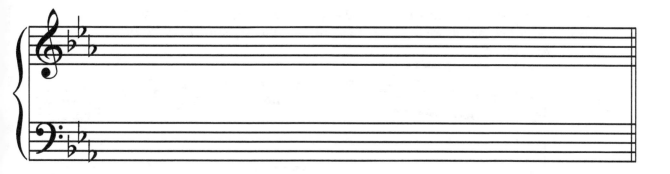

EXERCISE 7-H   *Analyzing First-Inversion Triads in Context*

Analyze each example on two levels.

1. J. S. Bach (1685–1750), "Herzliebster Jesu, was hast du verbrochen," BWV 244–3; "Als vierzig Tag' nach Ostern," BWV 266; "Das heiligen Geistes reiche Gnad," BWV 295.

2. Giuseppe Verdi, "Au sein de la puissance" from *Les Vêpres Siciliennes* (1855), Act 3. Perform it yourself: sing the melody while playing the accompaniment on piano, omitting the octave doublings in the bass if necessary.

Translation: Within the power, within the greatness.

3. C. P. E. Bach, Sonata no. 5 in A minor for Flute and Keyboard, Wq. 128, H.555 (1740). Perform it yourself: sing the flute melody while playing the continuo part on keyboard. *Hint: Do not be fooled by the key signature.*

EXERCISE 7-1   *Filling in the Blanks in Keyboard Style*

First, play each given outer-voice duet on piano to determine which harmonies are implied. Next, label the key and cadence(s) and analyze on two levels. Finally, add two inner voices to the upper staff to create a realization in keyboard style. Use neutral position for first-inversion tonic and dominant triads.

1.

2.

ASSIGNMENT 7.4

EXERCISE 7–J   *Dovetailing Short Paradigms into Longer Units*

In woodworking, a dovetailed joint overlaps two boards to connect them more strongly than if only their edges were to touch. In the exercises below, the third chord of a five-chord progression is the dovetailed joint: it is the end of the first three-chord paradigm and also the beginning of the second one.

First, play each three-chord paradigm on its own. Next, using the scale degrees of the five-note melody as a guide, decide which order the two paradigms need to be in and dovetail them to create a five-chord progression in keyboard style. Keep in mind that the melody is not in the same key as the model paradigms. Finally, notate and play the result, and analyze on two levels.

Sample:

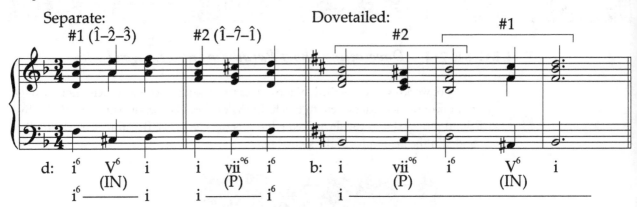

1.

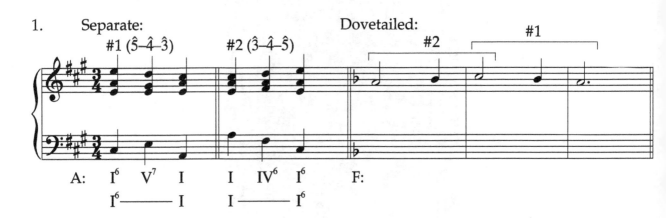

2.

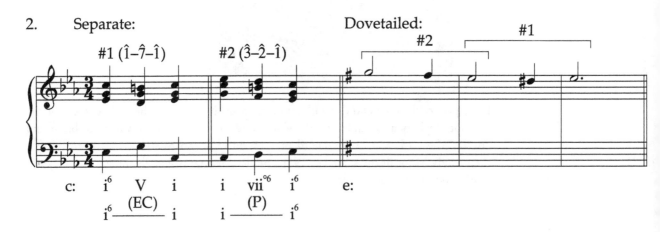

3.   Separate: Dovetailed:

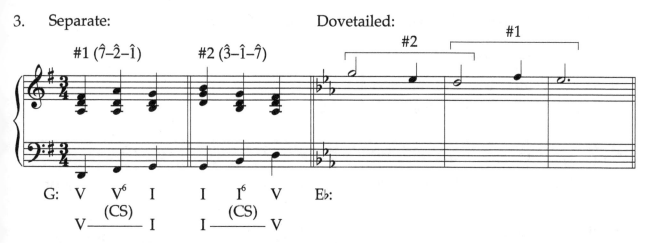

EXERCISE 7–K   *Harmonizing a Melody in Chorale Style*

Harmonize the given melody in chorale style with one chord per melody note. Work in this order:

1. Sing or play the melody to identify opportunities to employ the following short paradigms:
   - voice exchange between i and i⁶ (with or without a passing harmony in between)
   - outer-voice tenths on i and i⁶ with the bass descending the long way ($\hat{1}$–$\hat{6}$–$\hat{3}$)
   - dominant expansion (V–V⁶) with parallel tenths in the soprano ($\hat{7}$–$\hat{2}$)
2. Bracket and label these paradigms above the melody.
3. Add a bass line and a two-level analysis. Create strong soprano-bass counterpoint, keeping in mind that $\hat{1}$ and $\hat{3}$ are often each other's best match, forming a tenth or a sixth.
4. Fill in the inner voices in chorale style.

EXERCISE 7-L   *Analyzing First-Inversion Triads in Context*

Analyze on two levels.

1. Rosa Giacinta Badalla (1660–1710), Aria from *Vuò cercando*

   Translation: If the Dawn of Roses still blooms, do not disdain.

2. Marianna Auenbrugger (1759–1782), Sonata for Harpsichord or Fortepiano in E♭ major,
   Moderato

ASSIGNMENT 7.5

EXERCISE 7–M   *Matching and Composing with Short Progressions*

1. Draw lines to match each harmonic progression (in the left column) with the soprano scale-degree pattern that it can harmonize (in the right column).

Harmonies:	Soprano Scale Degrees:
1. I–V⁷–I	A. $\hat{3}$–$\hat{4}$–$\hat{5}$–$\hat{4}$–$\hat{3}$
2. I–I⁶–V⁷–I	B. $\hat{5}$–$\hat{5}$–$\hat{4}$–$\hat{2}$–$\hat{1}$
3. I–V–V⁶–I	C. $\hat{3}$–$\hat{2}$–$\hat{1}$–$\hat{7}$–$\hat{1}$
4. I–V⁶–I–V⁷–I	D. $\hat{1}$–$\hat{2}$–$\hat{3}$
5. I–vii°⁶–I⁶–V⁷–I	E. $\hat{3}$–$\hat{2}$–$\hat{5}$–$\hat{3}$
6. I–IV⁶–I⁶–V⁷–I	F. $\hat{3}$–$\hat{1}$–$\hat{7}$–$\hat{1}$
7. I–V–IV⁶–V⁶–I	G. $\hat{1}$–$\hat{2}$–$\hat{3}$–$\hat{2}$–$\hat{1}$
8. I⁶–V⁶–I	H. $\hat{1}$–$\hat{7}$–$\hat{1}$

2. Choose three of the matching pairs and put them in order to create a longer phrase that closes with an authentic cadence.
3. Realize the complete progression in a key and meter of your choice, using one of the sample textures below.
4. Analyze on two levels.

Sample Texture A	Sample Texture B
Voice: passing tones + chordal leaps	*Voice:* chordal leaps + lower neighbors
Right Hand: broken chords with lower neighbors in alto	*Right Hand:* repeated block chords
Bass: repeated notes	*Bass:* passing tones between root and third (*not* fifth)

Texture A: Texture B:

Your Composition:

EXERCISE 7-N   *Realizing a Figured Bass in Keyboard Style*

1. Analyze the figured bass on two levels.
2. Bracket the following three-chord paradigms and use them to fill in some soprano pitches:
   - voice exchange with a passing chord in the middle (two instances of this paradigm)
   - $\hat{3}$–$\hat{4}$–$\hat{5}$ in soprano with bass descending the long way ($\hat{1}$–$\hat{6}$–$\hat{3}$)
3. Fill in the rest of the soprano line, ensuring strong counterpoint with the bass.
4. Add the inner voices in keyboard style, using neutral position for each i⁶ and V⁶ chord.

EXERCISE 7–O   *Completing a Fragment*

Someone began this piece, but left it for you to finish. (The nerve!) Work in this order:

1. Decide which harmonies are implied by the bass line, and analyze it on two levels.
2. Bracket any harmonic paradigms that you find.
3. Sketch a soprano line that moves at the same rate as the bass. Use the three-note paradigms to help you select soprano pitches that form strong counterpoint with the bass.
4. Write the two inner voices, continuing the broken-chord figuration that is started.
5. Embellish your skeletal soprano line to create a florid melody. Employ passing tones, neighboring tones, and chordal leaps. Your melody will consist of quarter notes, eighth notes, and, if you wish, a few sixteenth notes.

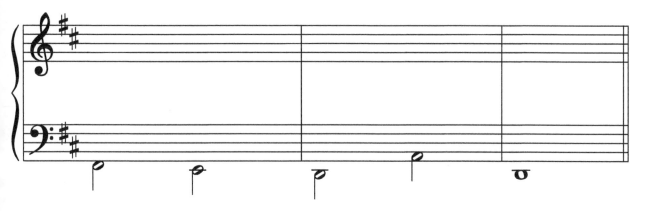

CHAPTER 8

Inversions of V⁷ and Leading-Tone Seventh Chords

ASSIGNMENT 8.1

EXERCISE 8–A   *Analyzing Inversions of V⁷*

In the following excerpts, the tonic is expanded with inversions of V⁷. Analyze on two levels.

1. Anna Amalia of Brunswick-Wolfenbüttel, "Das Veilchen" (1776)

Translation: "Oh!", thinks the violet. "If only I were the most beautiful flower in nature. Alas, just a little"

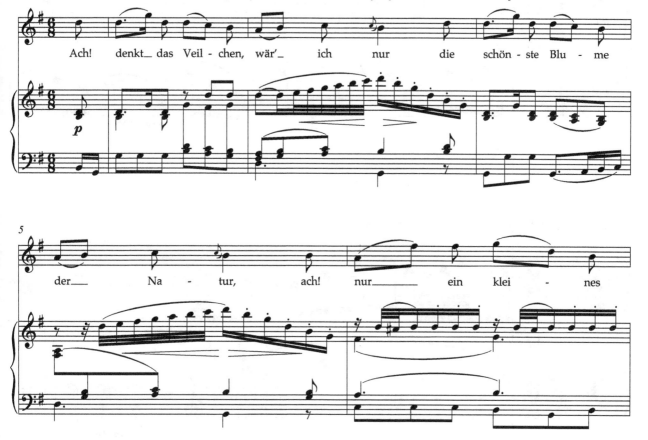

2. Henry Thacker Burleigh, "Till I Wake" (1915)

When I am dy - ing, lean o - ver me_____ ten-der-ly,

3. W. A. Mozart, Sonata in C major, K. 279 (1774), *Andante*

4. W. A. Mozart, Sonata in D major, K. 576 (1789), *Adagio*

5. Thomas Wiggins, *Sewing Song* (1889)

6. Fanny Hensel, Piano Trio, op. 11 (1847), *Allegro molto vivace*. Decide first which instrument is playing the bass voice.

7. W. A. Mozart, Sonata in F major, K. 547a (1788)

Var. IVa

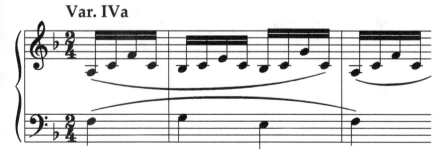

EXERCISE 8–B   *Transposing Short Paradigms*

Each short paradigm below illustrates a common usage of one inversion of V^7. Play each paradigm as written and then transposed to the two keys indicated. *Hint: Transpose just the two outer voices first, then the full chords.*

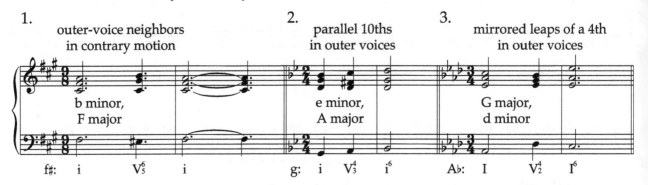

EXERCISE 8–C   *Realizing a Figured Bass in Keyboard Style*

First, analyze the figured bass on two levels. Next, bracket all three-chord paradigms that you notice. Two paradigms often overlap (or dovetail), with a single chord acting as the end of one paradigm *and* the beginning of the next one. Then, add a soprano voice, using the paradigms to guide you. Finally, add inner voices to the upper staff to create a keyboard-style realization.

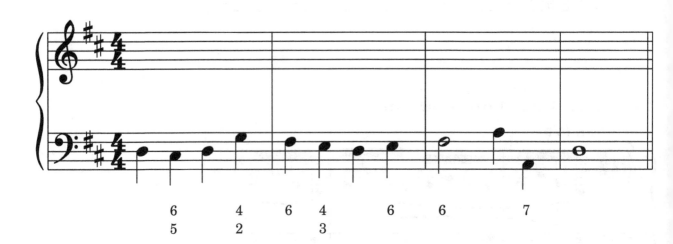

ASSIGNMENT 8.2

EXERCISE 8-D   *Completing Dominant Seventh Chords*

Three notes of a dominant seventh chord are provided. First, determine the root of the dominant seventh chord and write the name of the key in which it acts as V. Next, add the missing member of the chord to the upper staff to create a complete chord in keyboard style. Then, write the roman numeral and figured bass underneath each chord. Finally, play the chord on keyboard to check your work aurally.

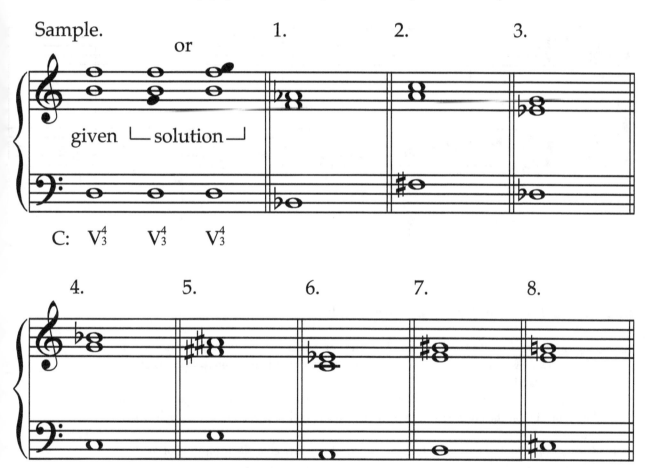

EXERCISE 8-E   *Realizing a Figured Bass in Chorale Style*

First, analyze the figured bass on two levels. Next, bracket all three-chord paradigms that you notice. Two paradigms often overlap (or dovetail), with a single chord acting as the end of one paradigm *and* the beginning of the next one. Then, add a soprano voice, using the paradigms to guide you. Finally, add inner voices to create a realization in chorale style.

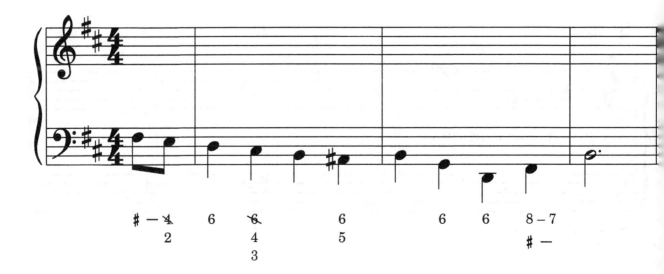

EXERCISE 8-F   *Analyzing Inversions of V⁷*

1. Ludwig van Beethoven, Piano Sonata no. 2 in A major, op. 2, no. 2 (1795), *Largo appassionato*. Analyze on two levels. In the second-level analysis, there two different interpretations of m. 3 that are both plausible:

   a. *As tonic (T):* The tonic function of the phrase continues through all of m. 3, giving way to dominant (D) on the downbeat of m. 4. This makes the first chord in m. 3 a neighboring chord.

   b. *As dominant (D):* The dominant function of the phrase arrives at the beginning of m. 3, making the last chord in m. 3 a passing chord that harmonizes a passing tone in the soprano voice.

   The decision has performance implications. Which one do you find more convincing? Why? Answer in a paragraph.

2. Josephine Lang (1815–1880), *Menuetto* from *Der trauernde Humor*. Analyze on two levels. The second-level analysis requires interpretation. When does the dominant function of the phrase begin? Which factors suggest the last measure? Which factors suggest the first complete measure? Answer in a paragraph.

Nicht zu rauch

3. Jean-Baptiste Loeillet (1680–1730), Sonata for Oboe in A minor, op. 5, no. 2, *Allegro*. Analyze on two levels.

EXERCISE 8–G   *Writing Inversions of V^7*

1. *Keyboard Style:* In D major, expand tonic using a neighboring V$_5^6$ chord. Write a total of three chords. Add bar lines if necessary. Analyze on two levels.

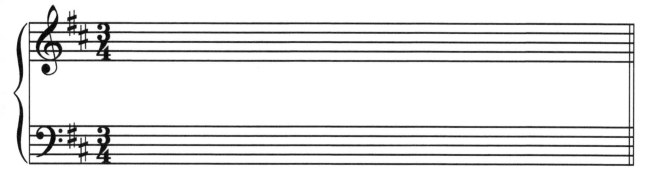

2. *Chorale Style:* In D minor, expand tonic using a passing V^4_3 chord. Write a total of three chords. Add bar lines if necessary. Analyze on two levels.

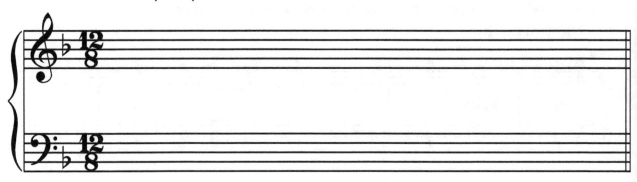

3. *Oboe/Bassoon Duet:* In F♯ minor, expand tonic using an incomplete-neighboring V^4_2 and then close with an authentic cadence. Continue in the texture that is started: lower neighbors in the bassoon (which carries the bass voice) and three-voice arpeggiations in the oboe.

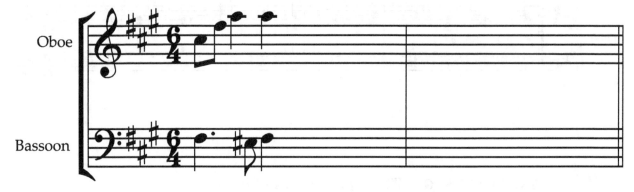

ASSIGNMENT 8.3

EXERCISE 8–H   *Writing Inversions of V⁷ in Rhythmically Active Textures*

1. Analyze on two levels based on the implications of the two outer voices. Then, add the missing inner voices in the broken-chord figuration that is started: alto voice on the beat, and tenor voice on the offbeat.

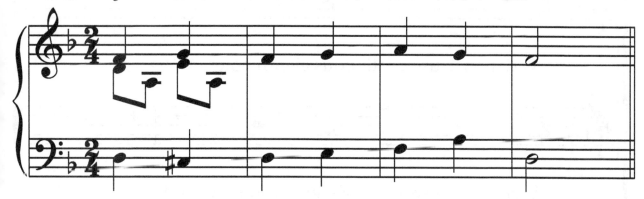

2. Realize the given roman numerals by continuing the block-chord waltz figuration that is started. The alto and tenor voices sound together on beats 2 and 3.

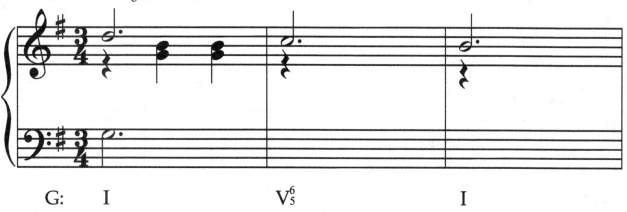

G: I   V$_5^6$ I

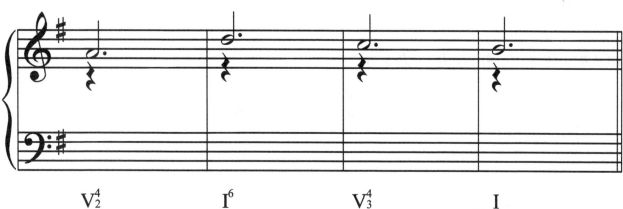

V$_2^4$ I^6 V$_3^4$ I

3. Using only I, I⁶, V, and inversions of V⁷, use the provided bass to analyze on two levels. Next, add three upper voices to the piano accompaniment in the figuration shown: soprano and alto on the beat, tenor on the offbeats. Finally, compose three different melodies that could be accompanied by the piano part that you write. Use the rhythmic guidance and the provided noteheads.

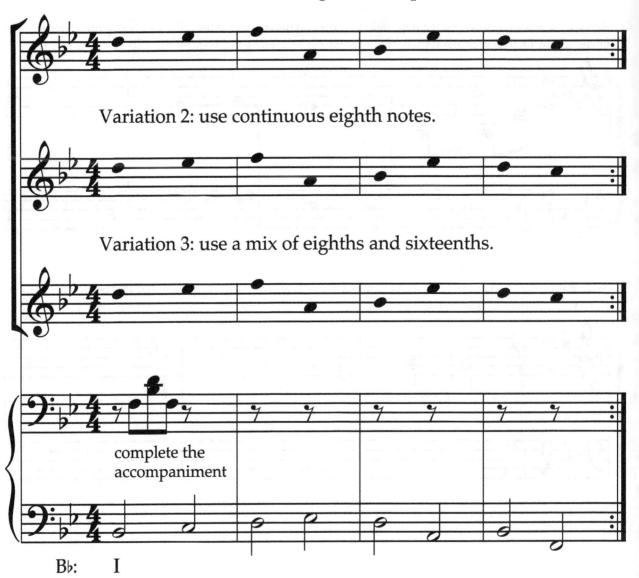

Variation 1: use a mix of eighths and quarters.

Variation 2: use continuous eighth notes.

Variation 3: use a mix of eighths and sixteenths.

complete the accompaniment

Bb: I

EXERCISE 8-1   *Analyzing a Passage*

Analyze on two levels the passage from the *Allegro ma non troppo* movement of Ludwig van Beethoven's Piano Sonata in G major, op. 49, no. 2 (1805). What is the key of this passage? Notice that both staves are in treble clef.

EXERCISE 8-J *Analyzing and Composing with Inversions of V⁷*

1. Use the given bass and soprano pitches to write one roman numeral for each measure. The possibilities are I, I⁶, V, and inversions of V⁷. Then, continue the figuration pattern begun in m. 1 to realize the four-voice broken-chord figuration for the entire phrase.

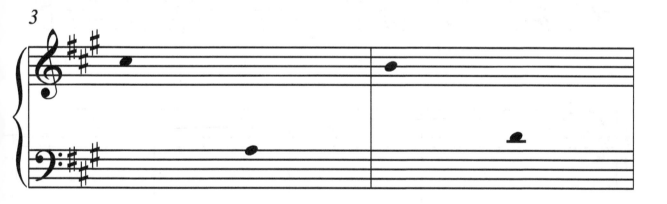

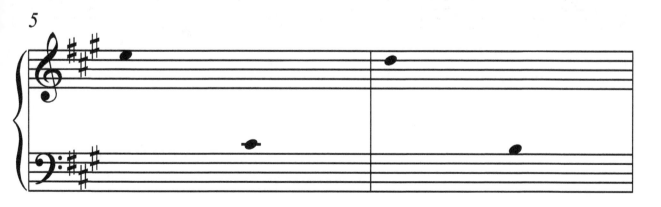

7

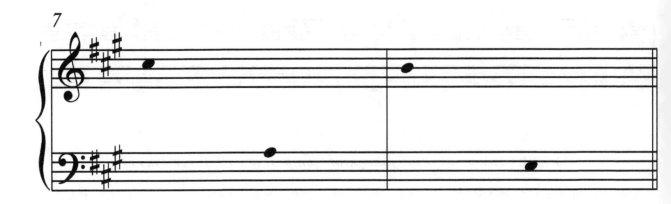

2. The given bass voice includes chordal skips, repeated notes, and passing tones. Begin by writing one roman numeral per measure to label the implied harmony. The choices are i, i^6, and inversions of V^7. Then, write the three upper voices in the broken-chord figuration pattern begun in m. 1.

5

EXERCISE 8–K   *Comparing Inversions of V⁷ and vii°⁷*

A subtle difference in shading can have a significant effect. Each tonic prolongation below is missing a single pitch in its second chord. Fill in that missing pitch in two different ways: (a) to create an inversion of V⁷, and (b) to create vii°⁷ or one of its inversions. Play both versions on keyboard while singing along with the voice that differs between the two versions. Analyze both versions on two levels.

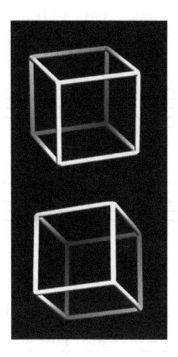

1. Fill in each gap to create an inversion of V⁷.

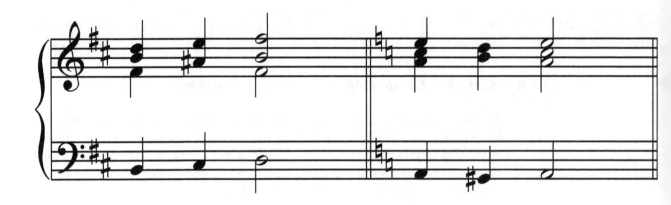

2. Fill in each gap to create vii°7 or one of its inversions.

EXERCISE 8–L   *Analyzing What Is and What Could Be*

First, analyze each excerpt using two levels. Next, circle the chordal seventh of each fully diminished seventh chord (vii°⁷ or one of its inversions). Then, in the space provided, renotate the passage by replacing each circled pitch so that the diminished seventh chord becomes an inversion of V⁷. Finally, analyze your recomposition on two levels.

1. Zenobia Powell Perry, *Teeta* from *Piano Potpourri* (1988)

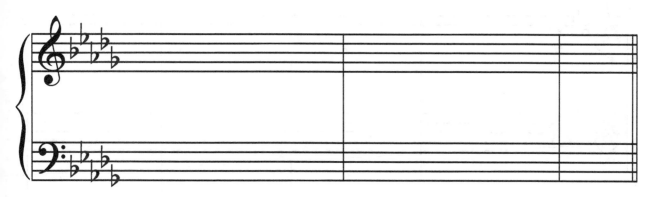

2 and 3. Franz Joseph Haydn (1732–1809), String Quartets:

op. 17, no. 5, Hob. III:29 (1771), *Adagio*

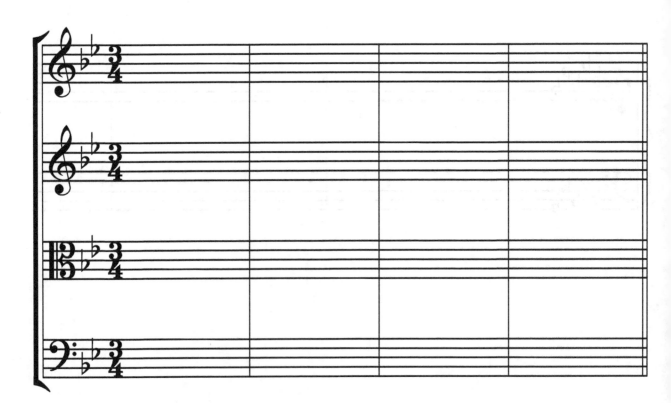

op. 9, no. 4, Hob. III:22 (1769), *Menuet*

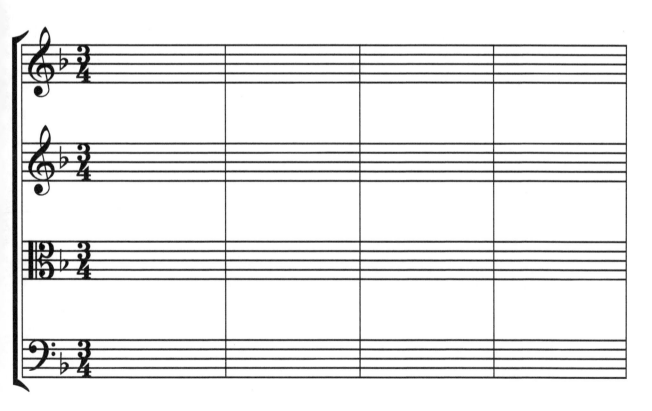

EXERCISE 8-M   *Realizing a Figured Bass*

Realize the figured bass in chorale style. Use harmonic paradigms to craft a soprano voice that moves mostly stepwise and makes strong counterpoint with the bass. Analyze on two levels.

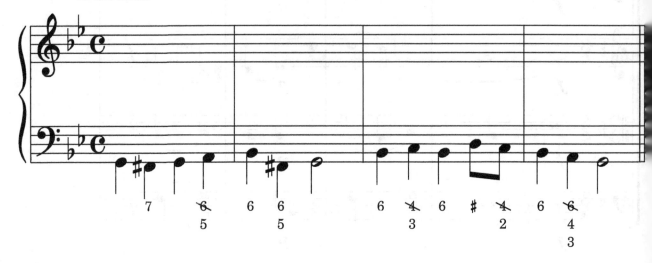

ASSIGNMENT 8.5

EXERCISE 8–N   *Analyzing Inversions of vii°⁷*

Analyze the following excerpts using two levels.

1. C. P. E. Bach, Sonata no. 5 in A minor for Flute and Continuo, Wq. 128, H.555 (1740)

2. Maria Szymanowska (1789–1831), "Se spiegar"

Translation: If I could explain, oh, God, my excessive pain.

si - vo mi - o do - lo - re

3. Christoph Willibald Gluck, "Pantomime" from *Alceste* (1767)

EXERCISE 8-O   *Composing from a Figured Bass*

Analyze on two levels. Then, realize the figured bass in keyboard style. Use a neutral position on each of the i⁶ and V⁶ chords. Finally, play your realization while singing along with the bass voice.

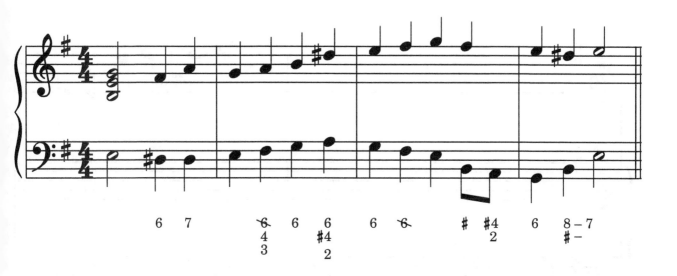

Now, convert your realization above into a short composition by doing the following:

- Notice that the bass voice is already written on the lowest staff, just adapted to the $\frac{12}{8}$ meter.
- Use your three upper voices above to create a broken-chord accompaniment on the middle staff: soprano and alto voices on the first and third eighths of each beat, and tenor on the second eighth.
- Fill in the missing measures of the violin melody on the upper staff. Use similar rhythms and lower neighbors so that the melody is coherent.

ASSIGNMENT 8.6

EXERCISE 8–P   *Analyzing Inversions of V⁷ and vii°⁷*

Analyze each passage on two levels.

1. Juan Bautista Alberdi (1810–1884), "La ausencia" from *Six Piano Pieces*

2. Jesús Castillo (1877–1946), *Fiesta de Pájaros*

3. Ludwig van Beethoven, Piano Sonata no. 5 in C minor, op. 10, no. 1 (1798), *Allegro*. The parenthesized embellishing tones that occur in the right hand in mm. 14–16 are called suspensions and are addressed in Chapter 10. The notes that *follow* them are chord tones.

EXERCISE 8-Q *Making a Quick Save*

Due to a grave photocopying error in haste before the first rehearsal, the piano part of this passage from the Rondo of Ludwig van Beethoven's Violin Sonata in D major, op. 12, no. 1 (1798), is missing most of its upper staff. The responsible violinist has her entire part, so the melody is shown, as is the bass line in the left hand of the piano. To salvage your professional reputation, here's what you need to do:

1. Analyze on two levels. Determine the implied harmonies by considering the two outer voices, which form familiar paradigms.
2. Circle the structural pitches of the violin part, which move at the same rate as the bass line. Keep in mind that the metrically accented notes are not always structural; there are some embellishing tones.
3. Fill in the right-hand part following the small fragment that managed to survive the disastrous smudge. Write repeated-note chords in the right hand, in keyboard style, which attack on every eighth note that is not already covered by the bass line.
4. Finally, ensure the accuracy of your last-minute save by singing the violin part while self-accompanying with the piano part. To make it more easily playable, omit the octave doublings in the bass and/or reduce the repeated right-hand chords to just a single attack on the beat.

Rehearsal begins shortly. Good luck!

CHAPTER 9

The Pre-Dominant Function and the Phrase Model

ASSIGNMENT 9.1

EXERCISE 9–A *Analyzing Pre-Dominant Chords*

Analyze each passage on two levels. Include the phrase model in your analysis.

1. Franz Joseph Haydn, Symphony no. 88 in G major, Hob. I:88 (1787), *Allegro*

2. John William Boone, *Spring: Reverie for Piano* (1885). Notice that both staves are in treble clef.

3. Maria Hester Reynolds Park, Violin Sonata, op. 13 (c. 1801)

EXERCISE 9–B   *Transposing Short Paradigms at the Keyboard*

Each paradigm illustrates a common usage of a pre-dominant chord. Play as written and then transposed to the two keys indicated. Transpose the two outer voices first, then the full chords. Sing along with the bass voice.

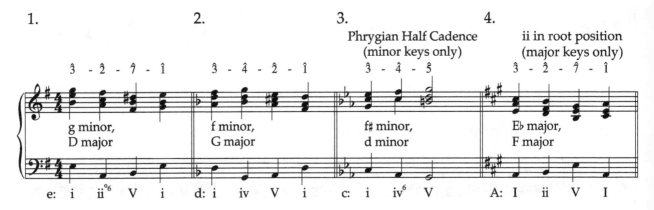

EXERCISE 9–C   *Harmonizing Melodies with Guidance*

At a piano or keyboard, harmonize each short melody in keyboard style. Work in the following order:

- Using the bracketed guides, add a bass voice and a two-level analysis. Use paradigms where possible and strive for strong soprano-bass counterpoint. Limit your choices to chords we have studied so far.
- Add the two inner voices to the upper staff.

Violin 1 and Viola: rhythmic unison with cello
Violin 2: upper neighbors

3.

ASSIGNMENT 9.3

EXERCISE 9–H   *Realizing a Figured Bass Using Harmonic Paradigms*

First, analyze the figured bass on two levels. Next, label each bracket with one of the following paradigms and use it to choose soprano pitches: voice exchange (two occurrences), parallel tenths (two occurrences), Phrygian HC (two occurrences), $\hat{1}$–$\hat{7}$–$\hat{1}$ bass, and a cadence with converging soprano ($\hat{2}$–$\hat{7}$–$\hat{1}$). Finally, fill in any gaps in the soprano voice and add two inner voices to the upper staff in keyboard style.

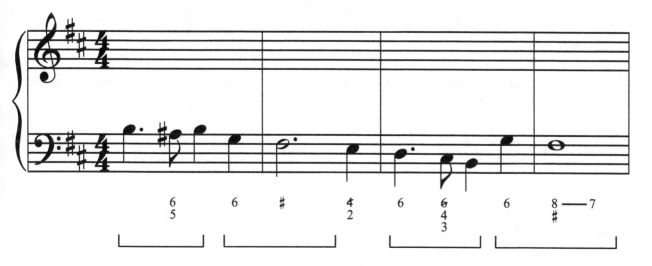

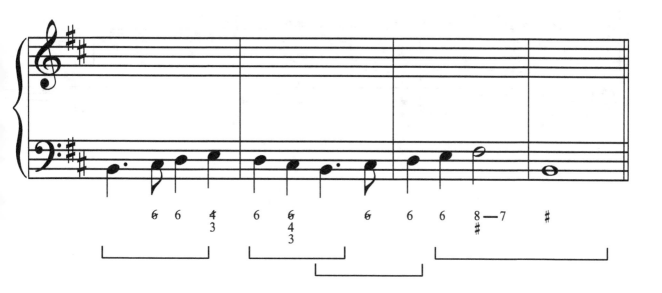

EXERCISE 9–1   *Analyzing and Reducing a Passage*

First, analyze the passage from W. A. Mozart's "Das Kinderspiel," K. 598 (1791) on two levels. Next, create and play a keyboard reduction consisting of one chord per measure (except in m. 6, which features 5–6 motion). To locate the upper voice of your reduction, circle one vocal pitch per bass note; make sure that the upper voice consists entirely of chord tones. Play your reduction while singing the vocal melody.

Translation: We children, we have a real taste for joy. We joke and tease people when we are playing, needless to say.

Reduction:

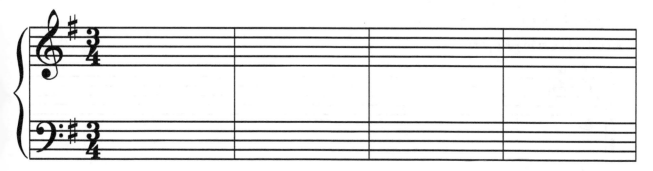

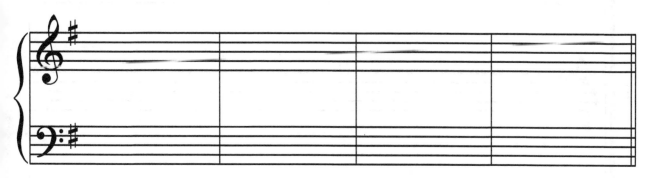

EXERCISE 9-J   *Cooking a Phrase Using a Recipe*

Compose a short, homophonic progression that features each list of ingredients. The lists are not in order; you need to order the events logically in order to create a phrase. Choose a meter, add bar lines, and choose rhythms that make structural harmonies more metrically accented than embellishing chords. Analyze on two levels.

1. In keyboard style, write a progression in D minor that:
    *   includes ii°^{6} as the pre-dominant
    *   expands tonic with an inversion of vii°^{7}
    *   includes a perfect authentic cadence

2. In open score (for SATB choir), write a progression in B minor that:
   • includes a Phrygian half cadence
   • expands the tonic with a voice exchange

Optional: add text to your phrase.

EXERCISE 9–K   *Analyzing a Phrase*

Analyze the passage from Estelle Ricketts's *Rippling Spring Waltz* (1893) on two levels.

ASSIGNMENT 9.4

EXERCISE 9–L   *Analyzing Pre-Dominant Chords*

Analyze each passage on two levels. Include the phrase model in your analysis.

1. Enrique Saborido, "Felicia" (transcribed for guitar by Pedro A. Iparraguirre) (1907)

2. Franz Joseph Haydn, String Quartet in E♭ major ("The Joke"), op. 33, no. 2, Hob. III:38 (1781). Ignore parenthesized pitches.

EXERCISE 9-M   *Harmonizing a Melody with Just a Bass Line*

First, decide how many phrases are in the melody, using rhythm and repetition as hints. Next, label each cadence. Then, write a bass line and roman numerals to harmonize the melody. Include at least one pre-dominant harmony in each phrase. Play the bass and melody together on keyboard to check aurally for strong counterpoint between the two voices.

EXERCISE 9-N   *Continuing Compositions That Someone Else Started*

Each phrase below is four measures long and closes with a half cadence. Compose the phrase that might *follow* each of the given ones: a four-measure phrase that ends with a PAC. Your phrases will begin like the given ones and match their basic character, harmonic rhythm, texture, and figuration. Analyze both the given and the new phrases on two levels.

1. Julie von Webenau, "Schäfers Klagelied" (1829). You do not need to compose the text for the vocal part in the second phrase. Just pitches and rhythms will be fine.

Translation: Then I follow the grazing herd. My little dog keeps them for me.

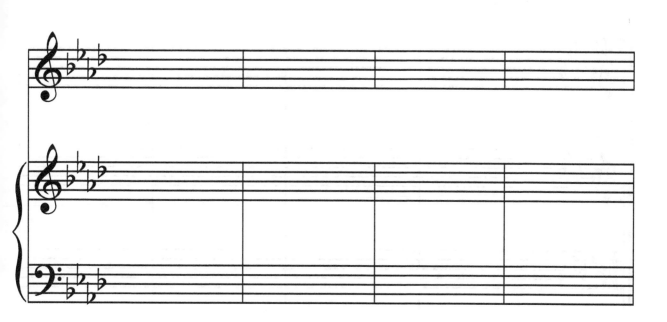

2. Antonio Vivaldi (1678–1741), Violin Concerto in C major, RV 176, *Largo*

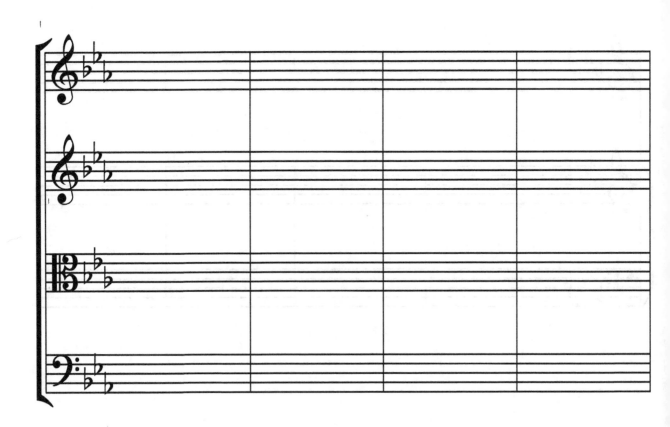

ASSIGNMENT 9.5

EXERCISE 9–O *Analyzing Passages*

Analyze each passage on two levels. Consider how many phrases are in each passage.

1. Franz Joseph Haydn, String Quartet in E♭ major ("The Joke"), op. 33, no. 2, Hob. III:38 (1781)

2. Franz Joseph Haydn, String Quartet in G major, op. 64, no. 4, Hob. III:66 (1790)

EXERCISE 9-P   *Reducing and Elaborating Phrases*

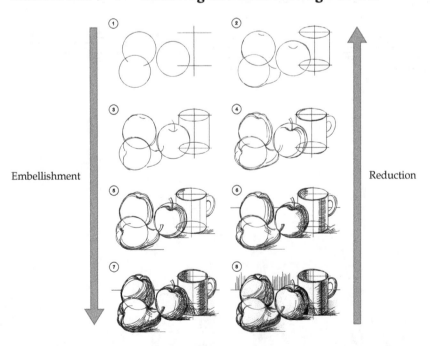

Below are two phrases in a three-voice texture: one in D minor that is fully realized, and one in B minor that is just a chordal sketch.

1. Reduce the D minor phrase to a three-voice chordal texture like the one shown in B minor. To do this, you will need to omit the embellishing tones (incomplete neighbors, passing tones, etc.).
2. Elaborate the B minor phrase using the same figuration strategy that is employed in D minor: two upper voices in compound melody with incomplete neighbors added to the lower one, all over a sustained bass.

Figurated Phrase in D minor:

Chordal Sketch in D minor:

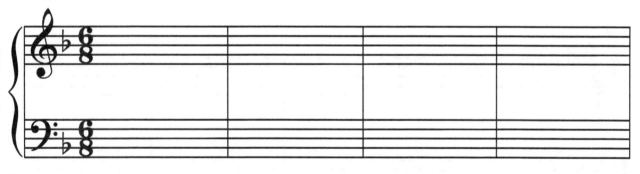

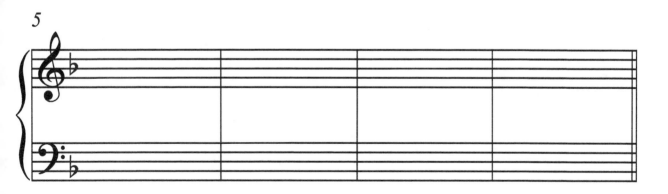

Chordal Sketch in B minor:

Figurated Phrase in B minor:

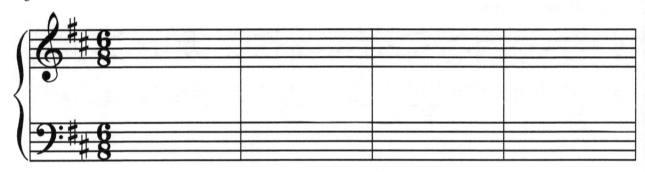

5

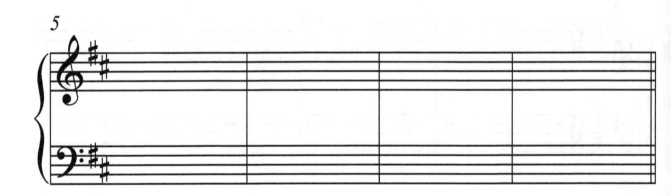

CHAPTER 10

Accented and Chromatic Embellishing Tones

ASSIGNMENT 10.1

EXERCISE 10–A *Creating and Resolving Suspensions in Two Voices*

Add a single upper voice in order to realize each suspension indicated by the figures. Your added voice will enter on a consonant preparation, tie into a suspension, and then resolve. Play your realizations at a piano or keyboard.

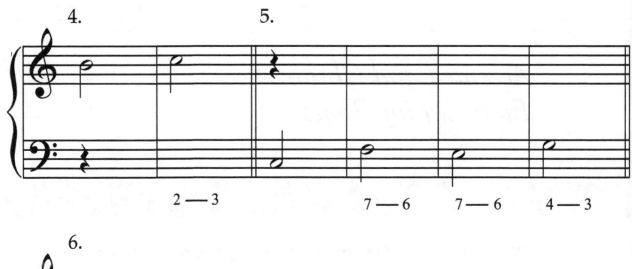

EXERCISE 10–B *Analyzing Embellishing Tones*

First, analyze each passage on two levels. Then, circle each embellishing tone and label its type. For each suspension, add figured bass (such as 9–8) and label the preparation (P), suspension (S), and resolution (R). A sample is provided.

Sample. Francis Johnson, *Citizen's Quadrilles* (1837), no. 3

1. Fanny Hensel, Piano Trio, op. 11 (1846), *Allegro molto vivace*

2. Ignacio Álvarez (1837–1888), *El canto de la tarde*. Note that each grace note acts as the bass note for its entire measure. Imagine each of the remaining pitches on the lower staff as sounding *above* a sustained version of that bass note.

3. John William Boone (1864–1927), *The Spring: Reverie for Piano. Hint: there is one bass note per measure.*

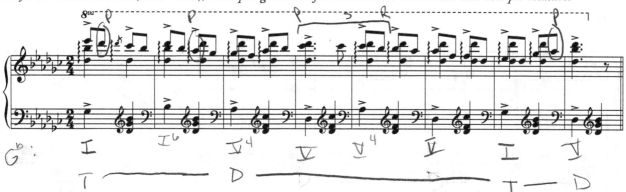

EXERCISE 10-C   *Detecting and Correcting Errors with Suspensions*

Each passage contains errors in suspension writing, listed below. Assume that all accented dissonances are attempts at suspensions. Add roman numerals, then label each error as follows:

NP: no preparation **DP:** dissonant preparation **NR:** not resolved correctly
ANT: anticipation

Finally, rewrite a corrected version with at least one correctly treated suspension.

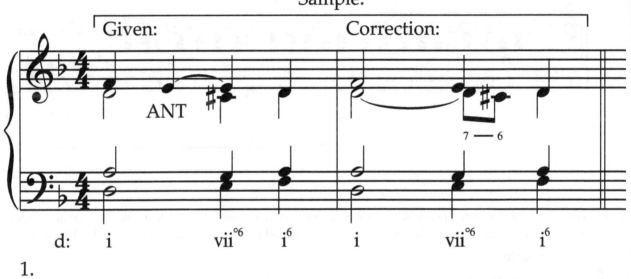

1.

2.

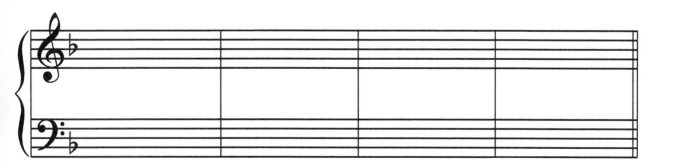

3.

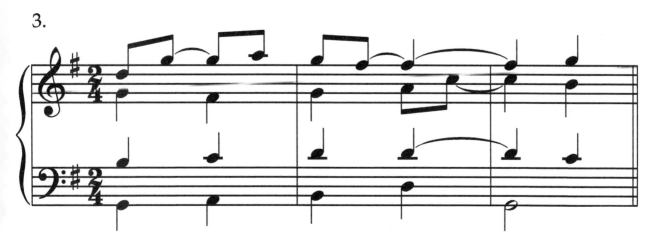

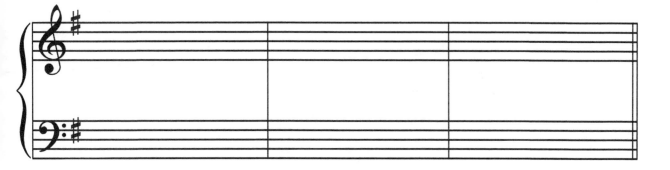

ASSIGNMENT 10.2

EXERCISE 10-D   *Adding Suspensions to Harmonic Paradigms*

First, play each harmonic paradigm on piano or keyboard as notated (without suspensions). Next, use the figured bass to determine which pitch(es) will be delayed by a beat or two. Circle those pitches. Finally, play the version with suspensions.

EXERCISE 10-E   *Analyzing Embellishing Tones*

First, analyze on two levels. Next, label all embellishing tones. For each suspension, label all three parts (P, S, and R) and its figured bass.

1. Ludwig van Beethoven, Piano Sonata in C minor, op. 10, no. 1 (1798), *Adagio molto*

2. Fanny Hensel, Piano Trio, op. 11 (1846), *Andante expressivo*. The analysis is started for you as a hint.

3. James A. Bland, *Oh, Lucinda* (1881)

4. Thomas Roseingrave (c. 1690–1766), Gavotte in D major for Flute and Continuo

EXERCISE 10-F *Adding Suspensions by Delaying Pitches*

First, play each progression and analyze it on two levels. Next, identify where a stepwise descent within a single voice can be delayed by one quarter note in order to create a suspension. Circle each pitch that will be delayed (at least four per progression). Finally, rewrite each passage with the suspensions added and labeled with figured bass (such as 4–3, 9–8, 7–6, or 2–3).

1.

2.

EXERCISE 10-G   *Realizing a Figured Bass in Keyboard Style*

Analyze the figured bass on two levels and realize it in keyboard style. Treat all suspensions correctly.

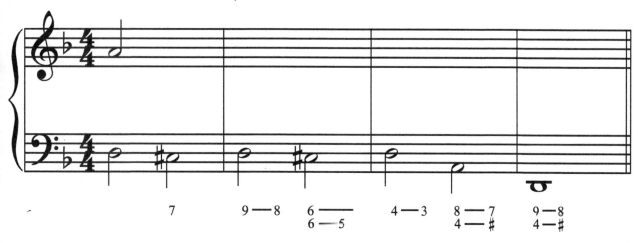

ASSIGNMENT 10.3

EXERCISE 10−H   *Analyzing and Recomposing Passages*

Analyze each passage on two levels and label all embellishing tones. Then, on the provided staves, rewrite a blander version of each passage by removing all or most of the embellishing tones and replacing them with consonances. The first recomposition is begun for you as a sample.

1. W. A. Mozart, Sonatina in C major, K. 545 (1788), *Menuetto*

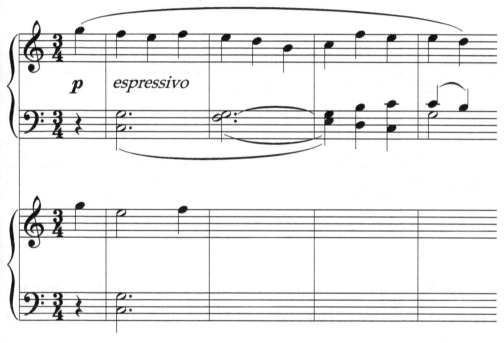

2. Pauline Duchambge, "Ronde des Pauvres" (1830). Recompose the vocal part only.

Translation: To the cries of poverty, to the accents of pleasure.

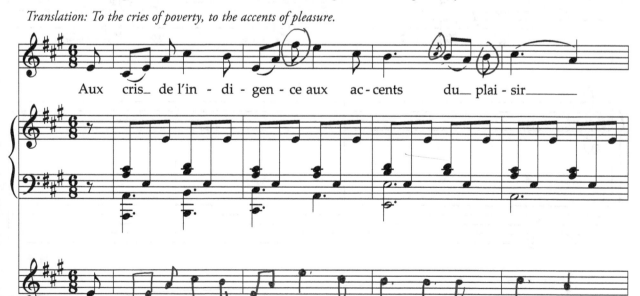

3. Anna Gardner Goodwin, *Cuban Liberty March* (1897)

4. Ludwig van Beethoven, Piano Sonata in A♭ major, op. 26 (1802), *Andante*

EXERCISE 10-1   *Realizing Figured Basses with Figuration*

First, analyze the figured bass on two levels. Then, realize it with the broken-chord figuration that is started for you. Each suspension needs to be prepared and resolved in the
same voice, even though there will not be any ties in the music. The sample demonstrates
how a broken-chord texture can imply suspensions.

Sample:

Exercise:

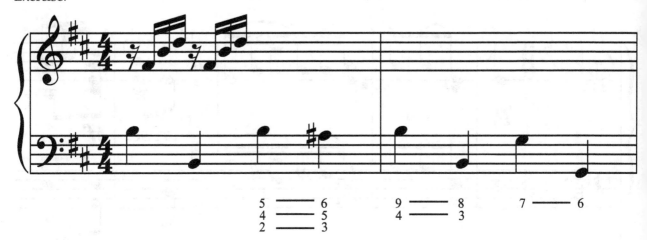

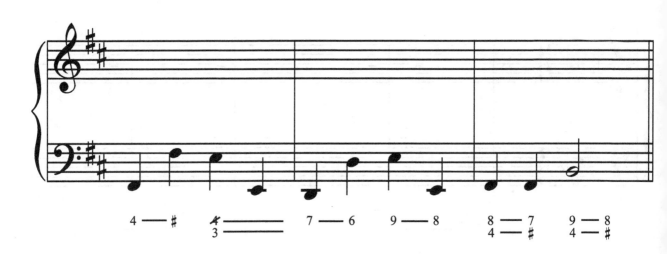

ASSIGNMENT 10.4

EXERCISE 10-J   *Writing Suspensions for String Quartet*

Analyze each figured bass on two levels. Then, realize it in open score for string quartet, treating suspensions carefully.

1.

2.

6   4—3 6   9—8 6   4—3 7   4—3
5

EXERCISE 10-K   *Analyzing Embellishing Tones*

Analyze each passage on two levels. Circle and label all embellishing tones.

1. Agustín Bardi (1884–1941), *Tinta Verde* for guitar

2. Agustín Bardi (1884–1941), *Tinta Verde* for guitar

3. Antonio Maria Barbieri (1892–1979), *Ave Maria*

   Translation: The Lord is with you.

4. Pyotr Ilyich Tchaikovsky, Symphony no. 4, op. 36 (1880), *Andantino in modo di canzona*

5. Alejandro Monestel Zamora, *Contemplation* (1914)

EXERCISE 10-L   *Enlivening a Homophonic Texture with Embellishing Tones*

Add as many passing tones, accented passing tones, neighboring tones, suspensions, and chordal leaps as you can to Arcangelo Corelli's Trio Sonata in G minor, op. 1, no. 10 (1681). Label all embellishing tones.

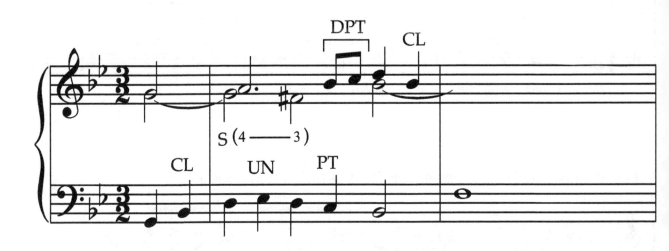

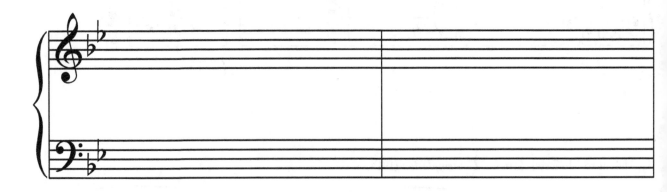

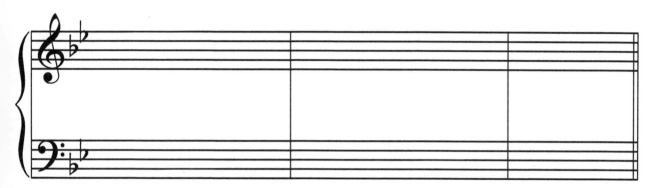

ASSIGNMENT 10.5

EXERCISE 10-M   *Creating Opportunities to Add Suspensions*

Adding suspensions to the phrases below will require more than just delaying some pitches by a beat. This is because there are relatively few descending steps within individual voices. When you rewrite each example, *insert* revoiced chords that jump higher than the preceding voicing, and thereby prepare a suspension that can *descend* stepwise into the following harmony. There are often multiple ways of doing this, as modeled in the sample.

Sample solutions:

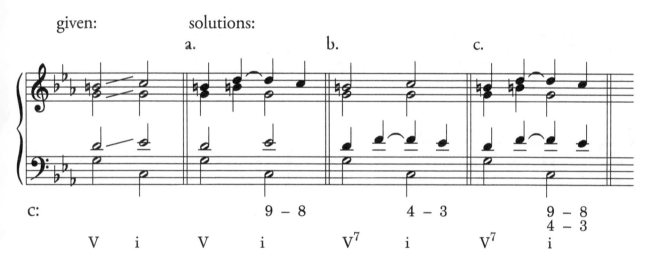

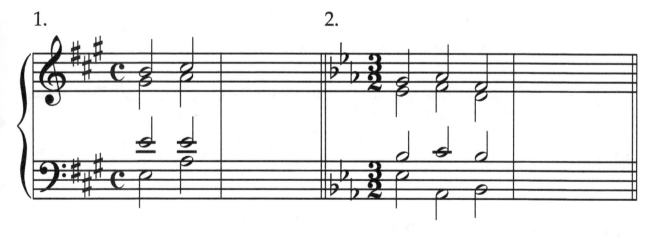

3.   **4.**

EXERCISE 10-N   *Analyzing Embellishing Tones*

Analyze the passage from Thomas Wiggins's *Sewing Song* (1889) on two levels. Circle and label all embellishing tones. *Hint: Think of the dissonances as resolving stepwise, even though the resolutions are not the pitches that sound immediately after.*

EXERCISE 10-O   *Framing a Structure and Then Adding Finishes*

Analyze each figured bass on two levels. Next, realize it homophonically in three voices. Some chords will need to be incomplete in order to prepare and resolve suspensions. Finally, create a more florid realization in open score by decorating the suspensions rhythmically as shown in the model.

Model:

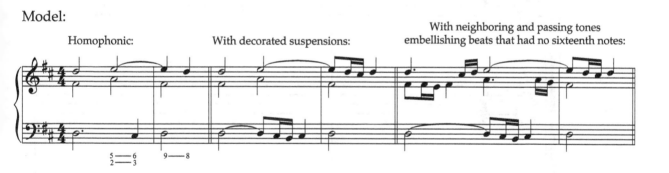

Homophonic realization in three voices:

1.

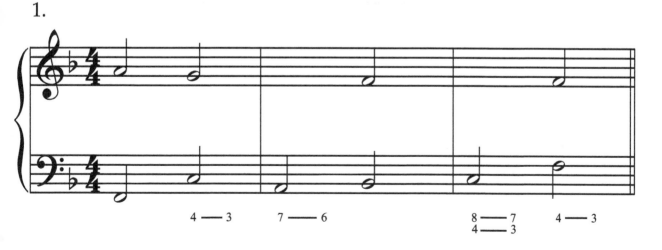

2.

Embellished version for two flutes and a bassoon:

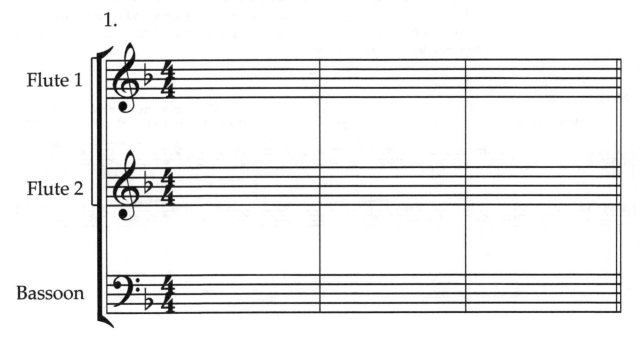

2.

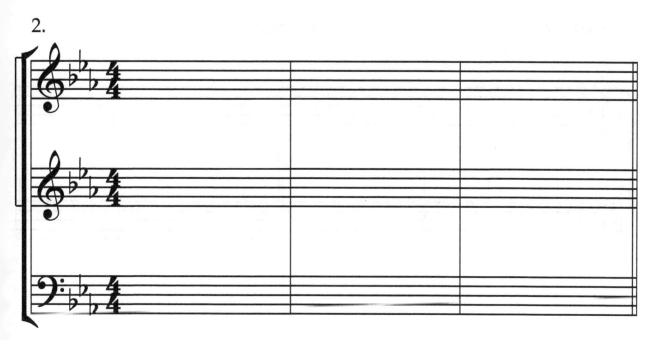

EXERCISE 10-P *Analyzing and Reducing a Passage*

Analyze the passage from Tekla Bądarzewska-Baranowska's (1834–1861) *J Skoven* on two levels. Label all embellishing tones. Then, in the space provided, rewrite a keyboard-style reduction without embellishing tones.

Original:

dolce con gravita

Rewritten with embellishing tones removed:

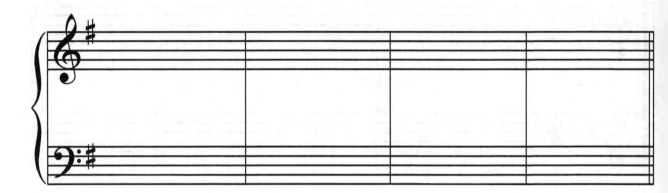

3. Samuel Coleridge-Taylor, Violin Sonata in D minor, op. 28 (1898), i

4. Harriett Abrams (c. 1762–1821), "Crazy Jane"

on that   spot   where last we   par - ted   on   that spot where first___ we met

5. "Amazing Grace"

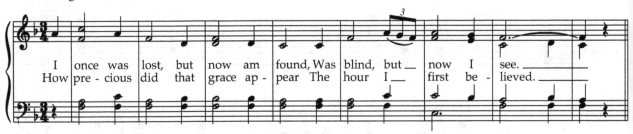

I once was lost, but now am found, Was blind, but _ now I see. ____

How pre - cious did that grace ap - pear The hour I _ first be - lieved. ____

6. W. A. Mozart, Piano Sonata in B♭ major, K. 570 (1789), *Adagio*

ASSIGNMENT 11.2

EXERCISE 11–D   *Writing Six-Four Chords in a Variety of Textures and Meters*

As you complete each writing task, choose your own meter and rhythmic values, adding bar lines as necessary. Ensure that each six-four chord is in an appropriate metrical position. Analyze on two levels.

1. In keyboard style, write I–P$_4^6$–I^6–IV–V$_{4-3}^{6-5}$–I in D major. Use harmonic paradigms to craft a soprano voice before you write the two inner voices.

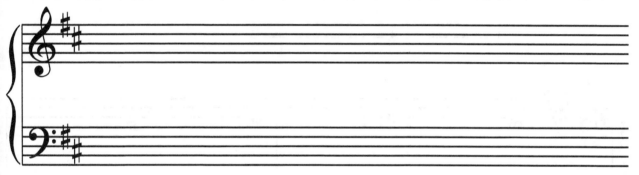

2. In chorale style, set the melody $\hat{5}$–$\hat{6}$–$\hat{5}$–$\hat{4}$–$\hat{3}$–$\hat{2}$–$\hat{1}$ in F minor. Include a plagal expansion of tonic as well as a cadential six-four chord.

3. Realize the figured bass by continuing the broken-chord figuration pattern that is started. Within each half measure, the upper staff includes: soprano, tenor, alto with a lower neighbor, soprano.

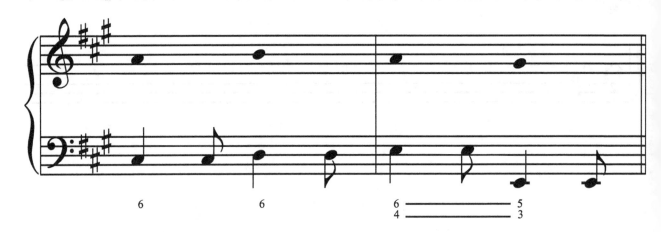

EXERCISE 11-E *Analyzing Six-Four Chords*

Analyze each passage on two levels.

1. Pyotr Ilyich Tchaikovsky, "Old French Song" from *Children's Album*, op. 39, no. 16 (1878)

2. Maria Teresa Agnesi Pinottini, Sonata for Harpsichord (c. 1745)

3. Robert Schumann, "Der Himmel hat eine Träne geweint," op. 37, no. 1 (1840). When do the circled B♭s in m. 3 resolve?

4. Jane Mary Guest (c. 1762–1846), "Marion"

5. Franz Schubert, "Gesang des Harfners III," D. 480, no. 3 (1822)

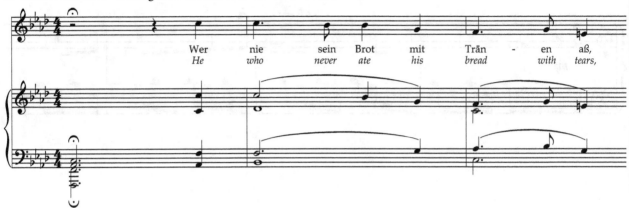

Wer   nie   sein Brot mit Trän - en aß,
He   who never ate his bread with tears,

ASSIGNMENT 11.3

EXERCISE 11–F   *What Can Go in the Middle?*

Each prompt shows two bass pitches or two soprano pitches, with a gap in the middle. Fill in each gap in three different ways: Each filling-in will use a different middle chord and a different texture. Model your three textures on the three shown in the sample. Analyze on two levels. Try to play what you write, however slowly.

Sample:

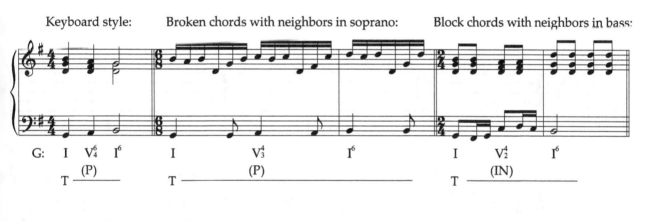

2.

b:

3.

D:

4.

B♭:

5.

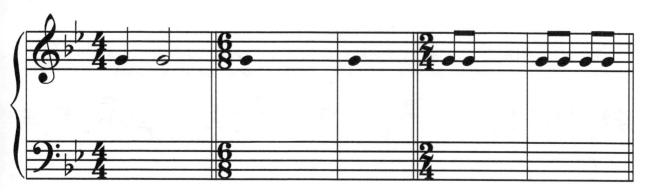

g:

6.

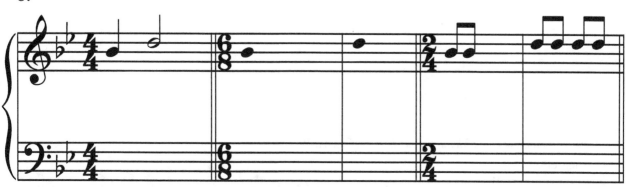

g:

EXERCISE 11-G *Analyzing Six-Four Chords*

Analyze each passage on two levels.

1. Juan Alais (1844–1914), *Zamacueca* for guitar. *Hint: Some bass notes are just passing <u>tones</u> and do not need roman numerals. Others are harmonized with passing <u>chords</u> and do need roman numerals.*

2. Maria Szymanowska, *Six Menuets Pour le Pianoforte* (1819), no. 1

ASSIGNMENT 11.4

EXERCISE 11-H   *Harmonizing Florid Melodies at the Keyboard*

First, sing or play each given melody. Next, harmonize it by adding roman numerals underneath. Aim for one or two chords per measure, and stick to the harmonic vocabulary that we have studied. Then, circle each melodic note that does not belong to the current harmony and label the type of embellishing tone. Finally, sing the melody while playing the bass line implied by the roman numerals that you add.

1. Henry Bishop and John Payne, "Home Sweet Home" (1823). Include a pedal six-four in your harmonization.

'Mid — pleas - ure and   pal - ac - es   though ___ we may   roam,

2. Marcello Tupinambá (1889–1953), "Mudança" from *Canções Brasileiras*. Include a cadential six-four chord.

3. Samuel Coleridge-Taylor, "A King Lived There in Thule" (1908)

A King there— lived in___ Thu - le, Was— faith - ful___ till the grave,___

4. Jonathan Spilman, "Flow Gently, Sweet Afton" (1837). Include a plagal motion.

1. Flow gen tly sweet Af ton, a - mong thy green braes; Flow

gen - tly, I'll sing thee a song in thy praise;

5. Ludwig van Beethoven, "Ich liebe dich," WoO 123 (1795). Include a cadential six-four chord. Treat the D♯ as a passing tone.

Translation: I love you as you love me, in the evening and in the morning. There has never been a day when you and I have not shared our sorrows.

Andante

Ich   lie - be dich, so   wie   du mich, am A - bend und am   Mor - gen, noch__   war kein Tag, wo

du   und ich   nicht   theil - ten uns' - re __   Sor - gen.

6. Joseph Bologne, String Quartet no. 4 in C minor, op. 1, no. 4 (1773)

p

7. W. A. Mozart, Violin Concerto no. 3 in G major, K. 216 (1775), *Rondeau.* Begin by deciding how many phrases there are.

(*f*)

EXERCISE 11-I   *Realizing a Figured Bass in Keyboard Style*

Analyze the figured bass on two levels. Then, realize it in keyboard style. Finally, play your realization while singing along with a voice of your choice.

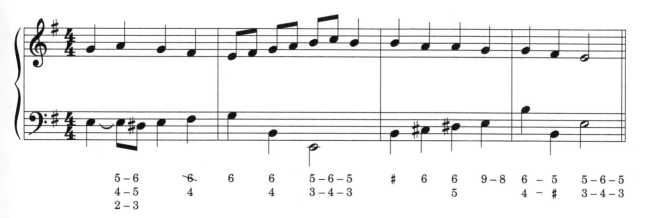

2. First, analyze the figured bass on two levels. Next, embellish the bass line into a cello part of continuous eighth notes by adding a combination of passing tones, neighboring tones, and chordal skips. Finally, write sustained block chords in the violin I, violin II, and viola parts.

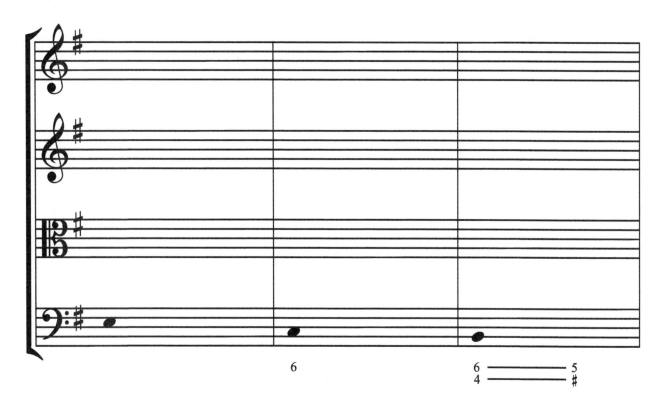

3. Use the roman numerals to create an accompaniment to the waltz melody given above. Write three quarter notes per measure: the bass note on beat 1, and the three upper voices on beats 2 and 3. Use strong voice leading.

4. Analyze on two levels. Then, write for a choir of four flutes. The bass line is given along with the start of the upper parts. Continue the figuration: a soprano voice (on the upper staff) decorated by lower neighbors, and two inner voices (on the middle staff) in the block chords shown.

ASSIGNMENT 11.6

EXERCISE 11–L *Analyzing Six-Four Chords and Plagal Motions*

Analyze each passage on two levels.

1. Jean-Marie Leclair, Trio Sonata in D major, op. 2, no. 8 (1728), *Allegro assai*

2. Barbara Strozzi, "Amore è bandito" (1657)

   Translation: No more loves, deceit, and fraud. Ah, ah, torments and rancor are no longer heard.

ni - ti gl'a-mo-ri l'in-gan-no e la fro-de, ah, ah,   ah, ah,   ah, ah, più non s'o-de tor-men-ti e ran-co - ri.

3. W. A. Mozart, Piano Sonata in C major, K. 330 (1783), *Allegro moderato*

4. W. A. Mozart, "Lacrimosa" from *Requiem*, K. 626 (1791), *Larghetto*

EXERCISE 11-M   *What Might Come Next?*

Below is a phrase from *Figarillo* by Argentine composer Juan Bautista Alberdi (1810–1884). First, analyze it on two levels. Then, compose the missing portion of the melody, following the given rhythm. Make sure that the two halves of the melody belong together.

1. Barbara Strozzi, "Chi brama in amore" (1657). Do not be misled by the key signature. What is the key of this passage?

Translation: Must not keep his suffering [inside his] heart.

2. George Frideric Handel, "Lascia ch'io pianga" from *Rinaldo* (1711), Act 2

Translation: Let me mourn my cruel fate.

La - scia   ch'io pian - ga

7

Mia   cru - da   sor - te

4   3   8

ASSIGNMENT 12.3

EXERCISE 12-G   *Writing Accompaniments and Composing Florid Melodies*

Realize each set of roman numerals by continuing in the figurated texture that is started for you. Then, compose a melody with the given rhythm, using a variety of accented and unaccented embellishing tones.

1. an *Andante* for violin and piano

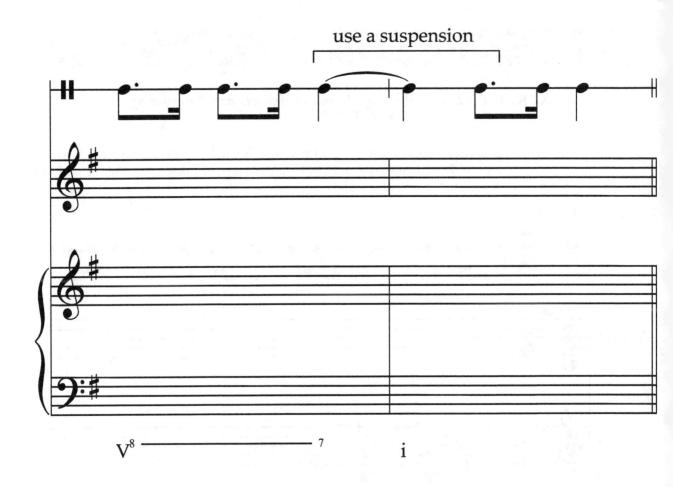

2. a slow nocturne for viola and piano

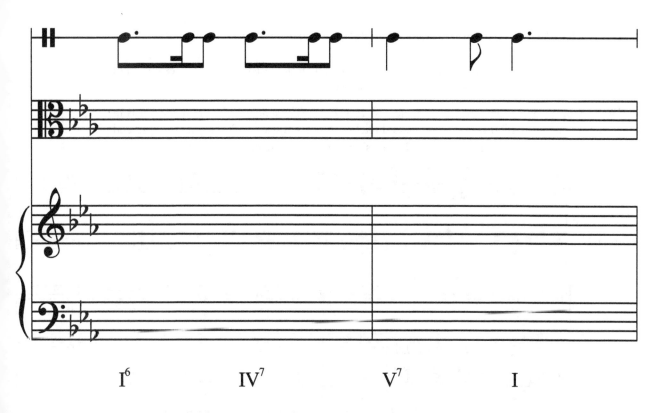

$$I^6 \qquad IV^7 \qquad V^7 \qquad I$$

EXERCISE 12-H   *Completing a Texture from a Figured Bass*

Shown below are the vocal melody and continuo part from a portion of one of J. S. Bach's (1685–1750) *Geistliche Lieder*. First, analyze on two levels. Then, realize the figured bass in keyboard style by adding two inner voices beneath the given melody on the upper staff. Finally, sing the vocal melody while playing your keyboard-style realization.

Translation: Up, up, my heart, with joy.

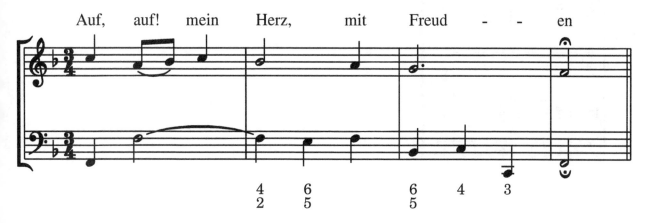

EXERCISE 12-1   *Reducing and Analyzing Passages in Open Score*

Analyze each passage on two levels. Label the preparation, dissonance, and resolution of each suspension and each pre-dominant seventh.

1. W. A. Mozart, Symphony no. 1 in E♭ major, K. 16 (1764), *Allegro molto*. Note that the horns in E♭ sound a major sixth lower than the notated pitches. A quick way to read that part is to pretend that it is in bass clef with three flats in the key signature, up one octave.

As part of your analytical process, complete and play this keyboard-style reduction of mm. 4–11, which takes the first oboe part as its upper voice. It will help you to notice that there are suspensions and pre-dominant sevenths that resolve across the bar line.

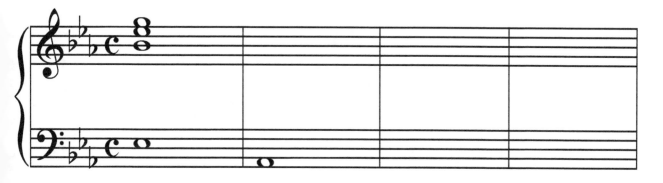

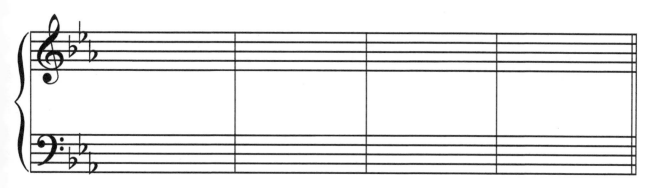

2. Joseph Bologne, String Quartet no. 4 in C minor, op. 1, no. 4 (1773)

ASSIGNMENT 12.4

EXERCISE 12–J   *Analyzing a Mix of Pre-Dominant Chords*

Analyze each passage on two levels. For each chord with a pre-dominant function, decide whether it acts as part of an embedded phrase model (EPM) or as the phrase's structural pre-dominant. If any pre-dominant harmonies are expanded, briefly explain how by annotating the score.

1. Mary Gossell, Suite in E major (2017), *Menuet I*

2. Robert Nathaniel Dett, *Ave Maria* (1930). *Hint: Treat the chord on the downbeat of m. 2 as lasting through the entire measure, connected by passing tones to the next chord on the downbeat of m. 3.*

   Translation: Hail Mary, full [of grace].

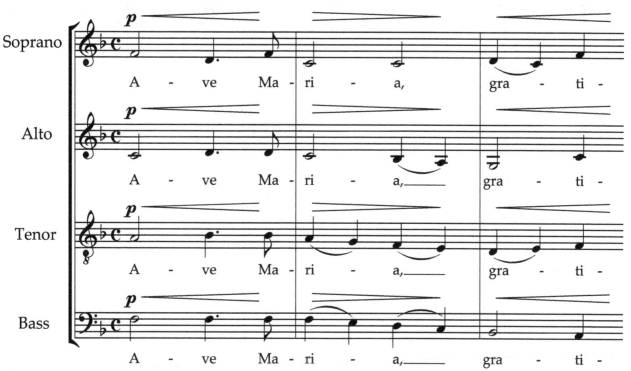

3. W. A. Mozart, Symphony in C major ("Linz"), K. 425 (1783), *Presto*

4. J. S. Bach, Flute Sonata in E♭ major, BWV 1031 (1730), *Siciliana*

5. W. A. Mozart, Symphony no. 30 in D major, K. 202 (1774), *Menuetto*

6. Luise Adolpha Le Beau, Sonata for Violin and Piano, op. 10 (1882), *Andante cantabile*

EXERCISE 12–K   *Realizing a Figured Bass in a Three-Voice Texture*

First, analyze the figured bass on two levels. Then, add just *two* upper voices to the upper staff in order to create a three-voice realization. As you choose your two upper voices, ensure that pre-dominant sevenths and suspensions are prepared and resolved. You will need to omit some chordal fifths. Some leaps are okay.

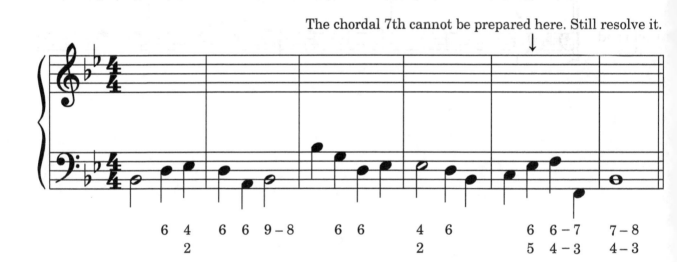

The chordal 7th cannot be prepared here. Still resolve it.

1. The bassoon part is provided. Add an upper voice in quarter notes for oboe. The harmonic rhythm is in quarter notes except at the very end.

2. The trumpet part is provided. Add a bass line in dotted quarter notes for trombone. The harmonic rhythm is mostly in dotted quarter notes.

EXERCISE 12–N   *Distinguishing Phrases from Subphrases*

Decide whether each passage consists of multiple *phrases* or just multiple *subphrases* within a single phrase. Support your interpretation in one to two sentences. Bracket phrases beneath the score with solid brackets and subphrases above the score with dashed brackets. Remember:

A *phrase* is a self-standing musical unit that contains harmonic motion (i.e., moving through tonic and dominant functions) and ends with a cadence.

A *subphrase* may contain a miniature harmonic motion (e.g., an EPM) and even a weak cadential gesture (e.g., a contrapuntal cadence), but it needs to be combined with one or more additional subphrases in order to form a complete phrase.

And not every rest is necessarily the end of either a phrase or a subphrase.

1. Philippe Courras, *Habanera*, op. 23 (1902)

2. W. A. Mozart, "Bei Männern" from *The Magic Flute*, K. 620 (1791), Act 1, Scene 7

Translation: A good heart is not lacking in men who feel love.

Andantino

Bei Män-nern, wel - che Lie - be füh len, fehlt auch ein gu - tes Her - ze nicht

3. Franz Joseph Haydn, Piano Sonata no. 35 in A♭ major, Hob. XVI:43 (1783), *Moderato*

ASSIGNMENT 12.6

EXERCISE 12–O   *Embellishing a Simple Texture*

1. Analyze the sample chorale-style phrase using roman numerals.
2. Study the elaboration, which implies the same progression, but is written for a solo instrument (such as viola or clarinet). Label each embellishing tone and answer these questions in two or three sentences: On what part of the beat does the bass note tend to fall? What is the balance between steps and leaps? Are the notes before and after each leap chord tones or embellishing tones?

Sample:

Given:

Elaboration:

3. Analyze the phrase below using roman numerals.
4. Elaborate it to create a phrase for a solo instrument. Be sure that only one pitch sounds at a time. Use your own written observations above as guidelines.

Your piece:

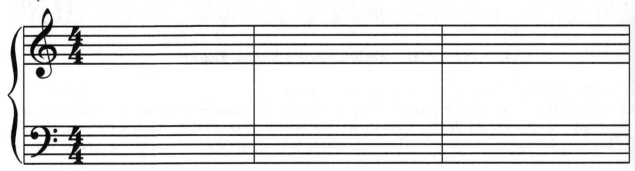

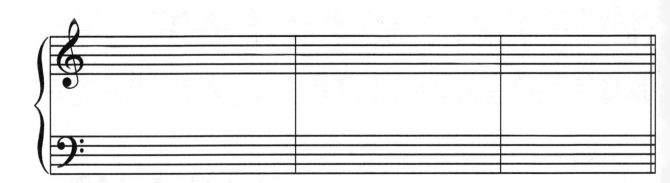

EXERCISE 12-P   *Analyzing Phrases*

Analyze each passage on two levels.

1. Franz Joseph Haydn, Piano Sonata no. 32 in G minor, Hob. XVI:44 (1771), *Allegretto*. Does this passage consist of one phrase or two phrases? Explain why in one sentence.

2. Julián Aguirre (1868–1924), *Estilo Argentino*, op. 44. Does this passage consist of one phrase or two phrases? Explain why in one sentence.

Translation: I don't care about the golden sun or that brilliant dew.

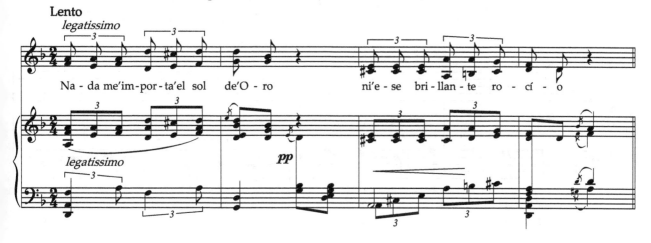

3. Franz Joseph Haydn, String Quartet in D major, op. 20, no. 4, Hob. III:34 (1772), *Un poco adagio affettuoso*. Before you analyze, play just the two outer voices.

EXERCISE 12-Q   *Realizing a Figured Bass*

First, analyze the figured bass on two levels. Next, craft a soprano voice, using the bracketed paradigms as hints. Finally, create a four-voice realization, maintaining the figuration that is begun for you: lowest three voices on the beat, and soprano after the beat.

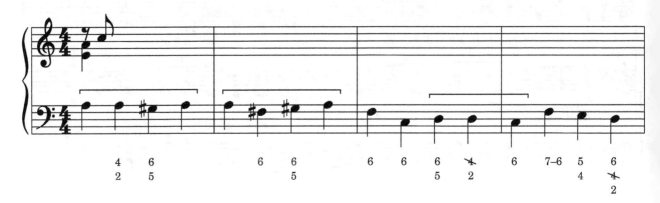

ASSIGNMENT 12.7

EXERCISE 12-R *Composing from Roman Numerals in a Variety of Textures*

Realize each set of roman numerals as specified.

1. Write homophonically for SATB choir. Incorporate four suspensions, and label the three parts of each of them. *Optional: Add text for the choir to sing on.*

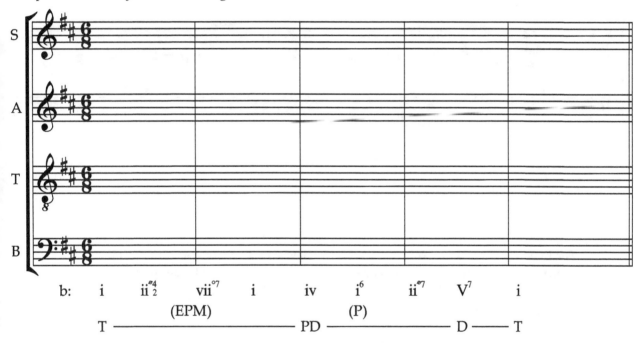

2. Write in keyboard style, but embellish the bass voice to feature continuous sixteenth notes. Keep the primary bass tones on the beat, and use a mix of passing tones, neighboring tones, double neighbors, and chordal skips and leaps.

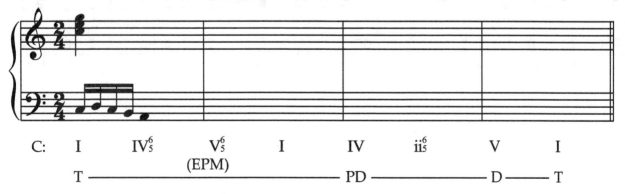

EXERCISE 12-S *Analyzing Phrases*

1. Clara Schumann, "Auf einem grünen Hügel" (1853). Analyze on two levels. How many cadences are there?

   Translation: I want to cry on the spot.

For Examples 2 and 3, in two sentences, explain how a single phrase comes to occupy so much musical time. Is it a single large-scale progression, or a series of more local progressions connected together?

2. Franz Schubert, "Die Sterne," D. 939 (1828)

   Translation: How the stars shine so brightly through the night! I've often woken up from a slumber because of it.

bin   oft   schon dar - ü - ber vom Schlum -mer er - wacht ._____

3. Franz Joseph Haydn, Piano Sonata in E♭ major, Hob. XVI:52 (1794), *Presto*

CHAPTER 13

The Submediant and the Step-Descent Bass

EXERCISE 13–A *Playing and Transposing Keyboard Paradigms*

Each paradigm illustrates the submediant triad in one of its typical contexts. Play as written and then transposed to the two keys indicated. *Hint: Transpose just the two outer voices first, and then the full chords.*

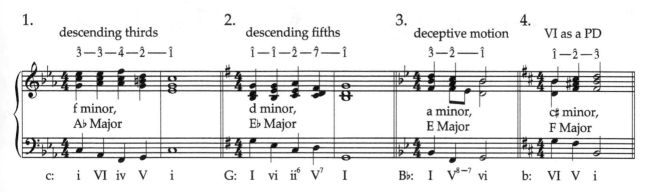

1. descending thirds
   $\hat{3}—\hat{3}—\hat{4}—\hat{2}—\hat{1}$
   f minor, Ab Major
   c: i VI iv V i

2. descending fifths
   $\hat{1}—\hat{1}—\hat{2}—\hat{7}—\hat{1}$
   d minor, Eb Major
   G: I vi ii⁶ V⁷ I

3. deceptive motion
   $\hat{3}—\hat{2}—\hat{1}$
   a minor, E Major
   Bb: I V⁸⁻⁷ vi

4. VI as a PD
   $\hat{1}—\hat{2}—\hat{3}$
   c# minor, F Major
   b: VI V i

EXERCISE 13–B *Analyzing Submediant Triads*

Analyze each passage on two levels.

1. Basile Barès (1845–1902), *La Creole*, op. 10. Label each embellishing tone in this passage.

2. Cecilia Maria Barthélemon, *Capture of the Cape of Good Hope* (1795), *Larghetto*

3. Amancio Alcorta (1842–1902), *Minué "Los Abrazos." Hint: This passage does not begin with a tonic chord.*

EXERCISE 13-C   *Harmonizing Melodic Fragments Using the Submediant Chord*

Harmonize each melody as instructed. End each harmonization with an authentic, half, or deceptive cadence. Analyze on two levels.

1. Write in keyboard style. Use the vi chord twice.

A:

2. Write in keyboard style. Use the VI chord once.

f#:

3. Write in chorale style. Use the VI chord once. There are several options for where to put it.

4. Write in keyboard style. Use one submediant triad and one cadential six-four chord. After harmonizing, add a time signature, rhythmic values, and bar lines so that each harmony occurs in
an appropriate metrical position.

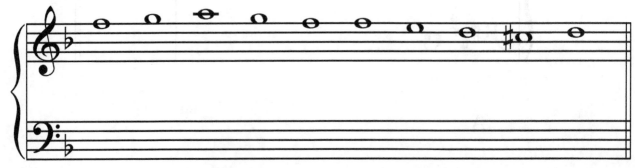

ASSIGNMENT 13.2

EXERCISE 13–D   *Analyzing Submediant Triads*

Analyze each passage on two levels.

1. W. A. Mozart, "Rex tremendae majestatis" from *Requiem*, K. 626 (1791)

Translation: King of tremdendous majesty.

(*excerpt continues on next page*)

2. Samuel Coleridge-Taylor, Sonata in D minor for Violin and Piano, op. 28 (1898)

3. Antonio María Barbieri (1892–1979), *Ave Maria*

   Translation: Hail Mary.

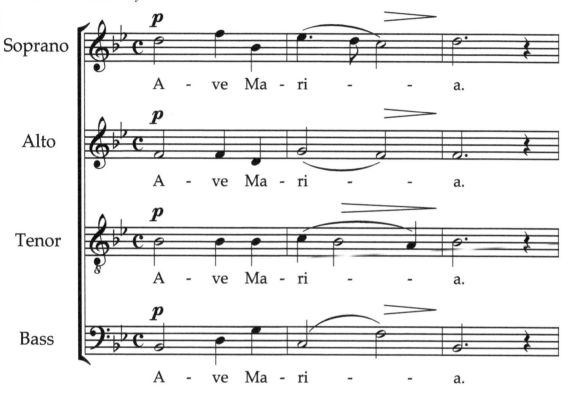

4. Frédéric Chopin, Nocturne in C minor, op. 48, no. 1 (1841). Before you analyze, circle the primary bass tones and primary melodic tones (which move in half notes throughout) and play this outer-voice duet on piano or keyboard.

ASSIGNMENT 13.3

EXERCISE 13–E   *Writing the Submediant Triad in a Variety of Textures*

1. Realize the given progression homophonically for SATB choir. Add a time signature, rhythmic values, and bar lines to place each harmony in a metrically appropriate position. Then, embellish the progression in two ways: In the bass voice, fill in each interval of a third by adding a passing tone. In any voice, add one suspension.

In A minor: 　　　i　　　vii°⁷　　　i　　　VI　　　iv　　　V^{6-5}_{4-3}　　　i

2. Realize the given progression in the figuration that is started, which consists of the following: In the *bass* voice, add a chordal leap on the second beat of each measure. Make sure that you do not leap downward to the chordal fifth, which would imply a six-four chord. (Chordal roots and thirds are clearest.) In the *upper voices*, notice the order of the broken-chord figuration within each measure: rest, tenor, alto with a lower neighbor, soprano, tenor, soprano. Use strong voice leading.

10

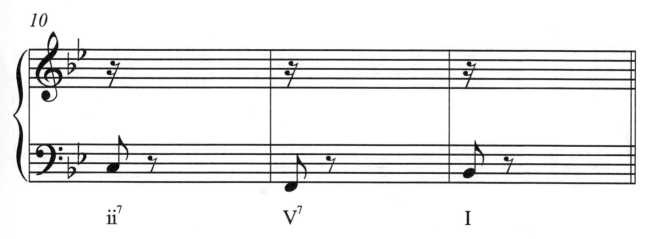

ii⁷   V⁷   I

3. Realize the given progression in the figuration that is started. On the *lower* staff, notice the order of the broken-chord figuration within each beat: bass, alto, tenor, soprano, alto, tenor. Use strong voice leading. On the *upper* staff, create a florid melody featuring a broad mix of embellishing tone types, including accented and chromatic ones. Use a mix of rhythmic values.

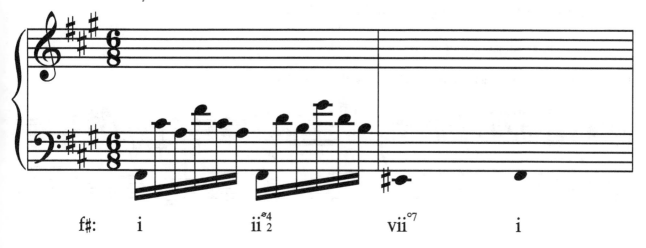

f♯:   i   ii°⁴₂   vii°⁷   i

3

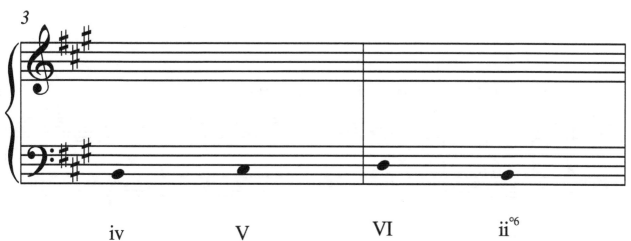

iv   V   VI   ii°⁶

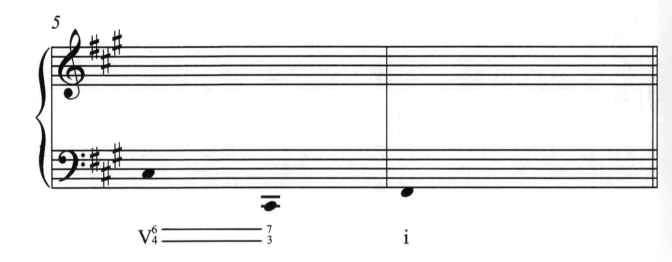

5

$V_4^6 \ ——————— \ ^7_3$ **i**

EXERCISE 13–F   *Analyzing Submediant Triads*

Analyze each passage on two levels.

1. Anna Amalia of Brunswick-Wolfenbüttel, "Das Veilchen" (1776)

2. Élisabeth Jacquet de La Guerre, Suite in G Major (1729), *Sarabande*

ASSIGNMENT 13.4

EXERCISE 13-G   *Cooking Phrases from Recipes*

1. In a minor key of your choice, write a homophonic progression in keyboard style that includes, *in this order*:
   - An embedded phrase model (EPM)
   - The VI chord in a descending bass arpeggiation
   - A pre-dominant that is expanded by voice exchange
   - A dominant chord that includes one suspension

Write the bass voice first, and incorporate paradigms where possible. Add a time signature, rhythmic values, and bar lines to place each harmony in its appropriate metrical position. Analyze on two levels.

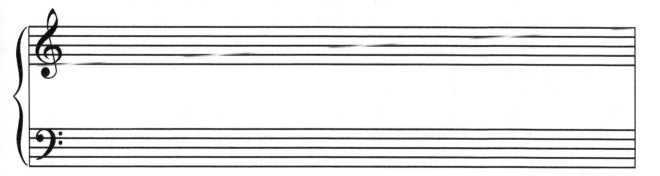

Maintaining your progression and your voice leading from the homophonic progression above, create a rhythmically active accompaniment for keyboard. In the *upper three voices*, use a broken-chord figuration. Activate the *bass* voice with a combination of passing tones, neighboring tones, and chordal leaps. Make sure that each chord lasts at least a few beats so that you have enough musical time for the broken chords.

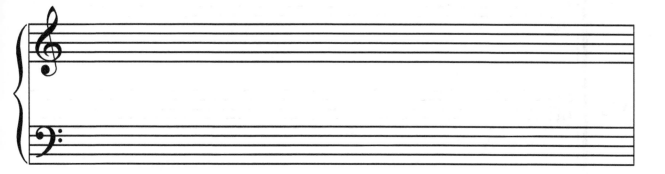

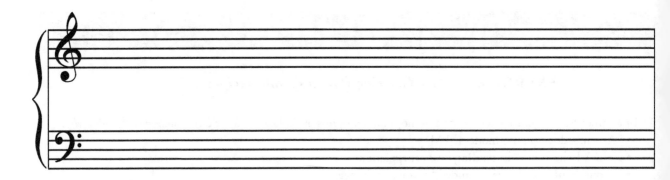

2. In a major key of your choice, write a homophonic progression for string quartet. Include each
   of the following ingredients, which are listed *out of order:*
   - A deceptive harmonic progression
   - A tonic expansion using a passing chord
   - A pre-dominant seventh chord
   - A descending fifths progression beginning on vi

   Begin by ordering them so that the progression makes harmonic sense. Write the bass voice first,
   and incorporate harmonic paradigms where possible. Analyze on two levels.

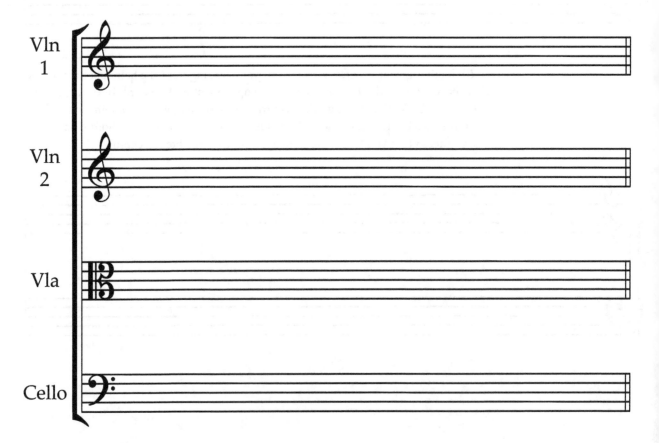

EXERCISE 13-H *Analyzing Submediant Triads*

Analyze each passage on two levels.

1. Julián Aguirre, *Fábulas* (1920). Circle and label each embellishing tone. Use the bass to decide when harmonies change.

Translation: Salicio used to play the zampoña all year long.

Sa - li - cio'u - sa - ba ta - ñer_____ La zam - po - ña to - do'el a - ño

2. Clara Schumann, *Easy Preludes for Students*, no. 2 (1895)

EXERCISE 13-I   *Writing a Step-Descent Bass in a Three-Voice Texture*

First, analyze the figured bass on two levels. Then, realize it in a three-voice texture: bass on the lower staff, and two voices on the upper staff. Omit the chordal fifth from seventh chords and, when necessary, from root-position triads as well.

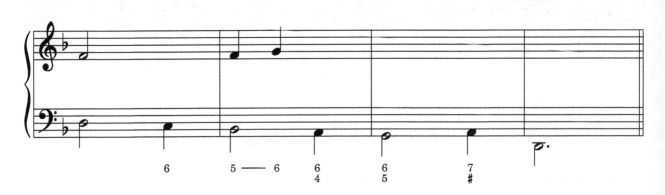

ASSIGNMENT 13.5

EXERCISE 13-J   *Analyzing Step Descents*

Analyze each passage on two levels and indicate whether each bass descends *directly* to V or *indirectly* past 5̂ to 4̂.

1. Samuel Coleridge-Taylor, Ballade in C minor, op. 73 (1907)

2. George Frideric Handel, "Thou Art Gone Up on High" from *Messiah*, HWV 56 (1741)

3. George Frideric Handel, Suite in G minor, HWV 432 (1720), *Sarabande*. In this example, the step descent occurs on the downbeat chords, elaborated by the metrically unaccented chords.

EXERCISE 13-K   *Analyzing, Reducing, and Varying a Passage*

1. *Analysis:* Analyze the passage from Arcangelo Corelli's Concerto Grosso no. 8 in G minor, op. 6 (posth. 1714), on two levels.

2. *Reduction:* On the two lowest staves provided on the following pages, write a keyboard-style reduction of the Corelli passage in dotted half notes. Select one primary bass tone and one primary melodic tone from each measure of passage above. Use your analysis and your skill with voice leading to fill in the two remaining voices.

3. *Variation:* Complete each melodic variation over Corelli's harmonic progression. As you continue each of the five beginnings, use similar rhythms and types of embellishing tones within the same variation. Record yourself playing your reduction on keyboard and use it as a backing track as you perform your variations on voice or an instrument of your choice.

Variation 1

Variation 2

Variation 3

Variation 4

Variation 5

Keyboard-Style Reduction

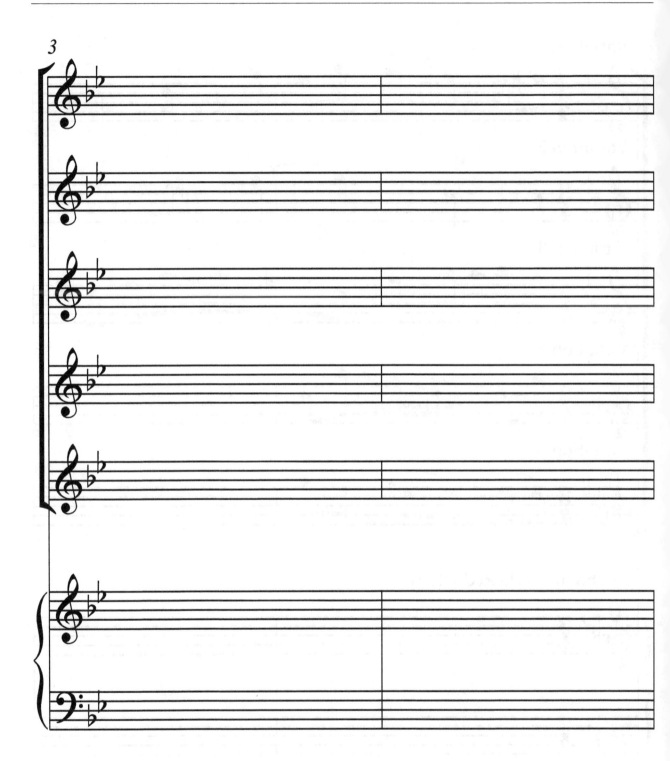

5

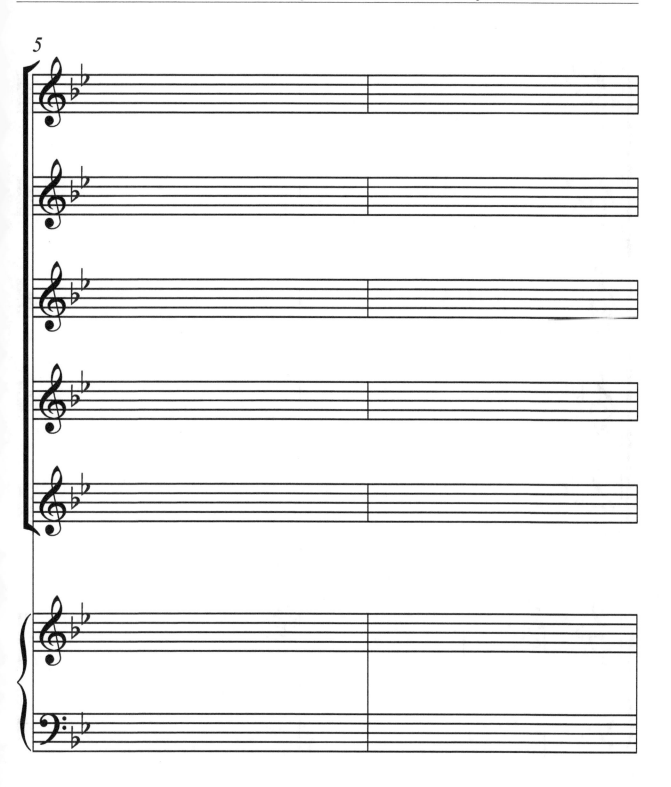

EXERCISE 13–L   *Analyzing a Passage*

Analyze the passage from Franz Schubert's Impromptu, op. posth. 142, no. 2, D. 935 (1827), on two levels. Circle and label each embellishing tone.

EXERCISE 13–M   *Composing Phrases Using the Submediant in a Variety of Ways*

First, play or listen to the sample phrase, analyze it on two levels, and study its broken-chord figuration pattern. Then, following the instructions, write two phrases of your own that use a similar figuration pattern.

After Robert Schumann, "Hör' ich das Liedchen klingen" from *Dichterliebe* (1840) (VI in a deceptive motion)

Adagio

1. In E minor, expand the tonic harmony using an embedded phrase model, and then use VI as the pre-dominant chord in a cadence.

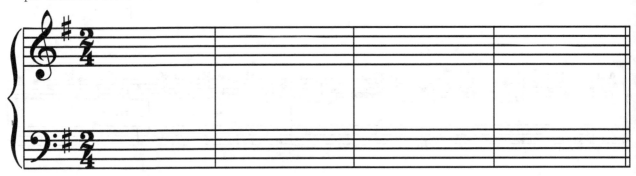

2. In C♯ minor, use VI as a bridge in a descending-thirds progression. Include a pre-dominant seventh chord and end with a cadence.

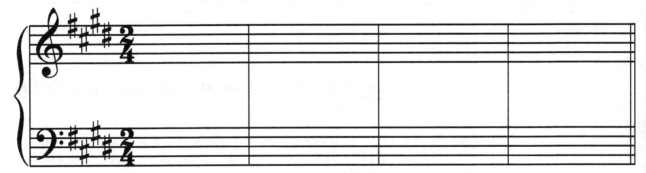

EXERCISE 13-N   *Analyzing a Passage*

Analyze the passage from the Prologue of Ruggero Leoncavallo's *Pagliacci* (1892) on two levels.

The Mediant and the Back-Relating Dominant

ASSIGNMENT 14.1

EXERCISE 14–A *Analyzing Mediant Chords*

Analyze each passage on two levels.

1. Laura Valborg Aulin, *Tondikter* for Piano, op. 7 (1882), ii

2. Amancio Alcorta (1842–1902), *Nocturno* for Flute and Piano

3. Arcangelo Corelli, Trio Sonata, op. 4, no. 5 (1694), *Gavotta*

4. Mary Harvey, "A False Designe to Be Cruel" (1653)

Men are too wise grown to ex-pire with bro-ken shafts,_____ and____ pain - ted fire.

5. Robert Schümann, *Davidsbündlertanze* (1837), no. 11

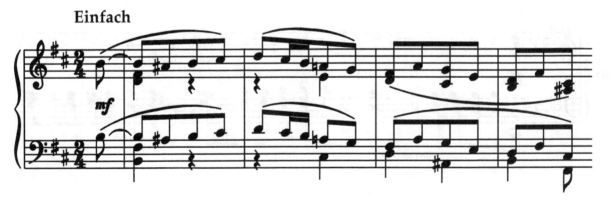

EXERCISE 14–B   *Playing and Transposing Keyboard Paradigms*

Each short paradigm below illustrates the mediant triad in one of its typical contexts. Play as written and then transposed to the two keys indicated. *Hint: Transpose the two outer voices first, and then the full chords.*

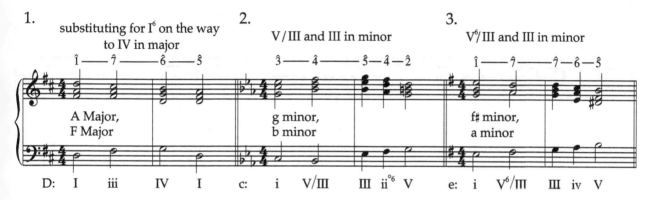

EXERCISE 14–C   *Writing Short Progressions in Keyboard Style*

Analyze each set of roman numerals or figured bass on two levels. Then, realize each example in keyboard style, starting with the given pitch in the soprano voice.

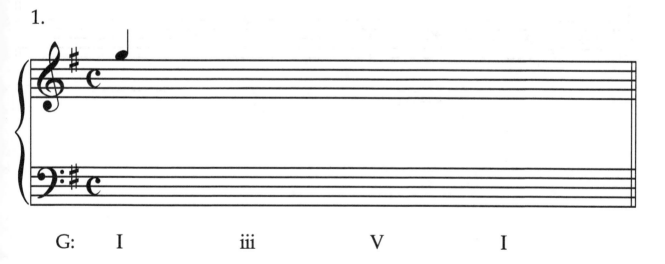

2.

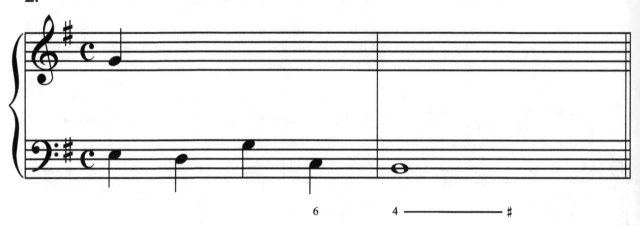

3.

ASSIGNMENT 14.3

EXERCISE 14–F   *Realizing a Figured Bass in a Three-Voice Texture*

Analyze the figured bass on two levels. Then, realize it in a three-voice texture, adding just two upper voices (both on the upper staff). You will need to omit the chordal fifth from seventh chords and some root-position triads. Make sure that inverted triads are complete.

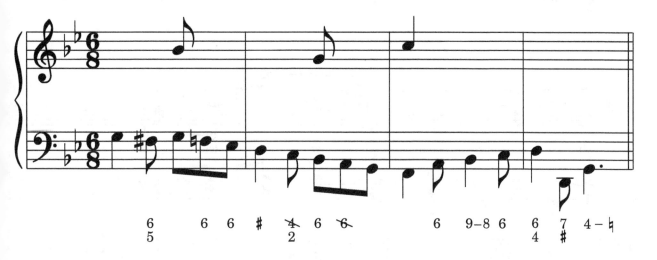

EXERCISE 14–G   *Analyzing Mediant Triads*

Analyze each passage on two levels.

1. Gustav Mahler, "Die zwei blauen Augen" from *Lieder eines fahrenden Gesellen* (1885), no. 4

   Translation: My beloved's two blue eyes sent me out into the wide world. I have to say goodbye to my most favorite place.

mich   in die   wei - te   Welt ge - schickt.   Da __ musst ich   Ab - schied

neh - - - men   vom   al - ler - lieb - sten   Platz!

2. José White, *La Bella Cubana* (1910)

ASSIGNMENT 14.4

EXERCISE 14–H   *Analyzing Mediant Triads*

Analyze each passage on two levels.

1. W. A. Mozart, Piano Sonata in A minor, K. 310 (1778), *Andante.* The second complete measure begins with a six-four chord. What type? *Hint: We have encountered this type of six-four chord many times before, but as an embellishment to the dominant chord.*

2. W. A. Mozart, Piano Sonata in C major, K. 330 (1783), *Andante cantabile*

$$\left(\begin{array}{c} \text{vii}^{\circ 6} \\ \text{of V} \end{array}\right)$$

3. On a separate sheet of paper, write three to four sentences comparing and contrasting the two Mozart passages above. What features do they share? How do they differ?

4. Eduardo Arolas (1892–1924), *Papas Calientes*

EXERCISE 14–1   *Contextualizing Submediant and Mediant Triads with Guidance*

First, play or sing the given melody. Next, harmonize it by adding a bass voice and roman numerals. Include at least one mediant triad and at least one submediant triad. *Hint: Measure 5 should be the end of a phrase. Which cadence type will work there?* Then, add two inner voices to the upper staff in order to create a keyboard-style realization.

Finally, embellish your harmonization from the previous page into a short piece for voice and piano. Model it after the samples below.

- For the upper staff of the piano (soprano/alto/tenor): block chords or broken chords
- For the lower staff of the piano (bass): repeated notes, chordal leaps between root and third, octave leaps
- For the voice part: chordal leaps, neighboring tones, and passing tones

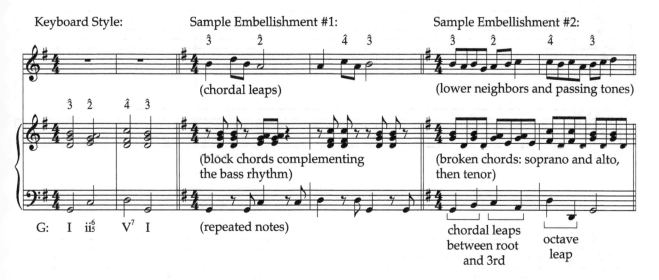

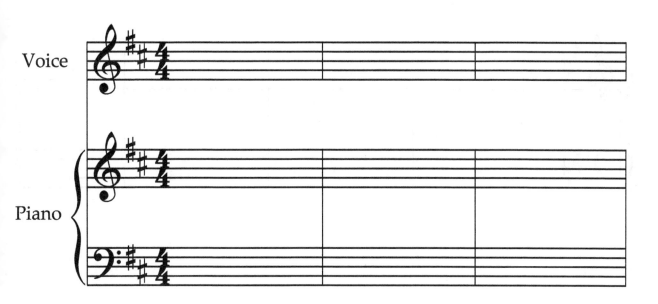

EXERCISE 14-K *Scavenging for Harmonic Paradigms in a Figured Bass*

First, play the outer voices in order to locate each paradigm listed below. Bracket and label each of them, and analyze the passage on two levels.

- two voice exchanges that expand the tonic
- a direct step-descent bass ending in a Phrygian HC
- a deceptive motion
- two cadential six-four chords
- V/III tonicizing III

Finally, add the missing inner voices to create a chorale-style realization. Include at least three suspensions.

CHAPTER 15

Periods

ASSIGNMENT 15.1

EXERCISE 15-A *Analyzing Periods*

After listening to each passage, draw a form diagram, label the form, and annotate the score to support your interpretation. You do not need to label every roman numeral, but do label the components of the phrase model and any cadences.

1. Francesca Lebrun, Violin Sonata in A major, op. 2, no. 5 (1780), *Rondo Allegro*

2. Joseph W. Postlewaite, *St. Louis Greys Quick Step* (1852)

3. Ludwig van Beethoven, Romance in F major for Violin and Orchestra, op. 50 (1798), *Adagio cantabile*

4. Luis Antonio Calvo, *Entusiasmo: Pasillo para Piano* (1909)

EXERCISE 15–B   *Composing an Eight-Measure Period from a Figured Bass*

Analyze with roman numerals. Then, add a time signature, bar lines, and rhythmic durations so that the figured bass lasts exactly eight measures (divided in half at the dotted line). Avoid making any chord excessively long or extremely short, and try to place embellishing chords in metrically unaccented places with the exception of cadential six-fours.

Next, place the bass voice on the lowest staff below and write a block-chord or broken-chord accompaniment in three voices on the middle staff. On the upper staff, compose a melody that fits the harmonic progression. Use embellishing tones to give the melody character. Choose whether your period will be parallel or contrasting, and craft the melody accordingly.

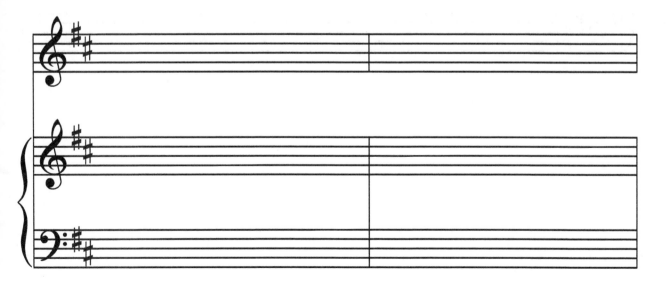

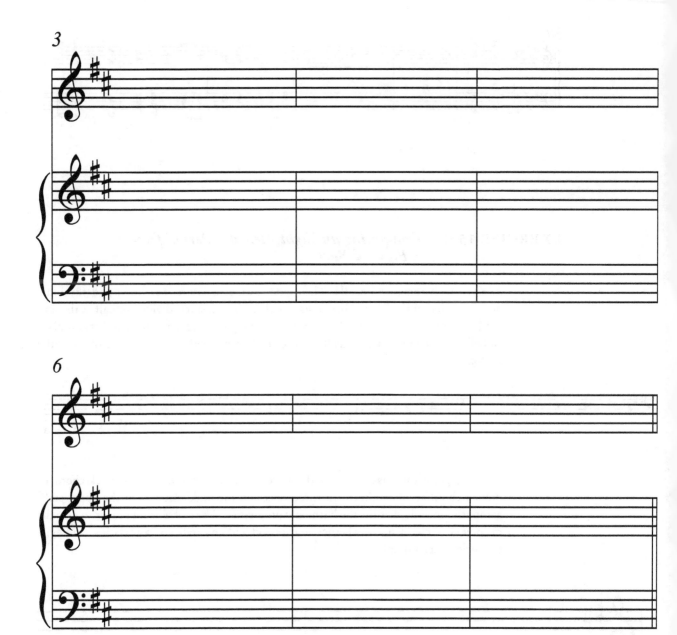

ASSIGNMENT 15.2

EXERCISE 15-C   *Harmonizing and Continuing a Melody*

- Play or sing each phrase and use its cadence to determine whether it would be more suitable as the antecedent phrase or the consequent phrase in a period.
- Compose the melody of the missing phrase on the blank staff.
- Label the two cadences, the period type, and the two phrases (antecedent and consequent).
- Harmonize the whole period by adding roman numerals (one or two chords per measure).

1. Robert Schumann, "Volksliedchen" from *Children's Pieces*, op. 51, no. 2 (1840)

Translation: When I go to the garden early in my green hat.

Wenn ich früh in den Gar - ten geh', in mei - nem __ grü - nen Hut,

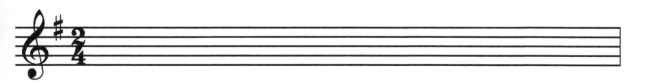

2. Marianna Auenbrugger, Sonata for Harpsichord or Fortepiano (1781), *Largo*

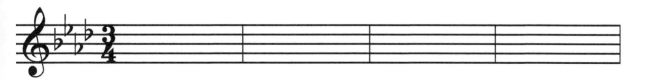

3. A. J. R. Connor, *American Polka Quadrilles*, no. 3 (1850)

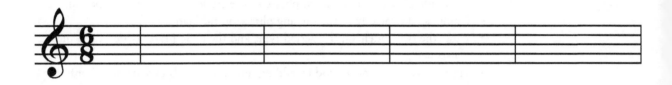

4. W. A. Mozart, Symphony in D major, K. 97 (1770), *Trio*

EXERCISE 15–D   *Analyzing Periods*

After listening to each passage, draw a form diagram, label the form, and annotate the score to support your interpretation. You do not need to label every roman numeral, but do label the components of the phrase model and any cadences.

1. Florence B. Price, *Adoration* (1951)

2. Ludwig van Beethoven, Piano Sonata no. 2 in A major, op. 2, no. 2 (1795), *Scherzo*

3. Nicanor Albarellos, *Valsa* for Guitar (1837)

ASSIGNMENT 15.3

EXERCISE 15-E   *Adding a Melody to Create a Period*

1. Play the provided block-chord accompaniment.
2. Label cadences, analyze on two levels, and label the period's tonal structure.
3. Craft a melody for trombone that creates a parallel period. Use the given noteheads as guides.
4. Sing your melody while self-accompanying on keyboard.

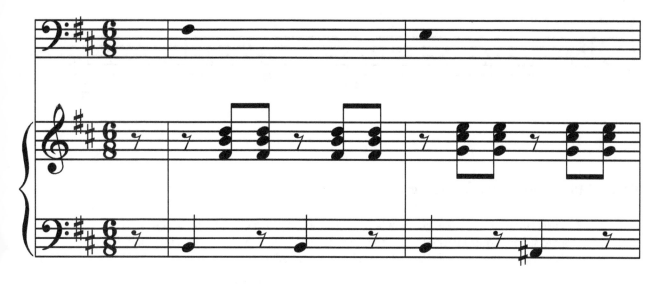

6

EXERCISE 15–F *Analyzing Periods*

After listening to each passage, draw a form diagram, label the form, and annotate the score to support your interpretation. You do not need to label every roman numeral, but do label the components of the phrase model and any cadences.

1. W. A. Mozart, Piano Sonata in C major, K. 330 (1782), *Andante cantabile*

2. Frédéric Chopin, *Grande Valse Brillante* in A minor, op. 34, no. 2, BI 64 (1833). How many true cadences (authentic or half) are in this passage? Remember that phrase markings on the score do not necessarily indicate complete tonal motions.

3. Robert Nathaniel Dett, *Inspiration Waltzes* (1903)

ASSIGNMENT 15.4

EXERCISE 15–G   *Composing Periods*

Maintaining the figuration pattern and harmonic rhythm of each given antecedent phrase, compose a consequent phrase. Label the period type and cadences, and analyze on two levels.

1. *Hint: Decide on how often harmonies change by sorting out which pitches in the Alberti bass act as bass tones. Play just those pitches with the left hand and the remaining bass-clef pitches with the right hand. Sing the melody.*

Antecedent:

Consequent:

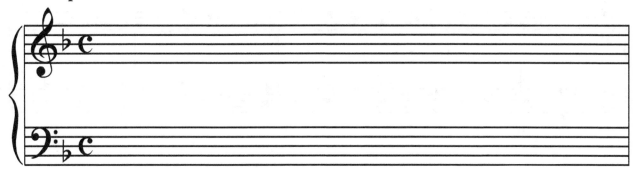

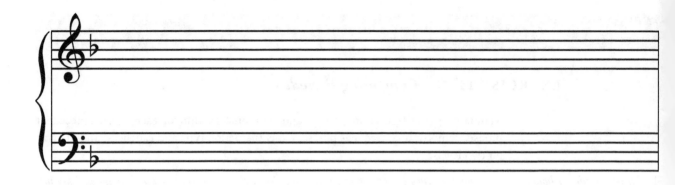

2. *Hint: Play the lower staff with two hands while singing the upper-voice melody.*

Antecedent:

Consequent:

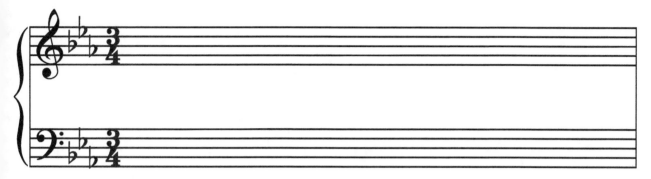

ASSIGNMENT 15.5

EXERCISE 15–H   *Composing an Eight-Measure Period from a Figured Bass*

Analyze with roman numerals. Then, add a time signature, bar lines, and rhythmic durations so that the figured bass lasts exactly eight measures (divided in half at the dotted line). Avoid making any chord excessively long or extremely short, and try to place embellishing chords in metrically unaccented places with the exception of cadential six-fours.

Next, place the bass voice on the lowest staff below and write a block-chord or broken-chord accompaniment in three voices on the middle staff. On the upper staff, compose a melody that fits the harmonic progression. Use embellishing tones to give the melody character. Choose whether your period will be parallel or contrasting, and craft the melody accordingly.

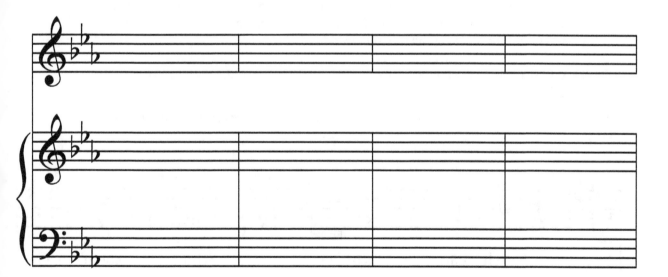

5

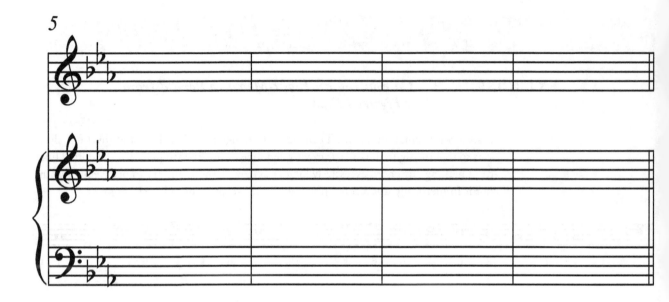

EXERCISE 15-1 *Completing the Keyboard Accompaniments of Two Periods*

Diagram and label the form of each passage, and analyze on two levels. Next, use the figured bass to complete the piano accompaniment, continuing the figuration pattern that is started for you. Sing and play your work.

1. After W. A. Mozart, *Abduction from the Seraglio* (1782), Act 2, Scene 1. Preserve the sixteenth-note motor throughout.

Translation: It is possible to win the hearts of young women through tenderness, flattery, courtesy, and jesting.

fäl - lig-keit__ und__ Scher - zen   er - o - bert man die__

Her - zen der gu - ten__ Mäd- chen   leicht,__

2. After W. A. Mozart, Violin Sonata in F major, K. 376 (1781). Preserve the eighth-note motor throughout.

CHAPTER 16

Sentences, Double Periods, and Asymmetric Periods

ASSIGNMENT 16.1

EXERCISE 16–A *Analyzing Small Forms*

After listening to each passage, label the key, any cadences, and form on the score. Then, draw a form diagram to show these details in a single picture. Include measure numbers.

1. Alejandro Monestel Zamora, *Contemplation* (1914)

2. Ludwig van Beethoven, Piano Sonata no. 3 in C major, op. 2, no. 3 (1795)

Allegro con brio

3. Joseph W. Postlewaite, *Veiled Prophet* (1880)

4. Franz Joseph Haydn, Symphony no. 101 in D major ("Clock") (1794), *Menuet*

EXERCISE 16-B *Harmonizing Sentential and Periodic Melodies*

- After singing or playing each melody, label its key, the cadence(s) it implies, and the number of phrases it includes.
- Provide a label for the form if applicable (such as sentence or PIP).
- Harmonize the melody by adding roman numerals and the phrase model (once per phrase) underneath. Label each embellishing tone in the melody. Finally, play your bass line while either singing or playing the melody.

Sample. W. A. Mozart, Bassoon Concerto in B♭ major, K. 191 (1774), *Rondeau*. Form: PIP

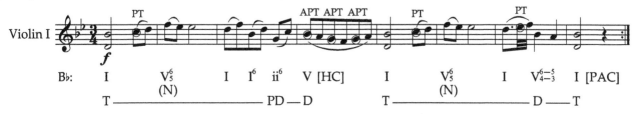

1. César Cortinas, *Preludio* (1913)

2. Franz Schubert, "Wiegenlied" ("Cradle Song"), op. 92, no. 2, D. 498 (1816)

Translation: Sleep, sleep, lovely, sweet boy. You are gently rocked by your mother's hand.

Langsam (Lento)

Schla - fe, schla - fe,   hol-der, sü - sser Kna - be,   lei - se   wiegt dich dei-ner Mut-ter Hand;

3. Franz Schubert, "An mein Klavier" ("To My Piano"), D. 342 (1816)

Translation: Gentle piano, gentle piano! What delights you create for me!

Mässig (Moderato)

Sanf - tes Kla-vier,   sanf - tes Kla-vier!   wel - che Ent-zück - ung - en schaf - fest du mir!

ASSIGNMENT 16.2

EXERCISE 16–C   *Analyzing Small Forms*

After listening to each passage, label the key, any cadences, and form on the score. Then, draw a form diagram to show these details in a single picture. Include measure numbers.

1. W. A. Mozart, Piano Trio in E major, K. 542 (1788), *Allegro*

2. Ludwig van Beethoven, Piano Concerto no. 3 in C minor, op. 37 (1800), *Allegro con brio*

3. Maria Szymanowska, March no. 3 from *Six Marches for Piano* (1819)

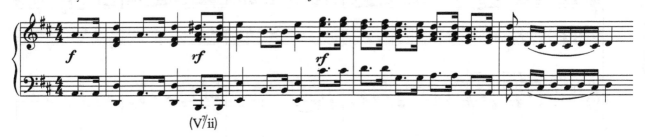

(V⁷/ii)

EXERCISE 16-D   *Harmonizing Sentential and Periodic Melodies*

- After singing or playing each melody, label its key, the cadence(s) it implies, and the number of phrases it includes.
- Provide a label for the form if applicable (such as sentence or PIP).
- Harmonize the melody by adding roman numerals and the phrase model (once per phrase) underneath. Label each embellishing tone in the melody. Finally, play your bass line while either singing or playing the melody.

Sample. W. A. Mozart, Horn Concerto in D major, K. 412 (1791), *Allegro*. Form: PIP comprised of two sentences, each with nesting.

1. Akiana Molina, Sonatina for Solo Violin, op. 5 (2007)

2. W. A. Mozart, Horn Concerto in D major, K. 412 (1791), *Allegro*

3. Robert Nathaniel Dett, "As His Own Soul" from *Eight Bible Vignettes* (1943). Treat the asterisked (*) pitches as accented embellishing tones.

ASSIGNMENT 16.3

EXERCISE 16–E   *Composing Sentences and Periods*

1. The first two measures of an eight-measure sentence are provided. Maintaining the same block-chord figuration on the lower staff, compose the rest of the phrase as follows:

    mm. 3–4: Use rhythms and melodic contours from mm. 1–2, adapted and re-harmonized to feature the given structural pitches in the melody.

    mm. 5–6: Increase the musical energy in three ways: (1) reach a climactic apex in the melody, (2) fragment the melodic material from mm. 1–2 into two one-measure units (m. 5 and m. 6), and (3) begin a harmonic progression that drives forward toward the cadence.

    mm. 7–8: Reach a cadence.

Play your phrase, or play the lower staff while singing the upper staff. Analyze your phrase on two levels.

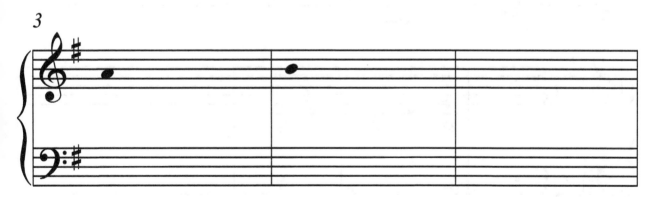

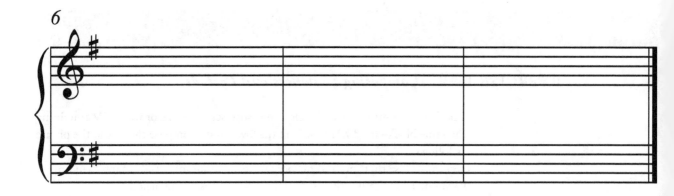

2. Using the given first measure, compose an eight-measure parallel interrupted period consisting of two four-measure sentences.
   - Plan the cadences that you need to reach in m. 4 and m. 8.
   - Craft a 1+1+2 sentence to comprise the antecedent phrase in mm. 1–4.
   - Decide how much of the antecedent phrase to repeat in the consequent phrase (mm. 5–8).
   - Rewrite the rest of the consequent to reach the appropriate cadence in mm. 7–8.

Play your accompaniment while singing the upper-voice melody. Analyze your period on two levels.

EXERCISE 16–F   *Analyzing Small Forms*

After listening to each passage, label the key, any cadences, and form on the score. Then, draw a form diagram to show these details in a single picture. Include measure numbers.

1. Scott Joplin, *The Chrysanthemum* (1904). *Hint: This passage includes three cadences in the home key (tonicized HC, PAC, and IAC, but not in this order) and one HC in a different key. Identify the key of each cadence (such as "PAC in E♭ major"). Do not be thrown off by the chromatic embellishing tones!*

2. José André, Sonatina for Piano (1918)

ASSIGNMENT 16.4

EXERCISE 16–G *Completing a Composition*

This unfinished passage for flute and piano consists of a two-measure introduction and an eight-measure parallel interrupted period.

1. Analyze the given piano accompaniment on two levels.
2. Compose the flute melody for the antecedent phrase (mm. 3–6).
3. Compose the consequent phrase (mm. 7–10), which will begin similarly to the antecedent but end more conclusively.

Consequent

EXERCISE 16–H   *Analyzing and Reducing Passages*

1. Ludwig van Beethoven, Piano Sonata in C minor, op. 10, no. 1 (1798), *Adagio*. After listening,
   label the key, any cadences, and form on the score. Then, draw a form diagram to show these
   details in a single picture. Include measure numbers.

2. W. A. Mozart, Symphony no. 40 in G minor, K. 550 (1788), *Molto allegro*. Listen, then perform
   it as follows:
   - *Sing* the first violin part in a comfortable vocal register.
   - *With your left hand,* play the bass part (which sounds an octave lower than it appears on
     the staff).
   - *With your right hand,* play the chords that sound in the divisi violas (omitting octave dou-
     blings).

After you perform the passage yourself, label the key, any cadences, and form on the score. Then, draw a form diagram to show these details in a single picture. Include measure numbers.

Sample of the opening of your keyboard reduction (played while singing the violin part):

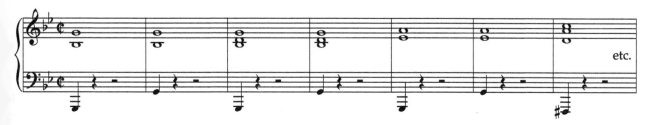

ASSIGNMENT 16.5

EXERCISE 16–I   *Harmonizing Sentential Melodies*

Each melody below is is a sentence. Label the cadence type that closes each melody, and harmonize the entire melody by adding appropriate bass notes and roman numerals.

1. Louise Reichardt, "Vanne felice rio" (1806)

Translation: Go to the sea, happy river. If only I could exchange my own fate with yours.

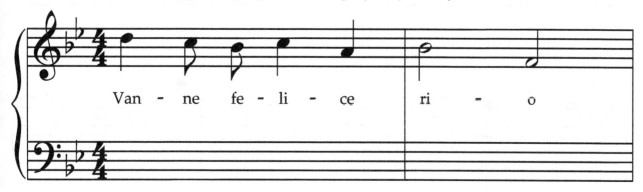

2. Robert Nathaniel Dett, *Magnolia Suite* (1912), i. Treat each asterisked pitch as an appoggiatura.

3. Maintain both the bass rhythm (quarter-eighth) and the harmonic rhythm (dotted quarters) throughout.

EXERCISE 16-J   *Analyzing Small Forms*

After listening to each passage, label the key, any cadences, and form on the score. Then, draw a form diagram to show these details in a single picture. Include measure numbers.

1. Franz Joseph Haydn, Piano Sonata no. 19 in E minor, Hob. XVI:47 (1765), *Allegro*

2. Juan Bautista Alberdi (1810–1884), "La Ausencia" from *Six Piano Pieces*

EXERCISE 16–K   *Crafting Musical Architecture*

You will compose two periods, following a design process not unlike what architects do with a building: Beginning with a list of what the periods need to do, you will sketch a floor plan for how to accomplish that, and finally realize the finer details.

THE PROGRAM: WHAT THE PERIODS NEED TO DO

First, read the three descriptions below, which list the features that particular periods need to contain. Label the tonal structure of each period as progressive, interrupted, continuous, or sectional.

Label for the Period's Tonal Structure	Phrase 1 (mm. 1–4)			Phrase 2 (mm. 5–8)		
	Begins on	Includes	Ends with	Begins on	Includes	Ends with
	I	an EPM, then a PD	HC	V	a deceptive motion	PAC
	i	indirect step descent leading to a PD	IAC	i	indirect step descent leading to an expanded PD	PAC
	i	ascending bass arpeggiation	Phrygian HC	i	descending bass arpeggiation, expanded PD	PAC

SCHEMATIC DESIGN: THE FLOOR PLAN OF EACH PERIOD

Next, choose two of the period descriptions above to bring to life through composition. Choose a different key for each of them and use the templates below to create tonal blueprints. These will include key signatures, time signatures, bar lines, a bass line with rhythms, roman numerals, cadence types, and labels for the period's tonal structure and melodic design.

Blueprint for Period A. Period type:

Blueprint for Period B. Period type:

DESIGN DEVELOPMENT: THE FINISHINGS

It is time to decide on the finer details: which type of wood for the floors, which shape for the windows, and, in your case, which figuration technique for the piano and some melodic embellishments for the upper voice.

Choose one of your two blueprints from the previous section to bring all the way to completion as a full-fledged piece. Study the repertoire sample below and emulate the piano's broken-chord figuration in your own period. Choose an instrument or voice for your melody and add the appropriate clef. Analyze and play your piece.

Isabella Colbran, "La speranza al cor mi dice" (1808)

Translation: I'll be happy again.

THE FINISHED PIECE

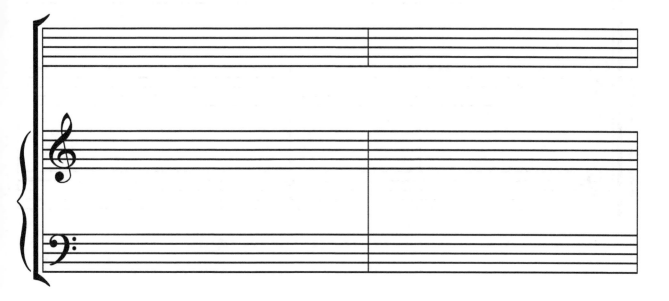

3

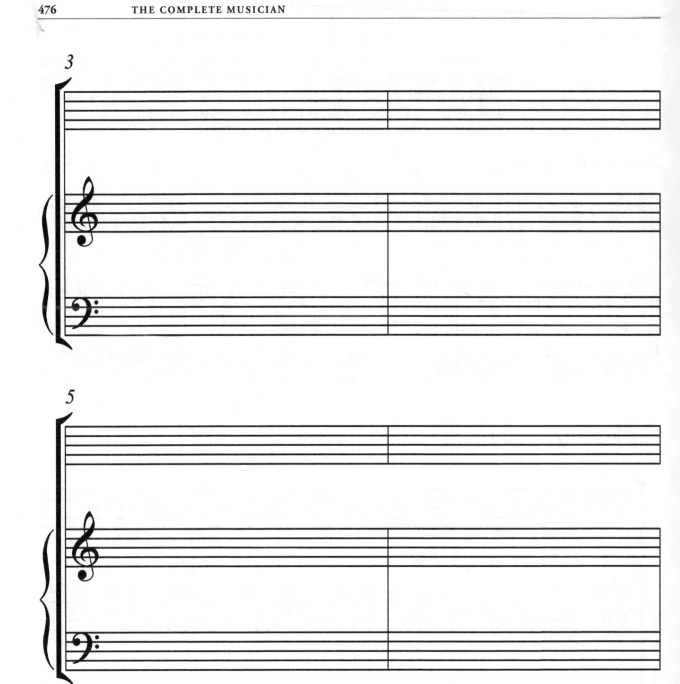

5

7

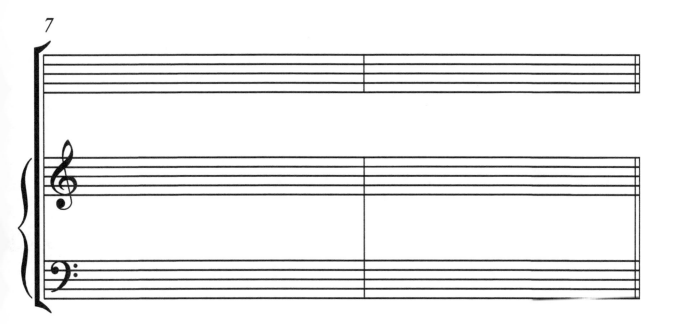

CHAPTER 17

Applied Chords

ASSIGNMENT 17.1

EXERCISE 17–A *Analyzing Applied Dominants in Short Passages*

Each excerpt provides a "snapshot" of one or more applied dominants in a short musical context. Look carefully at the indicated key of the passage, and then analyze with roman numerals.

1. Franz Joseph Haydn, String Quartet in E♭ major, op. 20, no. 1 (1772)

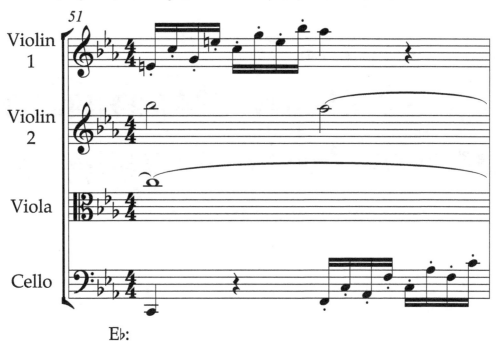

2. Louise Farrenc, Sonata no. 1 for Piano and Cello, op. 46 (1859)

3. L. Viola Kinney, *Mother's Sacrifice* (1909)

4. Franz Schubert, Piano Sonata in D major, D. 850 (1725), *Scherzo*

EXERCISE 17–B *Detecting Errors in Applied Dominants*

For parts 1 through 3, the roman numeral analysis and given key are correct, but the *chord spelling* is incorrect. Renotate the chord in the empty space to the right by correcting any missing or incorrect accidentals.

For parts 4 through 6, the notated pitches and given key are correct, but the *roman numerals* are incorrect. Renotate the roman numerals in the space below to match the pitches and given key.

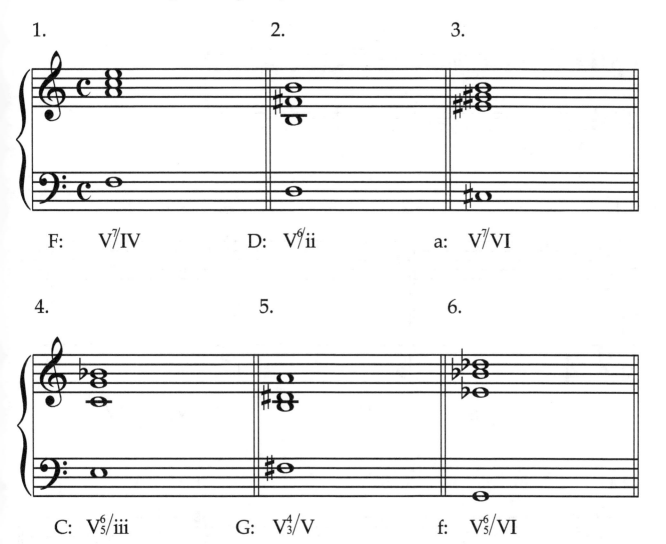

1.   2.   3.

F: V^7/IV D: V^6_5/ii a: V^7/VI

4.   5.   6.

C: V^6_5/iii G: V^4_3/V f: V^6_5/VI

EXERCISE 17–C *Playing and Resolving Applied Dominants*

Realize each progression in keyboard style. Use the provided soprano and the roman numerals as guides. The sample demonstrates a useful method:

a. Begin by determining the bass voice and playing the outer-voice duet.
b. Add the inner voices to the right hand, paying attention to voice leading.

Sample.

EXERCISE 17–D   *Resolving Applied Dominants at the Keyboard*

At the keyboard, fill in the blanks in the progressions below by resolving each applied dominant at the asterisk. Then, notate what you play. Be sure to resolve leading tones and chordal sevenths correctly. Analyze with roman numerals. *Hint: Ask yourself, "In what key is this chord a dominant?" That will tell you what chord follows in the blank.*

1.

2.

ASSIGNMENT 17.2

EXERCISE 17–E   *Analyzing Applied Chords in Context*

First, analyze all diatonic chords with roman numerals and provide a second-level analysis. Next, circle each applied chord and label it with a roman numeral. A sample analysis is provided. *Hint: Remember to use both your eye and ear to pinpoint chromatically altered tones as indicators of applied chords.*

Sample analysis: W. A. Mozart, String Quartet in E♭ major, K. 171 (1773)

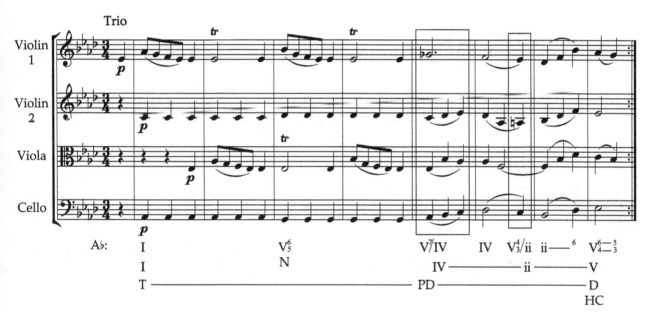

3. Louise Farrenc (1804–1875), *Valse Brillante*, op. 48. The chord in the sixth measure recurs later—but does it resolve in the same way both times? In addition to the harmonic analysis instructed above, diagram and label the phrase structure of this passage.

4. Ludwig van Beethoven, "Neues Liebe" (1809)

Translation: Lead me to her right now.

EXERCISE 17-F   *Realizing Short Figured Basses*

Realize each short figured bass in keyboard style. Determine what the applied chord is before you play, and attend to voice leading. Fragments of the upper voices are provided as a head start.

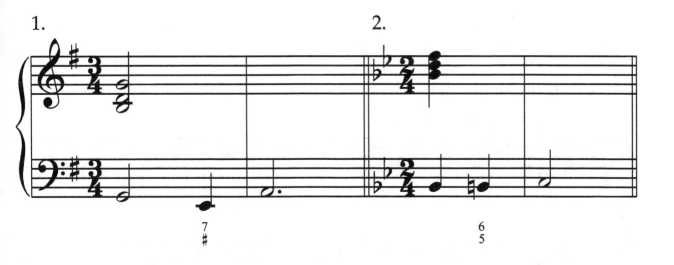

3.   **4.**

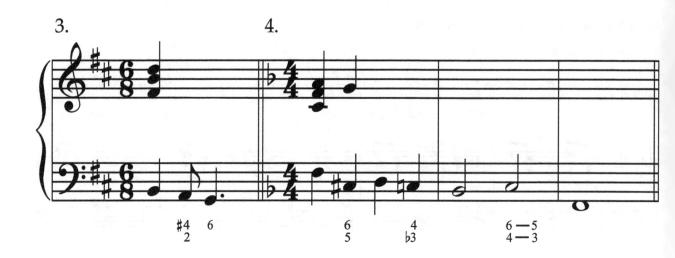

$\sharp4$ 6
2

6
5

4
$\flat3$

6 — 5
4 — 3

EXERCISE 17–G   *Playing and Transposing Keyboard Paradigms*

Play each progression in the given key, and then play and write it transposed to the additional keys listed. Follow these steps:

a.   *Bass:* Determine the scale degrees of the bass voice and transpose it to the new key.

b.   *Outer Voices:* Do the same with the soprano and play the outer-voice duet in the new key.

c.   *Four Voices:* Think about the harmonies and the right-hand chordal shapes in order to play all four voices transposed.

1.

C major (model)   F major

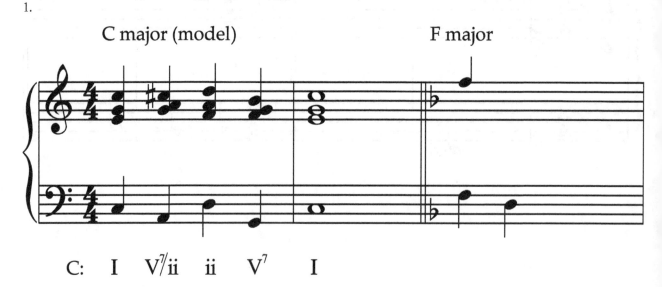

C: I   V⁷/ii   ii   V⁷   I

A major

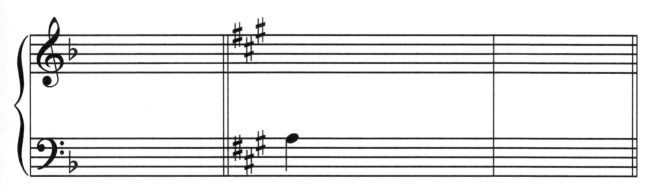

2.

G major (model)   Bb major

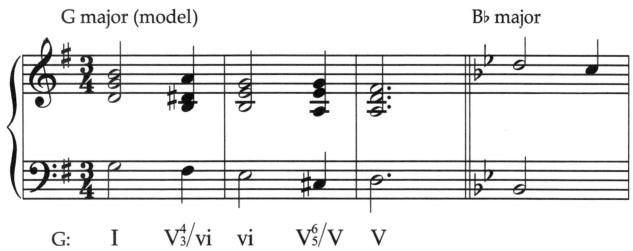

G: I   V$^4_3$/vi   vi   V$^6_5$/V   V

D major

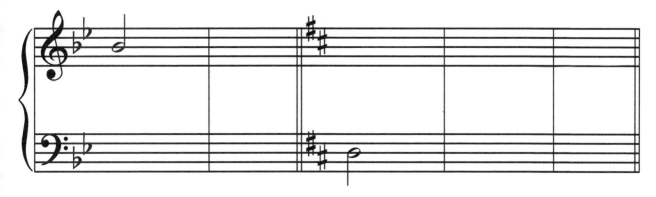

ASSIGNMENT 17.3

EXERCISE 17–H   *Analyzing Applied Dominants in Context*

Each example contains multiple applied chords. First, analyze all diatonic chords with roman numerals. Then, circle each applied chord and label it with a roman numeral.

1. Provide a second-level analysis as well.

2. Franz Schubert, Waltz in B♭ major from *German Dances and Ecossaises*, D. 783 (1823)

3. Mélanie Bonis, Suite en Trio for Flute, Violin, and Piano, op. 59 (1903), *Scherzo*

EXERCISE 17-I   *Analyzing and Resolving Applied Dominants*

First, analyze each applied dominant with a roman numeral. Then, write and analyze its resolution and play the whole progression on keyboard to check your work aurally. Resolve all tendency tones correctly. Keep in mind how each specific inversion resolves:

- V and V^7 resolve to a root-position chord with the bass leaping.
- V^6 and V$^6_5$ resolve to a root-position chord with the bass stepping upward.
- V$^4_3$ resolves either to a root-position chord with the bass stepping downward, or to a first-inversion chord with the bass stepping upward.
- V$^4_2$ resolves to a first-inversion chord with the bass stepping downward.

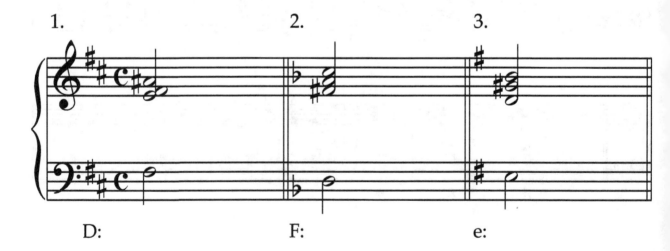

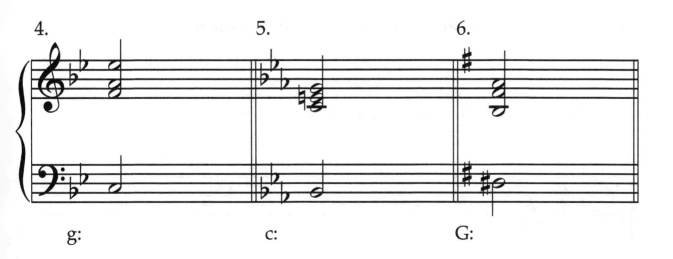

4.

5.

6.

g:

c:

G:

7.

8.

9.

10.

d:

f#:

E♭:

B♭:

EXERCISE 17–J   *Constructing Applied Dominants at the Keyboard*

Using the given roman numerals, harmonize the given soprano voice in keyboard style. Keep in mind that root-position V^7 chords are often incomplete (missing the chordal fifth), especially when the leading tone is in the highest voice. However, inversions of V^7 (i.e., V^6_5, V^4_3, and V^4_2) are always complete in a four-voice texture.

1.

F: I V^4_2 ⤳ IV^6 V^4_3 ⤳ V

2.

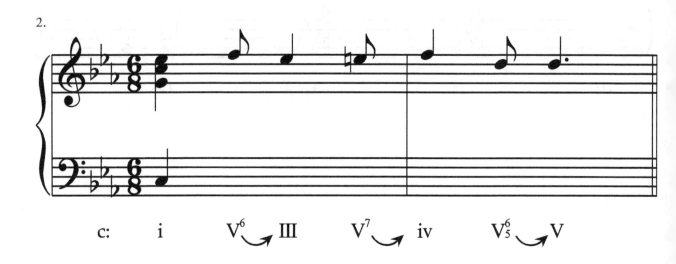

c: i V^6 ⤳ III V^7 ⤳ iv V^6_5 ⤳ V

ASSIGNMENT 17.4

EXERCISE 17–K   *Analyzing Applied Dominants in Context*

Analyze the following examples using two levels.

1. Edward Elgar, "Salut d'Amour" ("Love's Greeting"), op. 12 (1888). Diagram and label the form of this passage as well. *Hint: Not all chromatically raised notes are applied leading tones.*

2. Fanny Hensel, "Song for the Piano," op. 8, no. 3 (1826). One of the applied chords in this excerpt does not resolve as we would expect—which one? Does *anything* about its resolution conform to our expectations? *Do not be thrown off by the passage's many expressive accented embellishing tones.*

3. W. A. Mozart, String Quartet in F major, K. 158 (1772), *Allegro*. Diagram and label the form of this passage as well.

EXERCISE 17–L   *Self-Accompanying with Applied Dominants*

Use the given roman numerals to complete the piano accompaniment, maintaining the rhythmic pattern that is begun for you. When a harmony lasts for just two beats, you'll write the bass "oom" followed by just one right-hand "pah" rather than four. Keep voice leading in mind. Once you finish, sing the melody while accompanying yourself.

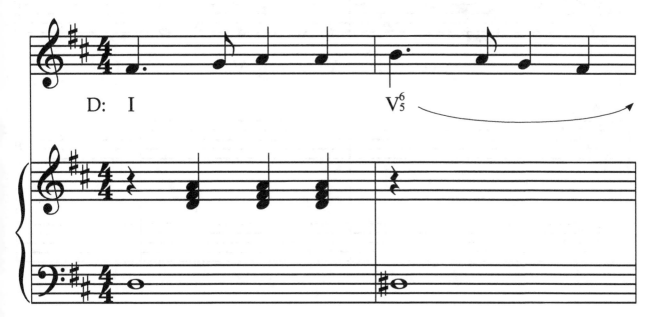

EXERCISE 17-M *Harmonizing Melodies with Applied Dominants*

In keyboard style, harmonize the given melody using one chord per melodic note. Consider voice leading and the proper resolution of tendency tones as you connect the chords. Some guidance is provided as a head start. Analyze your work on two levels.

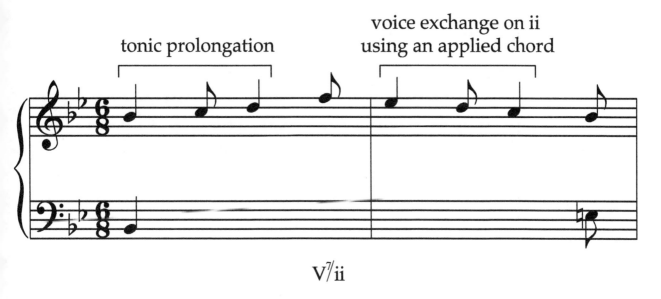

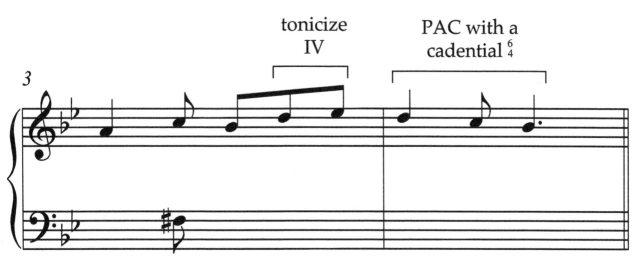

ASSIGNMENT 17.5

EXERCISE 17–N   *Analyzing Applied Chords in Context*

Analyze each passage on two levels.

1. Samuel Coleridge-Taylor (1875–1912), Sonata for Violin and Piano, op. 28. *Hint: Watch the clefs carefully on the lower staff and consider how long each chord lasts.* The first five measures are done for you.

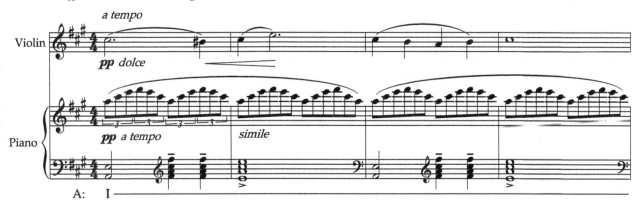

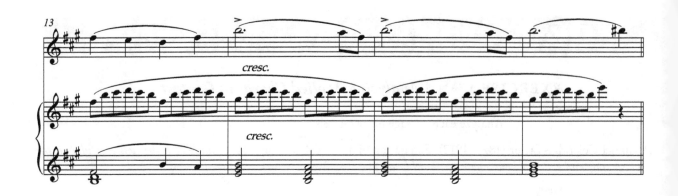

2. W. A. Mozart, "Agnus Dei" from *Requiem*, K. 626 (1791). Harmony and rhythm work together to lend weight to the emphasized syllables of the text. In a few sentences, elaborate on how this is accomplished.

Translation: Lamb of God who takes away the sins of the world.

3. Amancio Jacinto Alcorta (1805–1862), *Nocturno* for Flute and Piano

EXERCISE 17–O   *Resolving Applied Leading-Tone Chords at the Keyboard*

At the keyboard, fill in the blanks in the progressions below by resolving each applied leading-tone chord correctly at the asterisk. Then, notate what you play. Be sure to resolve each tendency tone. Analyze with roman numerals. *Hint: Ask yourself, "In what key is the root of this chord the leading tone?" That will tell you what chord follows in the blank.*

1.

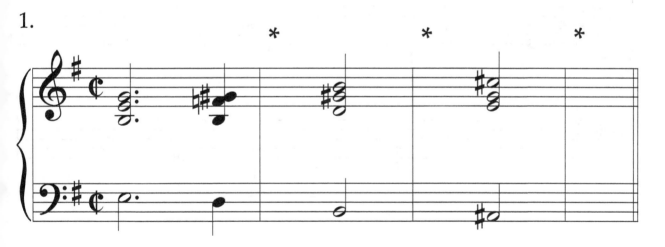

2.

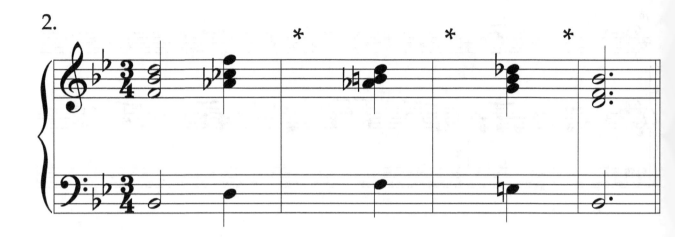

EXERCISE 17-P   *Adding Inner Voices*

In keyboard style—and at a keyboard!—realize the following figured bass, which includes applied leading-tone chords. The soprano voice is given. Analyze on two levels.

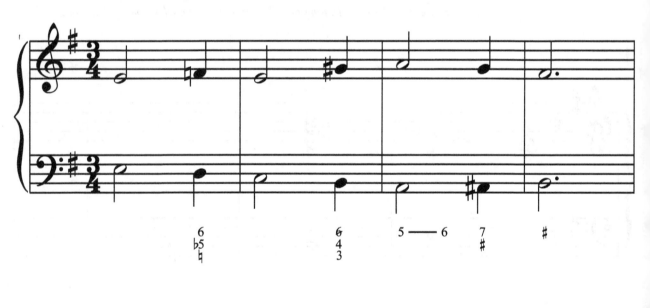

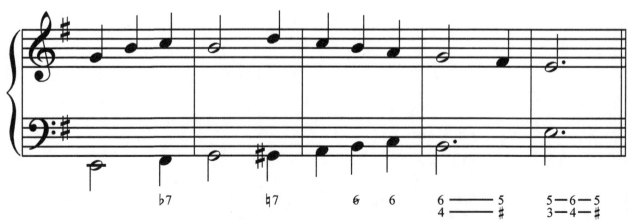

ASSIGNMENT 17.6

EXERCISE 17–Q   *Analyzing Applied Chords in Context*

Analyze each passage on two levels.

1. Joseph Bologne, String Quartet no. 4 from *Six String Quartets*, op. 1 (1773)

2. Mary Frances Allitsen, "The Lute Player" (1895)

A war-rior   like a prince at-tend-ed, Stay'd   his steed_ by the cas-tle walls.

3. Louise Farrenc, Violin Sonata no. 2, op. 39 (1850), *Allegro grazioso*

4. Scott Joplin, *Palm Leaf Rag* (1903). One of the applied chords in this passage is spelled enharmonically. See if you can determine its function by examining the context.

EXERCISE 17–R   *Playing and Transposing Keyboard Paradigms*

Each progression below contains one or more applied leading-tone chords. Play it in the given key, and then play and write it transposed to the additional keys listed. Some scaffolding is provided in the additional keys to guide your work. Follow these steps to transpose:

a. *Bass:* Determine the scale degrees of the bass voice and transpose it to the new key.
b. *Outer Voices:* Do the same with the soprano voice and play the outer-voice duet in the new key.
c. *Four Voices:* Thinking about the harmonies, play all four voices transposed.

1. 　　　C minor (model)　　　　　　　　　　　　A minor

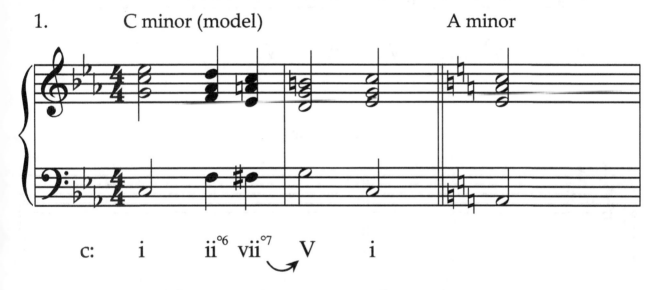

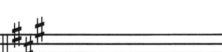

2.   D minor (model)   B minor

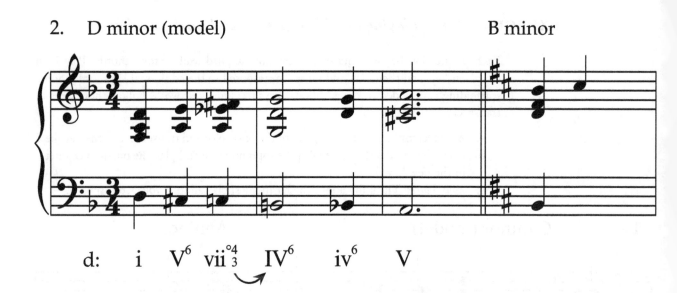

d: i   V⁶   vii°⁴₃   IV⁶   iv⁶   V

G minor

ASSIGNMENT 17.7

EXERCISE 17–S   *Spelling and Resolving Applied Leading-Tone Chords*

In keyboard style, write each applied leading-tone chord *and its resolution*. Keep in mind:

- vii°7 resolves to a root-position chord with the bass stepping upward.
- vii°$^6_5$ and vii°6 resolve either to a root-position chord with the bass stepping downward, or to a first-inversion chord with the bass stepping upward.
- vii°$^4_3$ resolves to a first-inversion chord with the bass stepping downward.

Be sure to resolve tendency tones correctly. Add the appropriate key signature and any necessary accidentals.

Sample.

Provided:

b: vii°7/V

Solution:

b: vii°7/V   V

1.   2.   3.   4.

e: vii°7/iv   D: vii°$^6_5$/ii   F: vii°6/iii   A: vii°$^4_3$/vi

EXERCISE 17–T   *Harmonizing Melodic Fragments*

In keyboard style, harmonize each melodic fragment using applied chords. Arrows indicate where applied chords should occur. Try to place applied chords on metrically *unaccented* beats and their resolutions on metrically *accented* beats. Work at a keyboard so you can check your work aurally. You are welcome to work out your ideas on this page, but notate your completed harmonizations on the next page.

A sample is provided.

Sample.

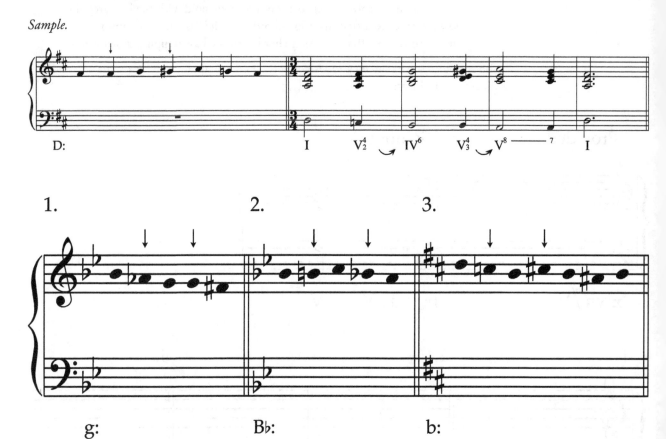

1.

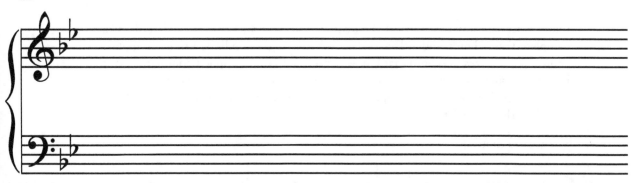

2.

3.

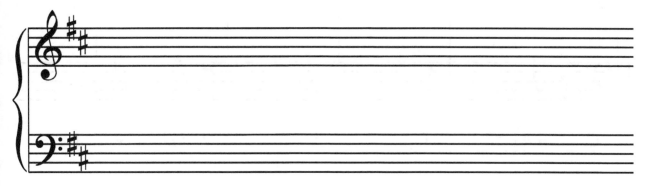

EXERCISE 17–U *Inserting Applied Chords*

Outer voices are provided for just the diatonic pillars of a phrase. In keyboard style, complete these chords and fill in each gap between these pillars, using an applied chord that tonicizes the chord that follows. Insert at least one applied dominant and at least one applied leading-tone chord into each phrase. Make sure you choose inversions and voicings that permit you to approach the given pillars with strong voice leading, including the resolution of tendency tones.

1. Insert three applied chords.

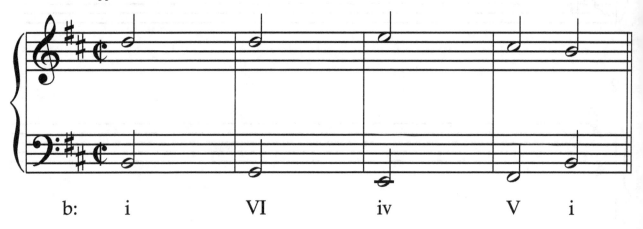

b: i   VI   iv   V   i

2. Insert four applied chords.

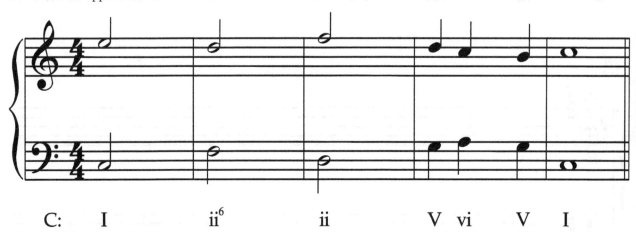

C: I   ii⁶   ii   V   vi   V   I

EXERCISE 17–V   *Analyzing an Extended Tonicization*

In this passage from Josephine Lang's "Am Wasserfall" from *Sechs Lieder*, op. 12 (1845), several applied chords work together to tonicize the same harmony. Analyze on two levels. You may find it useful to use the bracket notation.

Translation: It jumps up on the rocks and lifts itself back to pour down tears of unspeakable happiness.

ASSIGNMENT 17.8

EXERCISE 17–W   *Harmonizing Melodic Fragments*

In keyboard style, harmonize each melodic fragment using applied chords. Arrows indicate where applied chords should occur. Try to place applied chords on metrically *unaccented* beats and their resolutions on metrically *accented* beats. Work at a keyboard so you can check your work aurally. You are welcome to work out your ideas on this page, but notate your completed harmonizations on the next page.

A sample is provided for you:

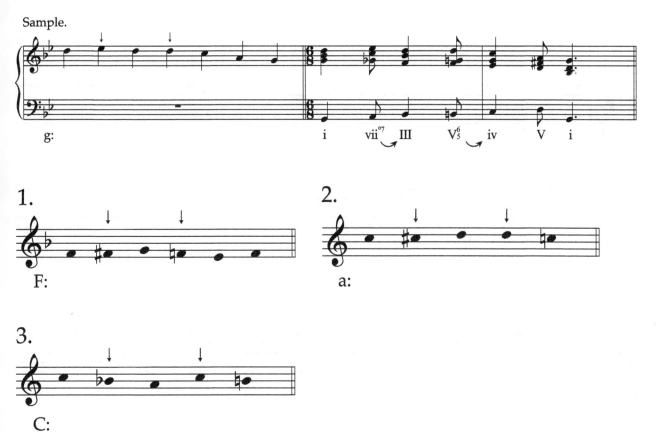

1.

2.

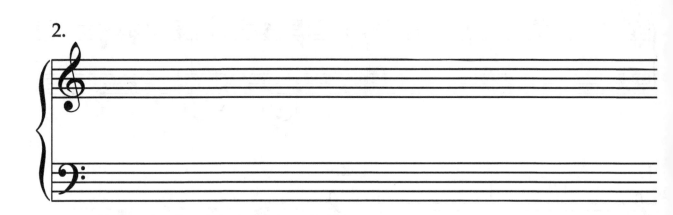

3.

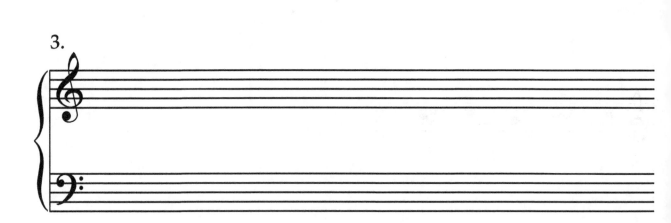

EXERCISE 17–X   *Composing with Applied vii°⁶ and vii°⁷*

Working in keyboard style—and at a keyboard!—complete the following progressions that incorporate applied vii°⁶ and vii°⁷ chords. First, complete the applied chords and resolve them. Then, compose an ending to the progression following the instructions in each example. Add bar lines as necessary. Analyze on two levels.

1.

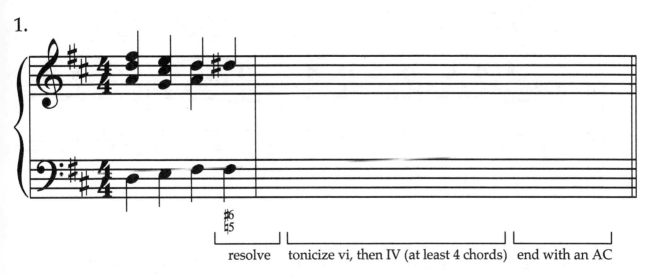

resolve   tonicize vi, then IV (at least 4 chords)   end with an AC

2.

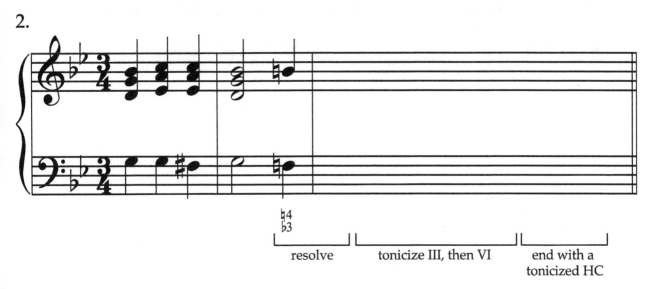

resolve   tonicize III, then VI   end with a tonicized HC

EXERCISE 17-Y *Analyzing an Extended Tonicization*

In this passage from Felix Mendelssohn's Cello Sonata no. 1 in B♭ major, op. 45 (1838), several applied chords work together to tonicize the same harmony. Analyze on two levels. You may find it useful to use the bracket notation. *Hint: Do not be misled by the circled F♯s, which are passing tones rather than applied leading tones.*

CHAPTER 18

Modulation

EXERCISE 18–A *Analyzing Modulations and Extended Tonicizations*

Each passage below features *either* a modulation *or* one or more extended tonicization(s). First, listen to the passage. Next, label the starting key and both the key and type of each cadence (e.g., HC: I, PAC: III). Finally, analyze the entire passage with roman numerals, including bracket(s) for any extended tonicizations or a clearly marked pivot chord for a modulation.

1. Louise Farrenc (1804–1875), Violin Sonata, op. 39, *Scherzo*

2. Robert Schumann, "Du bist wie eine Blume" ("You Are So Like a Flower") from *Myrthen*, op. 25 (1840), no. 24

Translation: You are like a flower, so sweet and beautiful and pure.

Du bist____ wie ei - ne Blu-me,   so hold und schön und rein;

3. Franz Joseph Haydn, Piano Sonata in E minor, no. 53, Hob. XVI:34 (c. 1779), *Vivace molto*

EXERCISE 18-B   *Listing Closely Related Keys*

List the five keys that are closely related to each given key. Use uppercase letters for major keys and lowercase letters for minor keys.

1. D major __ __ __ __ __

2. A♭ major __ __ __ __ __

3. E minor __ __ __ __ __

4. B♭ major __ __ __ __ __

5. F minor __ __ __ __ __

6. C♯ minor __ __ __ __ __

7. B major __ __ __ __ __

8. C minor __ __ __ __ __

9. D minor __ __ __ __ __

EXERCISE 18-C   *Selecting Pivot Chords*

Complete the table below in order to show a possible pivot chord for each modulation. A sample is provided.

	First Key	Second Key	Key Relationship	Pivot Chord	Roman Numeral in First Key	Roman Numeral in Second Key
Sample.	F major	C major	V	D minor	vi	ii
1.	E minor	G major		C major		
2.	A major		V		I	
3.	C minor	G minor				iv
4.		D major	III	E minor		
5.	A minor		v		III	
6.	E♭ major	B♭ major				ii
7.		F♯ minor	v	B minor		
8.		B major	V		E major	

ASSIGNMENT 18.2

EXERCISE 18-D *Analyzing Modulations and Extended Tonicizations*

Each passage below features *either* a modulation *or* one or more extended tonicization(s). First, listen to the passage. Next, label the starting key and both the key and type of each cadence (e.g., HC: I, PAC: III). Finally, analyze the entire passage with roman numerals, including bracket(s) for any extended tonicizations or a clearly marked pivot chord for a modulation.

1. Josephine Lang, *Charakterstücke*, op. 32 (1864), ii. What is the form of this passage? *Hint: What would the form be if it stopped after eight measures, and how do the last two measures relate to what has come before?*

2. Francis Johnson (1792–1844), "The American Girl"

3. Robert Schumann, "Talismane" from *Myrthen,* op. 25 (1840), no. 8

4. Ludwig van Beethoven, Piano Sonata no. 27 in E minor, op. 90 (1814)

Mit Lebhaftigkeit und durchaus mit Empfindung und Ausdruck

EXERCISE 18-E   *Filling in Missing Pivot Chords*

Each miniature phrase below expands the tonic in an original key and reaches a cadence in a different key. First, play the phrase on piano and label the two keys. Next, insert a pivot chord at the arrow. Finally, analyze the entire phrase with roman numerals.

3.

4.

ASSIGNMENT 18.3

EXERCISE 18–F   *Realizing Figured Basses that Modulate*

Realize each figured bass in the specified texture. In addition, analyze with roman numerals, including a clearly marked pivot chord. Play your work at the keyboard.

1. Chorale Style

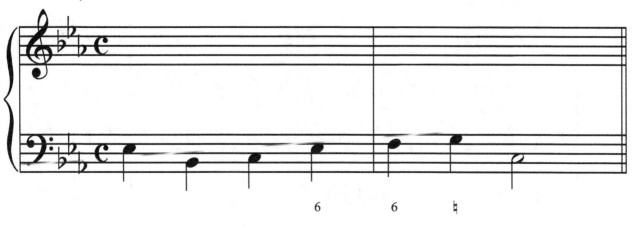

2. Keyboard Style

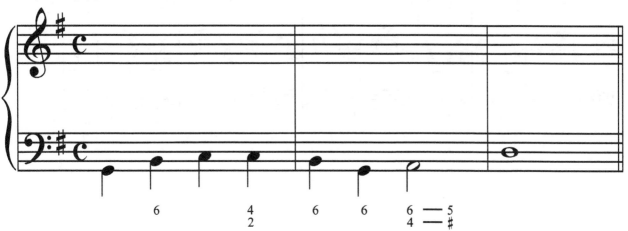

EXERCISE 18-G *Analyzing Modulations and Extended Tonicizations*

Each passage below features *either* a modulation *or* one or more extended tonicization(s). First, listen to the passage. Next, label the starting key and both the key and type of each cadence (e.g., HC: I, PAC: III). Finally, analyze the entire passage with roman numerals, including bracket(s) for any extended tonicizations or a clearly marked pivot chord for a modulation.

1. Johannes Brahms, *Hungarian Dance* no. 1, WoO 1 (1879)

2. Amy Beach, Three Compositions for Violin and Piano, op. 40 (1898), no. 3

3. Franz Joseph Haydn, Symphony no. 97 in C major, Hob. I:97 (1792), *Allegretto*

4.   Franz Joseph Haydn, String Quartet in E♭ major, op. 71, no. 3 (1793), *Andante con moto*

ASSIGNMENT 18.4

EXERCISE 18–H   *Writing Modulations*

Each example begins in G major and includes a vi (submediant) chord roughly halfway through what will become a complete phrase. Write each phrase as instructed.

1. Modulate to V using the given vi as a pivot chord. Reach an authentic cadence in the new key. Write in keyboard style.

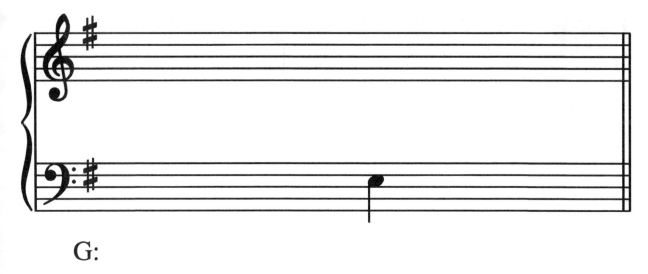

2. Remain in G major and reach an authentic cadence. Write in chorale style.

3. Modulate to iii using the given vi as a pivot chord. Reach an authentic cadence in the new key. Write in keyboard style.

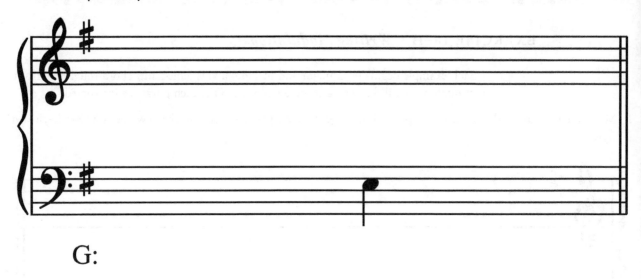

G:

4. Modulate to vi using the given vi as a pivot chord. Reach an authentic cadence in the new key. Write in chorale style.

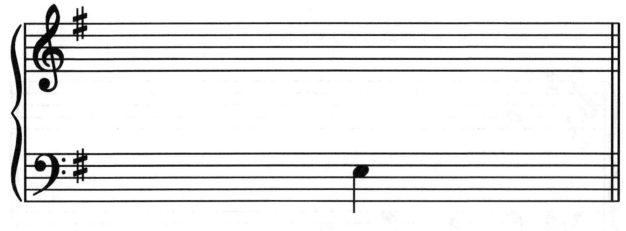

G:

EXERCISE 18-I   *Analyzing Modulations and Extended Tonicizations*

Each passage below features *either* a modulation *or* one or more extended tonicization(s). First, listen to the passage. Next, label the starting key and both the key and type of each cadence (e.g., HC: I, PAC: III). Finally, analyze the entire passage with roman numerals, including bracket(s) for any extended tonicizations or a clearly marked pivot chord for a modulation.

1. Samuel Coleridge-Taylor, "Lift Up Your Heads" (1892)

2. W. A. Mozart, Piano Concerto in G major, K. 453 (1784), *Allegretto*

ASSIGNMENT 18.5

EXERCISE 18–J   *Analyzing Modulations and Extended Tonicizations*

Each passage below features *either* a modulation *or* one or more extended tonicization(s). First, listen to the passage. Next, label the starting key and both the key and type of each cadence (e.g., HC: I, PAC: III). Finally, analyze the entire passage with roman numerals, including bracket(s) for any extended tonicizations or a clearly marked pivot chord for a modulation.

1. Maria Hester Park, Piano Sonata in C major, op. 7 (1796), *Allegro spirito*

2. Marianna Martines, Keyboard Sonata no. 3 in E major (1762), *Allegro*

3. Ludwig van Beethoven, Violin Sonata in A major, op. 12, no. 2 (1797), *Allegro piacevole*

4. Amy Beach, *Children's Album*, op. 36 (1897), no. 5

EXERCISE 18-K *Composing a Modulation*

The first two measures of an eight-measure parallel progressive period are provided. Compose the remaining six measures. Reach a HC: I in m. 4, restart on tonic at m. 5, introduce a pivot chord in m. 5 or m. 6, and reach a PAC: V in m. 8. Analyze the entire period with roman numerals.

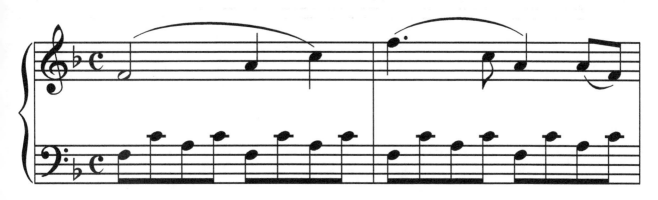

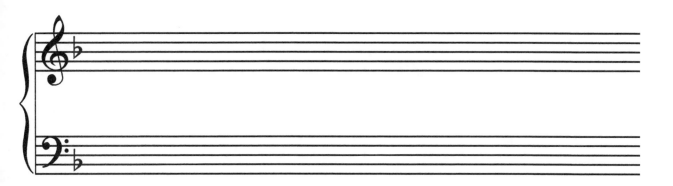

ASSIGNMENT 18.6

EXERCISE 18–L   *Playing and Analyzing Modulations
in a Two-Voice Texture*

First, listen to each passage and, if you can, play it at the keyboard. Next, label the starting key and both the key and the type of the cadence that ends the passage (e.g., PAC: V).
Then, analyze the passage with roman numerals, including a clearly marked pivot chord.
You will need to listen carefully and decide which harmonies are implied by the two-
voice texture, since there are seldom complete harmonies. Finally, label and diagram the
form of each passage.

1.

2.

3.

EXERCISE 18–M   *Harmonizing Melodies That Modulate*

Harmonize each soprano melody in keyboard style, following the instructions. Play your harmonizations on piano.

1. Begin in G minor and modulate to III. (You will need to use a few applied chords.)

2. Begin in D minor and modulate to III.

EXERCISE 18-N *Analyzing Modulation or Extended Tonicization*

Analyze the passage from Josephine Lang's (1815–1880) "Heimweh" from *Drei Klavier-stücke*. First, listen to the passage. Next, label the starting key and both the key and type of the cadence that ends the passage (e.g., HC: I, PAC: III). Finally, analyze the entire passage with roman numerals, including either bracket(s) for any extended tonicizations or a clearly marked pivot chord for a modulation.

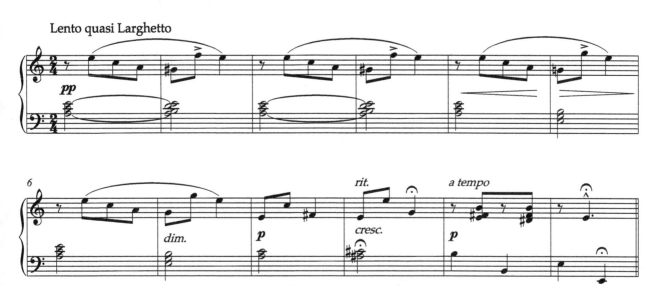

EXERCISE 18–O   *Realizing Figured Basses that Modulate*

Realize the first figured bass (part 1) in keyboard style and the second one (part 2) in
chorale style. Analyze with roman numerals, including a clearly marked pivot chord.
Play your realizations at the keyboard.

1.

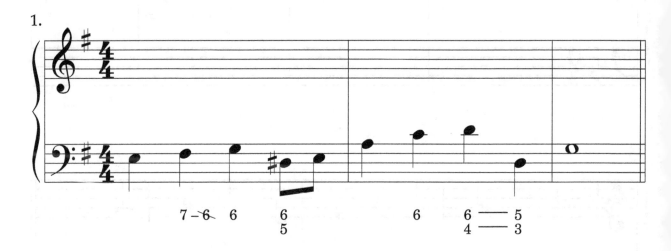

2.

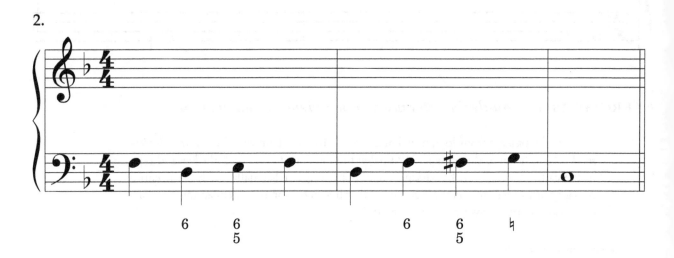

CHAPTER 19

Harmonic Sequences

EXERCISE 19–A *Playing, Completing, and Transposing Sequence Paradigms*

The outer voices and figured bass of several sequences are provided below. First, play the outer voices and bracket the model and copies of each sequence. Next, write in the two inner voices in keyboard style, using the figured bass as guidance. Then, label each chord's root with a letter name (such as C). Finally, play just the outer voices of each sequence transposed to the specified keys.

1. D2 (↓5,↑4)

   a. In major, all root position. Transpose to F major and A major.

   b. In major, with ⁶₃s. Transpose to G major and E♭ major.

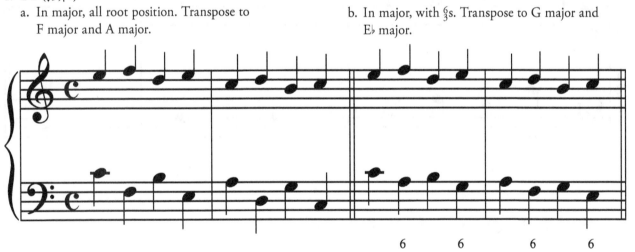

c. In minor, all root position. Transpose to G minor and E minor.

d. In minor, with $^6_3$s. Transpose to B minor and D minor.

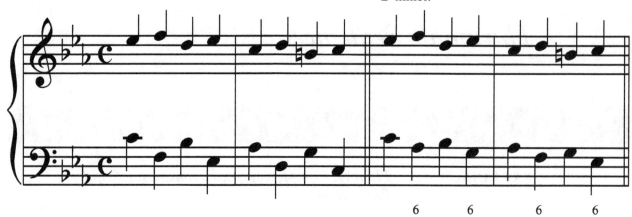

2. D3 (↓4,↑2)

a. In major, all root position. Transpose to D major and B♭ major.

b. In major, with $^6_3$s. Transpose to E major and F major.

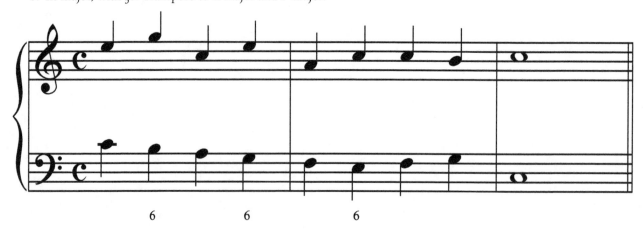

c. In minor, all root position. Transpose to A minor and F♯ minor.

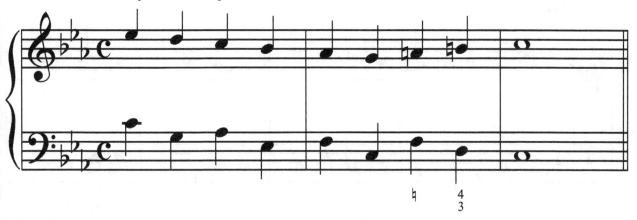

d. In minor, with ⁶₃s. Transpose to G minor and B minor.

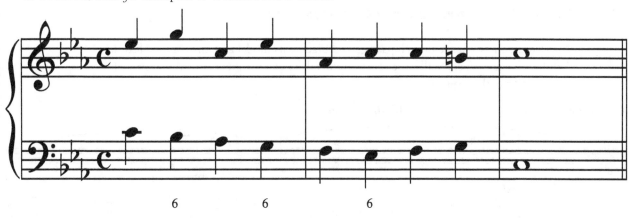

3. A2 (↓3,↑4)

a. In major, all root position. Transpose to D major and B♭ major.

b. In major, with ⁶₃s. Transpose to E major and F major.

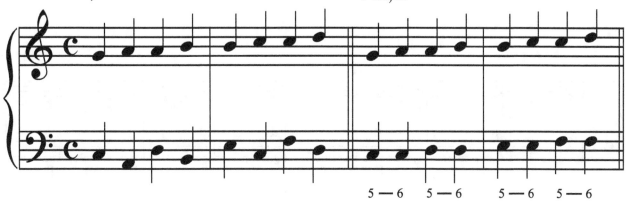

c. In minor, all root position. Transpose to A minor and F♯ minor.

d. In minor, with ♮s. Transpose to G minor and B minor.

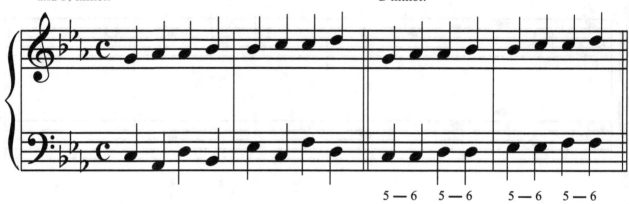

EXERCISE 19-B   *Analyzing Harmonic Sequences*

First, locate the sequence in each passage and bracket its model and any copies. Next, label the sequence type. Finally, use roman numerals to analyze any material that precedes and/or follows the sequence.

1. Pietro Mascagni, *Cavalleria Rusticana* (1890), *Interlude*

2.

3. Clara Schumann, Piano Sonata in G minor (1841–42), *Scherzo. Hint: There is just one harmony per measure. The metrically unaccented pitches on the lower staff are passing tones.*

ASSIGNMENT 19.2

EXERCISE 19–C *Analyzing Harmonic Sequences*

First, locate the sequence in each passage and bracket its model and any copies. Next, label the sequence type. Finally, use roman numerals to analyze any material that precedes and/or follows the sequence.

1. Marie Jaëll, *Impromptu* (1869). *Hint: Do not be thrown off by the many expressive accented and chromatic embellishing tones.*

2. C. P. E. Bach, Sonata in A major from *Sechs Sonaten für Kenner und Liebhaber*, Wq. 55 (1779)

3. W. A. Mozart, Serenade in C minor, K. 388 (1783), *Menuetto*. Before you analyze as instructed above, transcribe the following voices onto the provided staves as follows: the bassoon bass line onto the lower staff, and the two oboe parts onto the upper staff (Oboe 1 with stems up, Oboe 2 with stems down).

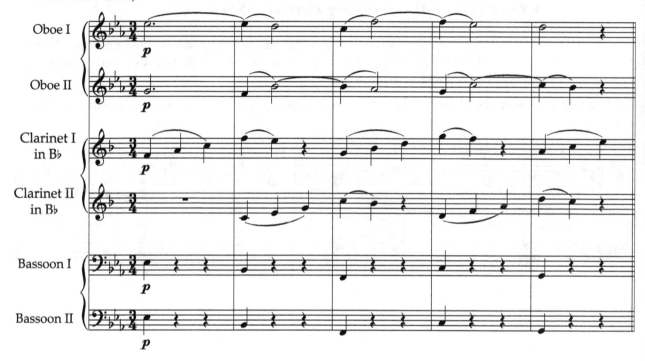

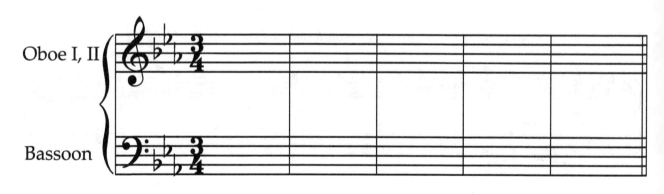

EXERCISE 19-D *Continuing Harmonic Sequences*

The beginning of each sequence is provided. First, play the given passage on keyboard and label the sequence type. Next, in keyboard style, write and play what comes next in the sequence by following the pattern strictly *at least* up through the beginning of the third measure (i.e., the fifth chord of the sequence). Finally, on a pre-dominant chord, break the sequence pattern and reach an authentic cadence.

1.

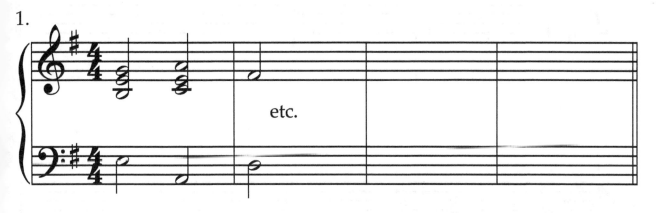

2.

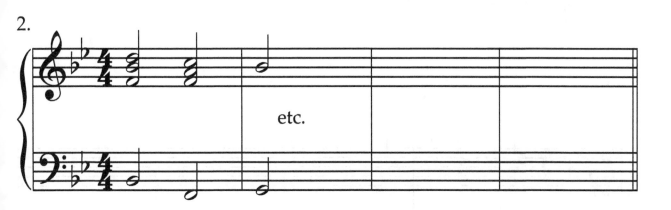

3.

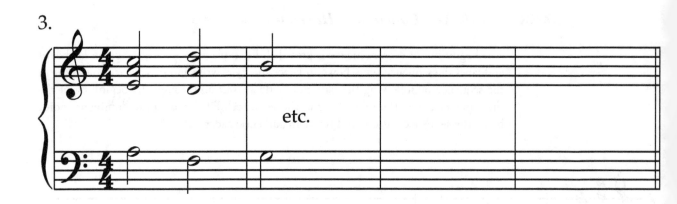

4.

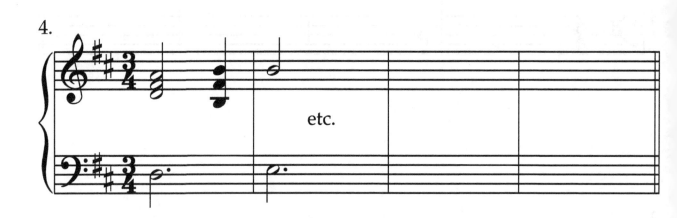

5.

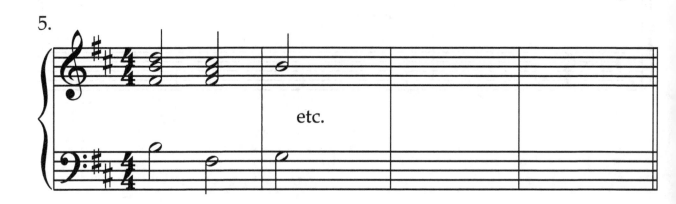

ASSIGNMENT 19.3

EXERCISE 19–E   *Analyzing Harmonic Sequences*

First, locate the sequence in each passage and bracket its model and any copies. Next, label the sequence type. Finally, use roman numerals to analyze any material that precedes and/or follows the sequence.

1. W. A. Mozart, Violin Concerto no. 2 in D major, K. 211 (1775), *Rondeau*. What is the key of this passage?

2.

EXERCISE 19–F   *Composing a Consequent Phrase*

The complete antecedent phrase of a period is provided along with just the figured bass of the consequent phrase. First, label the sequence type in the antecedent and the sequence type in the consequent. Next, continuing the block-chord figuration, realize the upper staff of the consequent phrase. Analyze and play your entire accompaniment. *Bonus:* Compose an upper-voice melody to sound above the keyboard accompaniment for the entire eight-measure period.

EXERCISE 19–G   *Adding a Single Inner Voice*

First, play the given outer voices. Next, use the figured bass to analyze the phrase, including bracketing and labeling its two sequences. Then, add a single inner voice to the upper staff in order to create a three-voice texture. Finally, play your three-voice realization. Keep in mind that you will need to omit some chordal fifths in a three-voice texture.

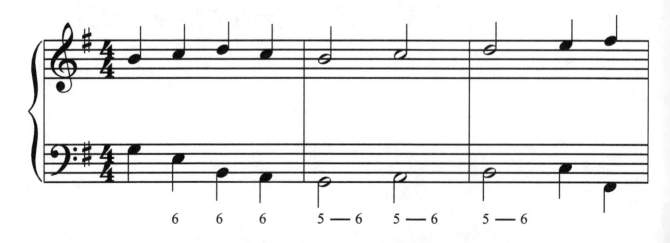

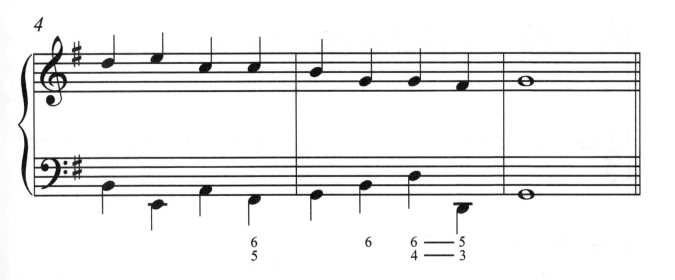

EXERCISE 19-H   *Continuing Figurated Harmonic Sequences*

First, label each sequence. Next, write the next three measures of music by following the sequential pattern strictly.

1. After J. S. Bach, Sonata for Flute in E♭ major, BWV 1031, *Allegro*

2. After Antonio Vivaldi, Sonata for Oboe in B♭ major, RV 34, *Allegro*

ASSIGNMENT 19.4

EXERCISE 19–1   *Harmonizing Melodies with Harmonic Sequences*

First, play or sing each given melody. Next, bracket the model (lasting two melody notes) and however many copies there are that follow the sequential pattern. Then, decide whether the sequence is A2, D2, or D3, and add the appropriate sequence label, bass voice, and inner voices in keyboard style. Finally, harmonize any non-sequential material at the end of the phrase in order to create a cadence. Once you finish, analyze the entire phrase and play what you write.

1.

Bb:

2.

g:

3.

D:

4.

b:

EXERCISE 19–J   *Analyzing Harmonic Sequences*

First, locate the sequence in each passage and bracket its model and any copies. Next, label the sequence type. Finally, use roman numerals to analyze any material that precedes and/or follows the sequence.

1. Arcangelo Corelli, Trio Sonata in D major, op. 4, no. 4 (1694)

2. George Frideric Handel, Trio Sonata in G minor, op. 2, no. 5, HWV 390 (1733), *Allegro*

3. W. A. Mozart, "Der Hölle Rache" ("Hell's Revenge") from *Die Zauberflöte* (*The Magic Flute*), K. 620
    (1791), Act 2, Scene 8

mehr,

ASSIGNMENT 19.5

EXERCISE 19-K   *Analyzing Harmonic Sequences in Solo Textures*

Each passage below contains either one or two sequences. After listening to the passage, bracket and label each sequence. You do not need to provide roman numerals for the other material.

1. J. S. Bach, Chaconne from Partita no. 2 in D minor for Solo Violin, BWV 1004 (1723)

2. Domenico Scarlatti, Sonata in D minor, K. 1 (transcribed for guitar) (1738)

3. W. A. Mozart, Flute Sonata no. 5 in C major, K. 14 (1764), *Allegro*

4. Johann Joachim Quantz, Flute Duet in A minor, op. 5, no. 5 (1759). How do mm. 9–16 relate
   to mm. 17–24?

ASSIGNMENT 19.6

EXERCISE 19–L *Analyzing a Modulating Harmonic Sequence*

First, listen to the passage from Antonín Dvořák's Cavatina from *Romantické kusy* (*Romantic Pieces*), op. 75, no. 1 (1887), *Allegro moderato*. Next, label the key in which it begins, and the key and type of the cadence that ends the passage. Finally, analyze the entire phrase, including the sequence and the modulation.

EXERCISE 19-M *Embellishing Harmonic Sequences*

Each model shows the outer voices of a harmonic sequence along with a florid realization of that same sequence in a specific meter. Play and study these models to see how neighboring tones, passing tones, and chordal leaps are deployed to create rhythmic interest.

Model #1: Arcangelo Corelli, Trio Sonata in B minor, op. 3, no. 4 (1689)

Model #2: Johann David Heinichen, Sonata in C minor for Oboe and Bassoon (1760)

Model #3: C. P. E. Bach, Flute Sonata in G minor, BWV 1020 (c. 1734)

Now, choose two of the outer-voice patterns below and realize each of them in a key and meter of your choice. Do at least one in the major mode and at least one in the minor mode. Based upon the models that you studied, ornament your sequences by incorporating embellishing tones.

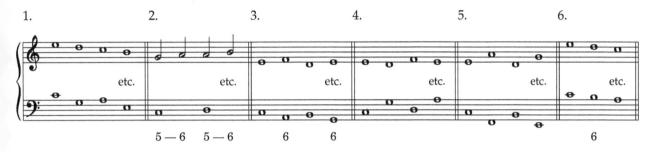

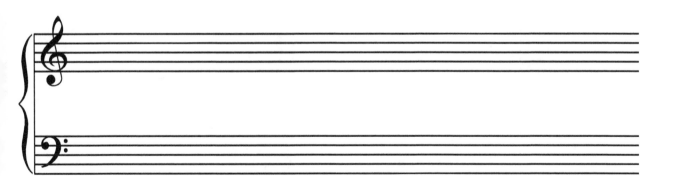

ASSIGNMENT 19.7

EXERCISE 19–N *Completing Harmonic Sequences That Include Diatonic Sevenths*

1. The beginning of a D2 (↓5,↑4) sequence with *alternating* diatonic sevenths is provided below. Continue the sequence by writing at least three more chords following the pattern, which alternates between a triad and a root-position seventh chord. Then, end the phrase with an authentic cadence. Analyze the entire phrase and play what you write.

2. Now, using the provided head start, write a D2 (↓5,↑4) sequence with *interlocking* diatonic sevenths. Aside from the first F major triad, each chord within the sequence will be a root-position seventh chord. Break the pattern at some point in order to reach an authentic cadence. *Hint: Keep in mind that you will need to omit some chordal fifths.*

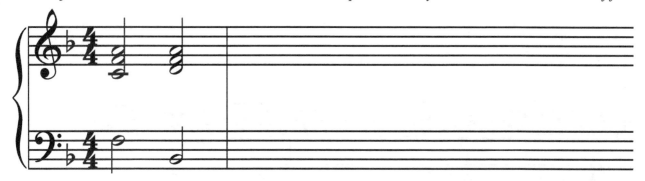

EXERCISE 19-O *Analyzing Harmonic Sequences That Include Seventh Chords*

First, locate the sequence in each passage and bracket its model and any copies. Next, label the sequence type, circle each chordal seventh, and label its preparation and resolution. Finally, use roman numerals to analyze any material that precedes and/or follows the sequence.

1. Louise Farrenc, Cello Sonata, op. 46 (1859), *Andante sostenuto*

2.

3. W. A. Mozart, Piano Sonata in F Major, K. 332 (1783), i

4. Mélanie Bonis, Églogue from *Five Pieces for Piano* (1897). In a few sentences, discuss how the sequence in this passage accomplishes a modulation. When, how, and to what key does it modulate?

ASSIGNMENT 19.8

EXERCISE 19–P   *Realizing a Figured Bass*

Realize the figured bass in chorale style by adding two inner voices. Analyze on two
levels, including bracketing and labeling each sequence.

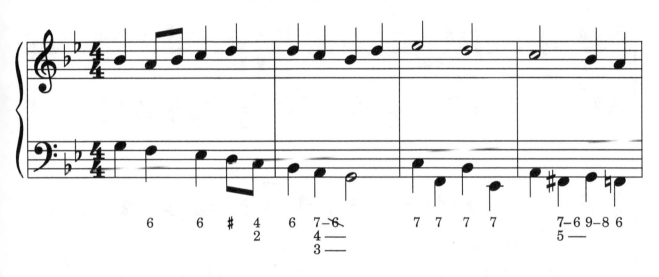

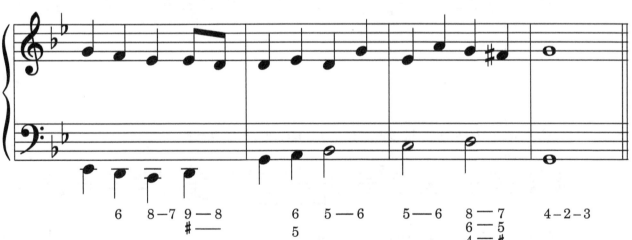

EXERCISE 19-Q   *Analyzing Harmonic Sequences That Include Seventh Chords*

First, locate the sequence in each passage and bracket its model and any copies. Next, label the sequence type, circle each chordal seventh, and label its preparation and resolution. Finally, use roman numerals to analyze any material that precedes and/or follows the sequence.

1. George Frideric Handel, "Pena Tiranna io sento al core" from *Amadigi di Gaula* (1715)

2. Jean-Marie Leclair (1697–1764), Violin Sonata in G major, op. 1, no. 5, *Allegro*

3. Pyotr Ilyich Tchaikovsky, Symphony no. 4 (1878), *Andantino*

4. George Frideric Handel, Concerto Grosso in B♭ major, op. 3, no. 2, HWV 313 (1734), *Largo*

ASSIGNMENT 19.9

EXERCISE 19-R *Adding Inner Voices to Applied-Chord Sequences*

The outer voices and figured bass of two applied-chord sequences appear below. First, play the given voices on keyboard. Next, label the sequence type, and bracket and label the model and any copies. Then, add two inner voices to create a keyboard-style realization. *Note:* Asterisks indicate the locations of applied chords to help you. When an applied chord is not possible because it is followed by a diminished triad, a diatonic chord sounds instead.

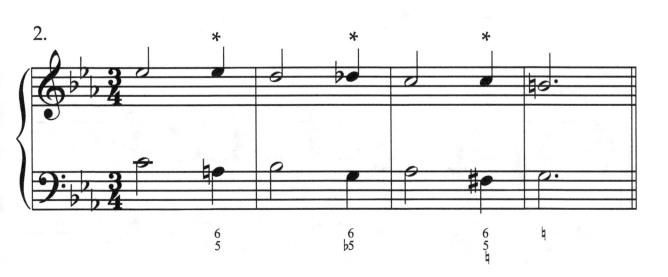

EXERCISE 19–S *Adding Applied Chords to Harmonic Sequences*

Shown below are just the diatonic pillars of applied-chord sequences—that is, the first chord, third chord, fifth chord, etc. First, label the sequence type, and bracket and label the model and any copies. Next, following the instructions, insert applied chords into each sequence. Finally, play the sequences at the keyboard.

1. add applied V$^6_5$

2. add applied V$^4_3$

3. add applied vii°7

EXERCISE 19–T   *Analyzing Applied-Chord Sequences*

After listening to each example, label the sequence type, and bracket and label the model and any copies. Finally, provide roman numerals for the remaining chords in each example.

1.

2.

3.

4. Clara Schumann, *Caprice en forme de Valse*, op. 2, no. 2 (1832). *Hint: The sequence enters subtly.
It actually starts in the third measure even though aspects of the first two measures are similar. The
key of this passage is A major.*

ASSIGNMENT 19.10

EXERCISE 19–U   *Analyzing Applied-Chord Sequences*

After listening to each example, label the sequence type, and bracket and label the model and any copies. Finally, provide roman numerals for the remaining chords in each example.

1. Eugène Dédé, *Douleur et Gaîté* (1886)

2. Fanny Hensel, "Die Mainacht," op. 9, no. 6 (1850). *Translation: I wander sadly from bush to bush.*

3. Clara Schumann, Polonaise, op. 1, no. 2 (1831). *Hint: The sequence pattern actually breaks during the first copy after the model.* Explain in a sentence how the pattern is *almost* maintained after that.

EXERCISE 19–V *Completing Applied-Chord Sequences*

First, play the given beginning of an applied-chord sequence. Next, determine the type of applied-chord sequence and label it. Then, write what comes next in the sequence, at least through the beginning of the third unit (the fifth chord), and break the sequence to close with either an authentic cadence or a half cadence. Finally, play your work on piano.

1.

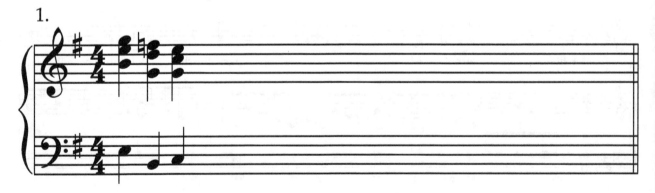

2.

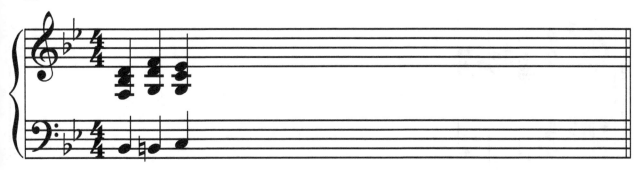

3.

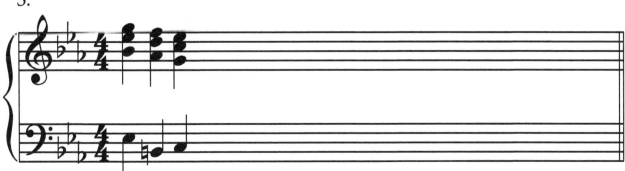

4.

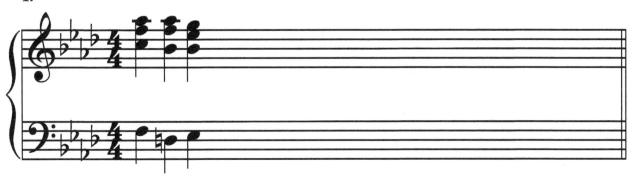

5.

ASSIGNMENT 19.11

EXERCISE 19-W *Adding Upper Voices to Bass Lines*

Each bass line implies an applied-chord sequence. First, study the diatonic pillars (every other chord) to notice the overall motion of the sequence. In keyboard style, write the upper voices of those chords first, using the first chord as a guide. Next, insert a specific applied chord in between the diatonic pillars, using the given bass notes as guides.

1.

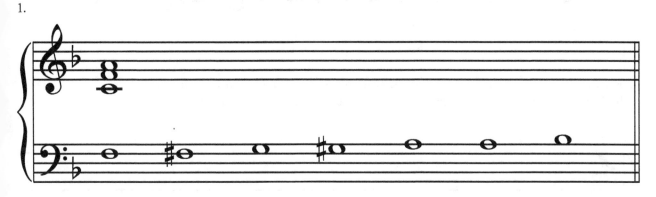

F:

2.

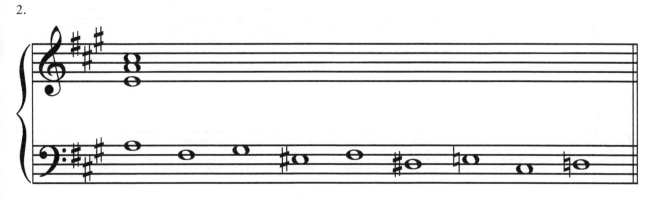

A:

3. Notice that this sequence breaks in order to reach a half cadence.

C:

4. Finally, choose one of the three sequences that you realized above, and embellish it with a broken-chord figuration of your choice. Choose a time signature, add bar lines, and determine rhythmic values.

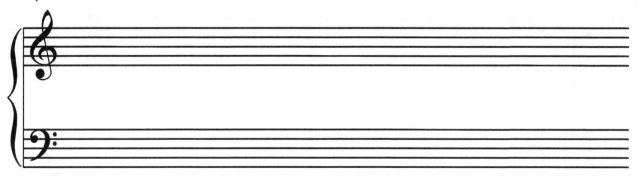

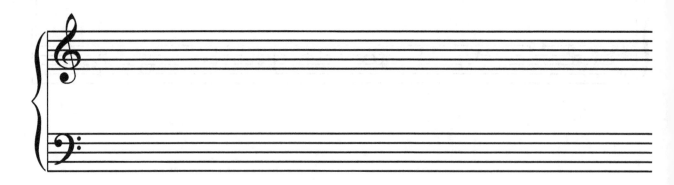

EXERCISE 19-X *Analyzing Applied-Chord Sequences*

After listening to each example, label the sequence type, and bracket and label the model and any copies. Finally, provide roman numerals for the remaining chords in each example.

1. Antonio Vivaldi, Concerto Grosso in C minor, op. 9, no. 11, Ryom 198a (1727), *Allegro*

2. Franz Schubert, Sonata in A major, D. 664 (1819), *Allegro*

ASSIGNMENT 19.12

EXERCISE 19-Y   *Continuing Figurated Applied-Chord Sequences*

Using the sequence label and the roman-numeral analysis as guides, write the next two copies (four measures) of each applied-chord sequence. Begin by determining what the four additional chords are. Your continuation will connect smoothly to the provided cadence.

1. A2 (↑4,↓3) with applied V_5^6 chords

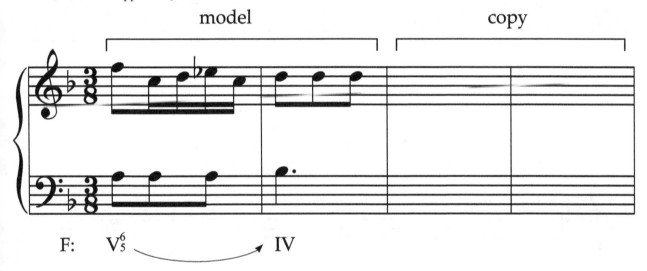

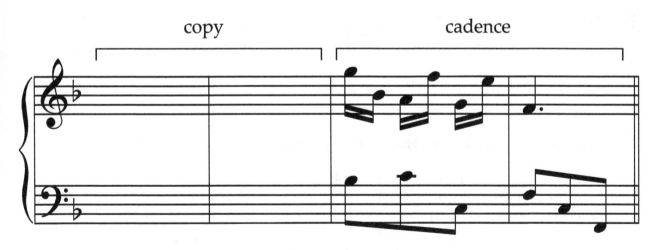

2. D3 (↑3,↓5) with applied V_3^4 chords

EXERCISE 19–Z   *Continuing Applied-Chord Sequences in Compound Melody*

Each passage provides just the model of an applied-chord sequence from the two minuets of J. S. Bach's Suite No. 1 for Solo Cello (c. 1720). The lower staff shows an implied bass line that does not sound in performance. Following the given guidance, write the next two copies of each sequence (four measures) in both the implied bass line and the cello part. Preserve the melodic and rhythmic shapes to make the sequence as strict as possible.

1. A2 (↑4,↓3) sequence with applied V$^6_5$ chords

G: V$^6_5$ ⌢→ IV   V$^6_5$ ⌢

↘V   V$^6_5$ ⌢→ vi

2. D2 (↓5,↑4) sequence with applied V^7 chords

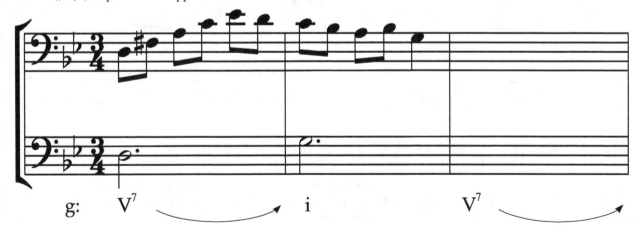

g: V^7 ⌢→ i   V^7 ⌢→

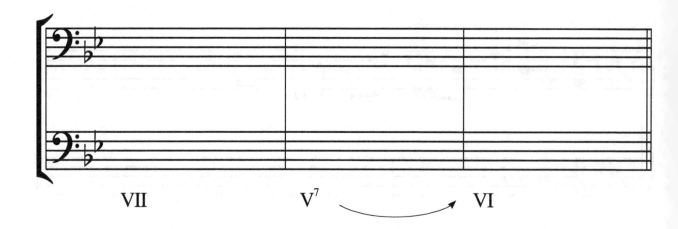

EXERCISE 19–AA   *Analyzing Modulating Sequences*

Bracket and label the modulating sequence in W. A. Mozart's Divertimento in B♭ major, K. 254 (1776), *Allegro assai*. Analyze the non-sequential material with roman numerals. Finally, write a few sentences explaining how, when, from which key, and to which key the sequence modulates.

CHAPTER 20

Binary Form and Variations

ASSIGNMENT 20.1

EXERCISE 20-A *Analyzing Short Binary Forms*

First, listen to each piece multiple times. Next, label all cadences on the score. Then, label the form and draw a detailed form diagram that shows cadences, keys, sections, embedded smaller forms (such as sentences and periods), and other details that you find important. Finally, answer the accompanying questions.

1. Joseph Bologne, String Quartet, op. 1, no. 6 (1773), ii. What motivic technique is used in the first three measures?

2. Daniel Gottlob Türk (1750–1813), "Evening Song." What is the form of mm. 1–8 on their own? How does Türk achieve both unity and contrast between the two reprises? What key is tonicized in mm. 9–10?

3. Carl Maria von Weber, *Six Écossaises*, no. 2, J. 30 (1802). Analyze the first reprise with roman numerals. Is there a cadence at m. 4? Why or why not? Where does the repeated-note melodic material of the second reprise come from? Contrast the texture of the first reprise with that of the second reprise.

ASSIGNMENT 20.2

EXERCISE 20-B *Analyzing Binary Forms*

First, listen to each piece multiple times. Next, label all cadences on the score. Then, label the form and draw a detailed form diagram that shows cadences, keys, sections, embedded smaller forms (such as sentences and periods), and other details that you find important. Finally, answer the accompanying questions.

1. Tekla Bądarzewska-Baranowska (1834–1861), *I Skoven* (*Into the Woods*). What elements of mm. 1–8 provide interest even though this passage contains just a few harmonies? Double-neighbor motions are a central feature of the piece; circle at least five instances of them. Finally, in a paragraph, explain how we can discern the piece's binary form even though there are no repeat signs.

2. Franz Joseph Haydn, Sonatina no. 4 in F major, Hob. XVI:9 (1758), *Scherzo*. Add upward stems to the pitches that participate in the melodically fluent (i.e., stepwise) descent that spans the entire first reprise.

ASSIGNMENT 20.3

EXERCISE 20–C   *Analyzing Two Duets in Binary Form*

First, listen to each piece multiple times. Next, label all cadences on the score. Then, label the form and draw a detailed form diagram that shows cadences, keys, sections, embedded smaller forms (such as sentences and periods), and other details that you find important. Finally, answer the accompanying questions.

1. W. A. Mozart, Duet for Two Violins in G major, K. 487 (1786). Label the pivot chord of the modulation that takes place during the first reprise.

2. Johann David Heinichen (1683–1729), Duet. What motivic technique takes place in mm. 1–3? What type of cadence ends the first reprise? What key is tonicized at the start of the second reprise?

Vivace

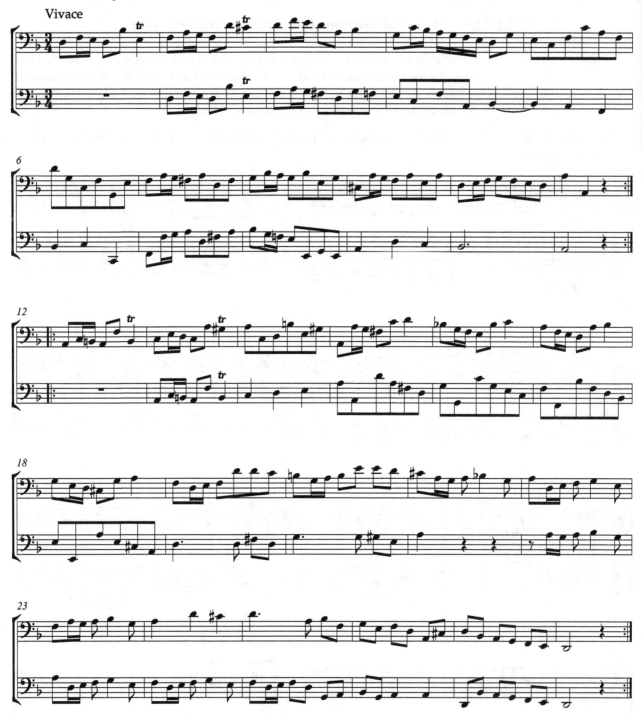

ASSIGNMENT 20.4

EXERCISE 20-D *Analyzing Sidney Lambert's* **Murmures du Soir,**
op. 18 (1876)

First, listen to the piece multiple times. Next, label all cadences on the score. Then, label the form and draw a detailed form diagram that shows cadences, keys, sections, embedded smaller forms (such as sentences and periods), and other details that you find important. Finally, answer the following questions: What is the form of mm. 1–4 on their own? What is unusual about the key that ends the first reprise, and which other key might we have expected at this point in the form? Which keys are tonicized during the second reprise?

ASSIGNMENT 20.5

EXERCISE 20-E   *Analyzing Robert Schumann's Romance in B♭ Minor, op. 28, no. 1 (1839)*

First, listen to the piece multiple times. Next, label all cadences on the score. Then, label the form and draw a detailed form diagram that shows cadences, keys, sections, embedded smaller forms (such as sentences and periods), and other details that you find important. In addition, analyze mm. 1–8 with roman numerals, label any harmonic sequences that you encounter in the piece, and write a sentence describing the harmonic function of C major in mm. 13–16.

EXERCISE 20–F *Analyzing François Couperin's Concert Royal no. 1 in G Major for Flute, Oboe, and Basso Continuo (1772),* **Menuet**

First, listen to the piece multiple times. Next, label all cadences on the score. Then, label the form and draw a detailed form diagram that shows cadences, keys, sections, embedded smaller forms (such as sentences and periods), and other details that you find important. Finally, answer the following questions: What is the motivic relationship between the winds and the continuo in mm. 1–2? When in the first reprise does the bass line imitate the winds' melodic material *in augmentation*? When in the *second* reprise does the melodic material from the opening of the *first* reprise return *in inversion*?

ASSIGNMENT 20.6

EXERCISE 20–G   *Analyzing Isabella Colbran's "Già la notte s'avvicina" (1821)*

First, listen to the piece multiple times. Next, label all cadences on the score. Then, label the form and draw a detailed form diagram that shows cadences, keys, sections, embedded smaller forms (such as sentences and periods), and other details that you find important. Finally, consider the translation of the piece's text and write one to two paragraphs discussing how the details of Colbran's musical setting depict poetic images or sentiments.

Translation:

(first reprise)	(second reprise)
The night is already approaching.	*One cannot claim to be delighted*
Come, oh Nice, my beloved	*without having stood on these sands,*
to breathe the fresh breezes	*now that a slow zephyr*
from the placid sea.	*gently undulates the sea.*

ASSIGNMENT 20.7

EXERCISE 20–H   *Analyzing Variations*

Shown below are the initial themes and first few variations of three variation sets. First, listen to each example in its entirely. Next, label and diagram the form of the theme on its own, and label the variation set as either sectional or continuous. Then, write a paragraph describing which musical elements from the theme (such as harmony, melody, rhythm, or texture) remain constant or just minimally changed in the variations, and which are substantially varied.

1. George Frideric Handel, Keyboard Suite XVI in G major, HWV 222 (c. 1722), *Gavotte*

Theme

Variation 1

Variation 2

2. W. A. Mozart, Variations in C major on "Ah, vous dirai-je, Maman," K. 265 (1785)

THEMA

VAR. I

VAR. II

VAR. III

VAR. VIII

3. George Frideric Handel, Keyboard Suite no. 3 in D minor, HWV 428 (1720), *Air*

Air

1. Variation

2. Variation

3. Variation

4. Variation

5. Variation

ASSIGNMENT 20.8

EXERCISE 20–I *Analyzing Variations*

Shown below are the initial themes and first few variations of two variation sets. First, listen to each example in its entirely. Next, label and diagram the form of the theme on its own, and label the variation set as either sectional or continuous. Then, write a paragraph describing which musical elements of the theme (such as harmony, melody, rhythm, or texture) remain constant or just minimally changed in the variations, and which are substantially varied.

1. Franz Schubert, Impromptu in B♭ Major, D. 935 (1827)

2. Tomaso Vitali (1663–1745), Chaconne in G minor

CHAPTER 21

Modal Mixture

EXERCISE 21–A *Analyzing Short Passages*

First, play or listen to each example. Then, analyze on two levels, including labeling any cadences. Draw an asterisk (*) above each modal mixture harmony.

1.

2. *Hint: Beware that this passage contains applied chords as well as modal mixture chords.*

3. Valérie Boissier, *Trois Études*, no. 1 (1870). In two sentences, describe how the texture changes after the first beat of the second measure.

EXERCISE 21-B   *Transposing Short Paradigms at the Keyboard*

Each paradigm illustrates a common usage of modal mixture. At the keyboard, play each paradigm as written and then transpose to the two keys indicated. Transpose the two outer voices first, then the full chords. Sing along with the bass voice as you play.

Cadential Progressions:

1. transpose to C major and G major

2. transpose to F major and A major

Embedded Phrase Models:

3. transpose to G major and E♭ major

4. transpose to D major and B♭ major

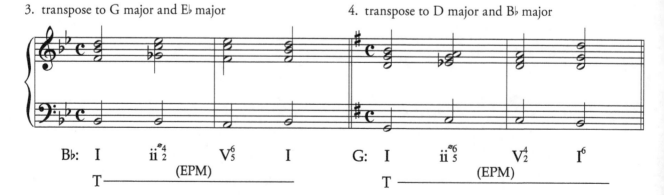

EXERCISE 21–C   *Adding Modal Mixture*

The given phrase contains no modal mixture. First, play it and analyze with roman numerals. Then, add the necessary accidental(s) to at least *three* diatonic chords in order to convert them to modal mixture chords that share their same function. Play your new version, write the changed roman numerals underneath the original ones, and add a second-level analysis that is shared by both versions.

ASSIGNMENT 21.2

EXERCISE 21–D *Analyzing Short Passages*

First, play or listen to each example. Then, analyze on two levels, including labeling any cadences. Draw an asterisk (*) above each modal mixture harmony.

1. J. S. Bach, Chorale, "Vater unser im Himmelreich," BWV 90 (1723). *Hint: The passage does not begin with a tonic chord. Determine the key by identifying the type of cadence that ends the phrase.*

2. Laura Netzel, Cello Sonata, op. 66 (1899), ii, *Cantabile ma non troppo lento. Hint: The piano's grace note near the end of the passage is a harmonically important bass note.*

3. Franz Schubert, "Jägers Liebeslied," D. 909, no. 2 (1827)

Mässig geschwind (Allegro moderato)

4. Julia Perry, "How Beautiful Are the Feet" (1946). The second half of this passage is full of accented embellishing tones that makes the appearance of modal mixture especially poignant. Circle and label each of them.

EXERCISE 21–E   *Writing Modal Mixture from a Variety of Prompts*

In addition to completing each writing task as instructed, analyze on two levels, including labeling any cadences.

1. First, decide which harmonies are implied by the bass voice and write roman numerals. Include *three* modal mixture chords. Then, realize the progression in *keyboard style* following the given head start. Play what you write.

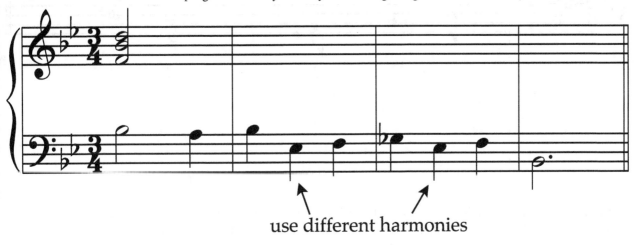

use different harmonies

2. First, analyze the figured bass on two levels. Then, realize it in *keyboard style* following the given head start. Plan your soprano voice so that the phrase concludes with a perfect authentic cadence. Play your realization.

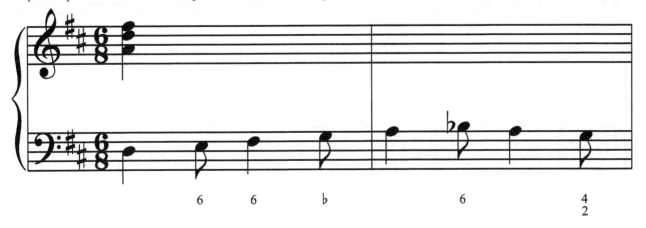

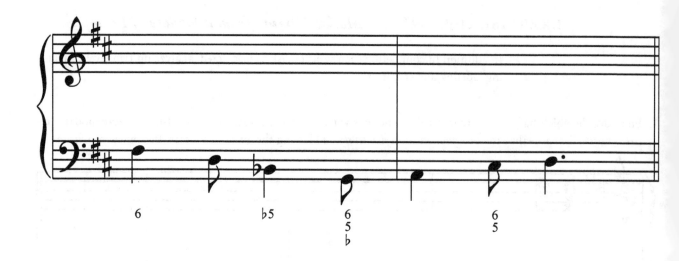

6   ♭5   6   6
                                    5   5
                                    ♭

3. Realize the roman numerals by continuing the broken-chord figuration that is started. Preserve strong voice leading among the four voices even though they do not all sound simultaneously. Play your realization.

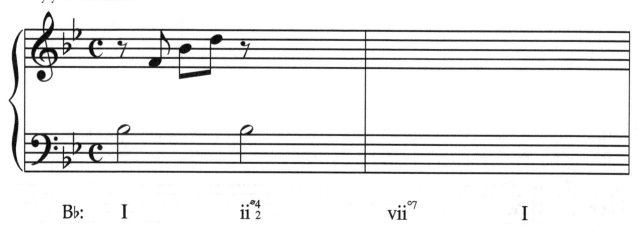

B♭:   I   ii°⁴₂   vii°⁷   I

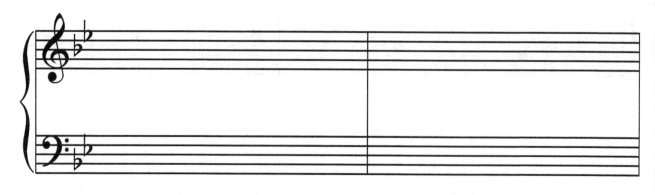

iv   iv⁶   V⁴ ——————— 3

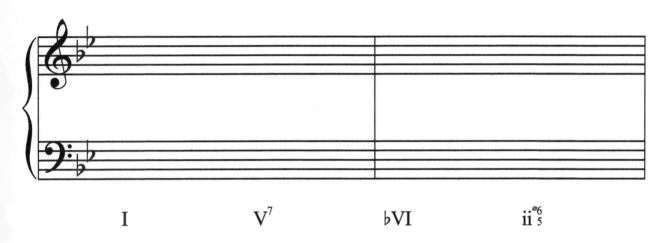

$$I \qquad\qquad V^7 \qquad\qquad \flat VI \qquad\qquad ii^{\varnothing 6}_{5}$$

$$V^{6}_{4} \underline{\qquad} \flat 6 \underline{\qquad} {}^{5}_{3} \qquad\qquad I^{5}_{3} \underline{\qquad} {}^{\flat 6}_{4} \underline{\qquad} {}^{5}_{3}$$

ASSIGNMENT 21.3

EXERCISE 21–F   *Analyzing Texted Music That Includes Modal Mixture*

Analyze each passage on two levels, including labeling cadences, and draw an asterisk (*) above each modal mixture chord. In addition, study the text of each passage and answer the questions in a paragraph.

1. José Maurício Nunes Garcia (1767–1830), "Beijo a mão que me condena." How does the role of D♭ in this passage differ from the role of its enharmonic equivalent, C♯? Which type of harmony is each of these enharmonically equivalent tones part of, and how does each of them resolve? Could you connect this contrast to the sentiments expressed by the text of the passage?

Translation: I'm a disgrace for loving so much without being loved. I'm unhappy.

2. Isabella Colbran (text by Pietro Metastasio), "Povero cor tu palpati" (1805). A small melodic motive (6̂–5̂) is bracketed in the first measure. How many more times does it sound in the passage? How does that motive, along with the dynamics and rhythm, emphasize the appearance of modal mixture? Speculate on what meaning this and other features of the music might give to the passage's text.

Translation: My poor heart, you throb so. How right you are to tremble.

3. Franz Schubert, "Das Zügenglöcklein," D. 871 (1826). With respect to the home key, what roman numeral is tonicized in the sixth through eighth measures of the passage? Within this tonicized key, what scale degree is the F♭ that appears melodically? How does E♮, the enharmonic equivalent of that F♭, behave in the *home* key? (See the end of the eighth measure.) When the downward tendency of the F♭ is replaced by the upward tendency of E♮, what aspect of the text might be conveyed?

Translation: If he is one of the happy ones who shares the joys of pure love and friendship, grant him yet bliss under this sun where he gladly [tarries].

Lieb' und Freund schaft theilt,   gönn' ihm noch die Won - nen   un - ter die-ser Son - nen,

cresc.

gönn' ihm noch die Won - nen   un - ter die-ser Son - nen,   wo___ er__ ger - ne

f

EXERCISE 21-G *Realizing a Figured Bass*

First, analyze the figured bass on two levels. Then, realize it in *keyboard style* following the given head start. Play your realization.

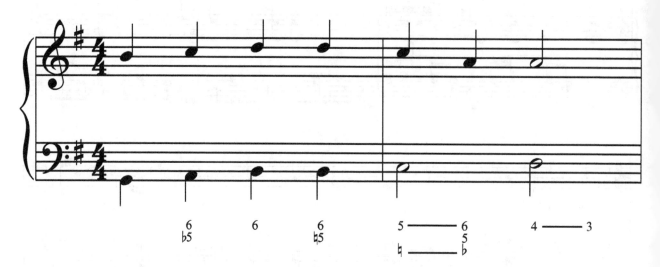

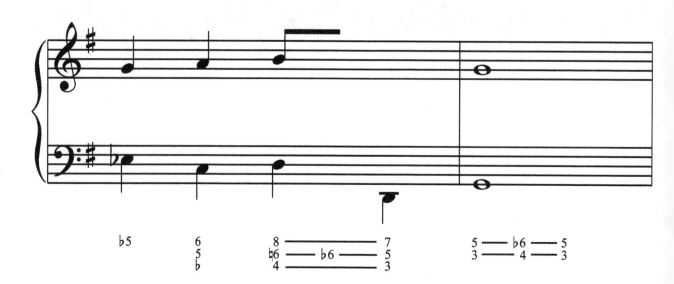

ASSIGNMENT 21.4

EXERCISE 21–H   *Analyzing Chromatic Step Descents*

First, play or listen to each example. Then, analyze on two levels, including labeling any cadences.

1. Play this passage at the keyboard before you analyze it.

2. Ludwig van Beethoven, Piano Sonata no. 28 in A major, op. 101 (1816), *Lebhaft. Marchmässig.*

EXERCISE 21-I   *Writing Progressions with Modal Mixture*

Realize each progression in the specified texture and major key. Begin with the specified scale degree in the soprano. Add key signatures, time signatures, bar lines, and rhythmic values as necessary.

1. In chorale style: I–III♯–ii^6–V^7–♭VI

2. In keyboard style: I–VI♯–IV–V–I

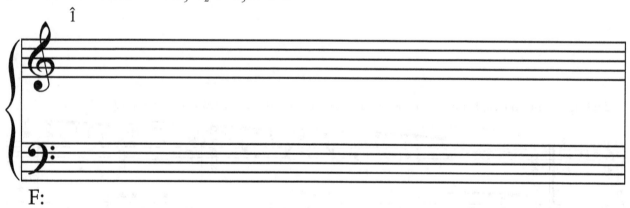

Eb: G:

3. With broken chords: I–♭VI–ii$^{ø6}_5$–V$^4_2$–I^6–V$^6_5$/iv–iv–I

F:

EXERCISE 21-J *Investigating When Modal Mixture Enlivens Repetition*

First, label each cadence, and label and diagram the form of each passage. Next, analyze on two levels. Finally, write a paragraph answering each set of questions.

1. Hélène Tham, *Eight Piano Pieces* (1894), no. 3, *Allegretto marcia*. Chromaticism enlivens the second phrase by *reharmonizing* the repeated melody. Discuss three moments where the harmony differs between the two phrases.

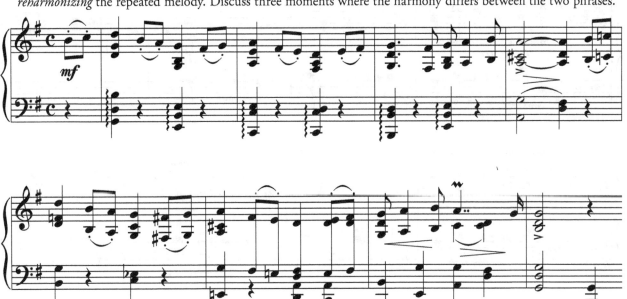

2. Maria Szymanowska, *Six Menuets* (1819), no. 3. The passage ends with a tiny melodic embellishment in the bass involving modal mixture, marked with an accent. Can you point out at least *two* earlier events (also accented) that foreshadow this modal mixture? Be sure to consider enharmonic equivalents.

Moderato

3. Franz Schubert, Piano Sonata in D major, D. 850 (1825), *Allegro vivace*. Compare the initial statement in m. 1 to its repetition in m. 5. What harmony is tonicized in m. 3? How about in m. 7? We have omitted the end of the second phrase: what kind of harmonic event would you expect to happen, and *when*?

ASSIGNMENT 21.5

EXERCISE 21-K   *Realizing a Figured Bass*

First, analyze the figured bass on two levels. Then, realize it in *keyboard style* following the given head start. Play your realization.

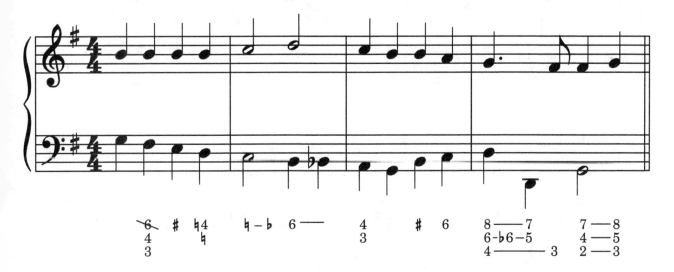

EXERCISE 21-L   *Exploring Chromaticism and Text Expression*

Label cadences and roman numerals in this passage from Fanny Hensel's (1805–1847) "Abendbild" from *Fünf Lieder*, op. 10. Then, after studying the text, write one or two paragraphs answering these questions: How might Hensel's harmonies express the sentiment of *leaning toward*? What aspect of the text might be expressed by the evaded cadence four measures before the end of the passage, and the slowing of the vocal rhythms right up until the grand pause?

Translation: [As evening peacefully sinks down upon the land,] the lovely one [Nature] smiles like a slumbering child in its father's arms as he, full of love, leans toward her. His divine eyes linger on her, and his breath blows across her face.

EXERCISE 21-M   *Analyzing a Larger Score*

Analyze the passage from W. A. Mozart's Clarinet Quintet in A major, K. 581 (1789), *Allegro*, on two levels. Be sure to show the contrapuntal function played by the chords in the fourth and sixth measures. *Hint: Remember that the Clarinet in A sounds a minor third lower than it reads.*

EXERCISE 21-N   *Cooking Phrases from Recipes*

Following the given prompts, compose short phrases on separate manuscript paper. Choose your own meter and write a time signature, bar lines, and rhythmic values accordingly. Analyze and play what you write.

1. D major: In keyboard style, expand tonic with an embedded phrase model that includes modal mixture. Then, reach a deceptive cadence on ♭VI.

2. A major: In a broken-chord figuration for piano, begin with a chromatic step-descent bass. Then, reach a PAC that incorporates at least one additional modal mixture harmony. Once you finish the accompaniment, add a single-line melody (for a voice or instrument of your choice) that incorporates at least two appoggiaturas.

3. E major: For string quartet in open score, write a sustained, chorale-like progression that features at least three modal mixture harmonies and at least three suspensions.

ASSIGNMENT 21.6

EXERCISE 21–O *Analyzing Instrumental Passages*

First, play or listen to each example. Then, analyze on two levels, including labeling any cadences.

1. Ludwig van Beethoven, Violin Sonata no. 9 in A major, "Kreutzer," op. 47 (1803), *Adagio sostenuto.* One of the decisions that you need to make is *how long* the key of A major lasts. When does C major take over? Answering this will help you to contextualize the many applied chords and modal mixture harmonies.

2. Francisca Chiquinha Gonzaga, *Grata Esperança* (c. 1886). This passage contains several chromatically altered pitches. Which ones participate in modal mixture? Which ones participate in tonicization? Are any of them just embellishing tones?

EXERCISE 21–P   *Analyzing Texted Music*

Analyze each passage on two levels, including labeling cadences if there are any. Then, answer the questions in a paragraph.

1. Maria Malibran, "Il Silfo" (text by Bocella) (1846). Is there a musical change (e.g., some kind of shrinking or compression) that might represent the closing of flowers? Is there anything in the music that might portray the *rootedness* of the flowers to the soil, against which they strive upward (in the voice), trying to open?

Translation: And already at night, the flowers are closed.

2. Johannes Brahms, "Sind es Schmerzen" from *Magelone-Lieder*, op. 33, no. 3 (1865). How does the middle system of this passage convey both the *falling* of tears and the *darkness* surrounding the narrator? Then, in the last system, what feature(s) of the music capture the bleak stasis of extinguished desire?

Translation: Oh, and when my tears fall down, it is dark all around me. If no desires return, [the future lacks hope].

CHAPTER 22

Chromatic Modulation and Text-Music Relations

ASSIGNMENT 22.1

EXERCISE 22–A *Analyzing Chromatic Modulations*

Each phrase below includes a chromatic pivot-chord modulation. First, play or listen to the phrase. Next, analyze with roman numerals, including a clearly marked pivot chord with a roman numeral showing the relationship of the new key to the original key. A sample analysis is provided for you.

Sample analysis:

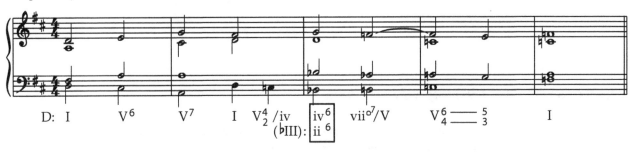

1.

2.

3.

EXERCISE 22–B   *Inserting a Pivot Chord*

Each phrase below establishes the tonic in *one* key and reaches a cadence in a *different* key. Add an appropriate chromatic pivot chord in the blank, which will function as a *modal mixture harmony in the original key* and as a *diatonic harmony in the new key*. Analyze the completed phrase with roman numerals, including a clearly marked pivot chord with a roman numeral showing the relationship of the new key to the original key. Play the finished phrase at the keyboard.

1.

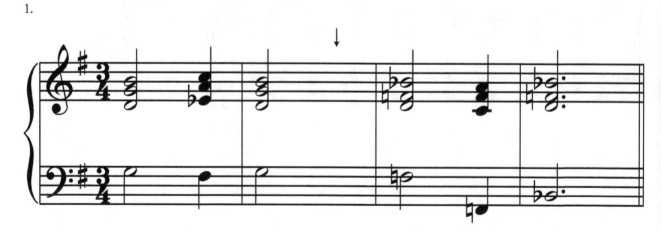

2.

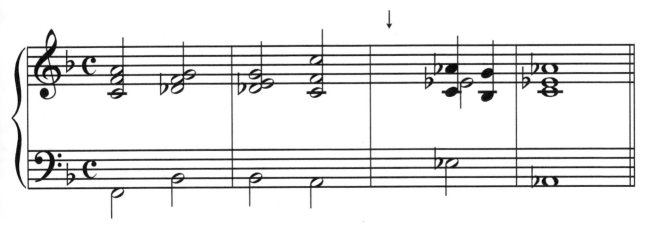

EXERCISE 22-C   *Realizing a Figured Bass*

First, analyze the figured bass with roman numerals, including a clearly marked pivot chord with a roman numeral showing the relationship of the new key to the original key. Then, using the provided soprano pitches and doubling guideline as head starts, realize the figured bass in keyboard style. Play your realization.

Double the 3rd

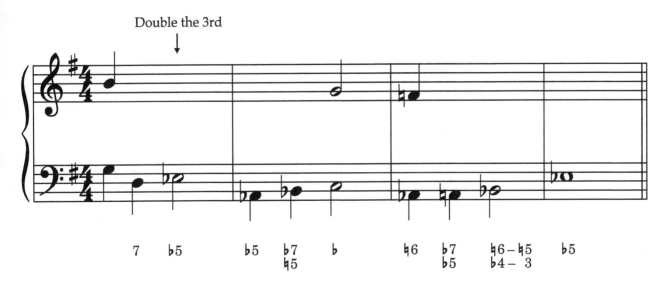

ASSIGNMENT 22.2

EXERCISE 22–D   *Analyzing Chromatic Pivot-Chord and Common-Tone Modulations*

Each passage includes a modulation to a chromatically related key. First, label the starting and ending keys and add a roman numeral showing the relationship of the new key to the original key. Next, label cadences. Then, determine whether the modulation uses a pivot chord or a common tone, and label it accordingly.

1. Josephine Lang (1815–1880), *Arabeske* from *Drei Klavierstücke*

2. From later in the same piece:

3. Frédéric Chopin, Etude in A♭ major, op. 10, no. 10 (1829). *Hint: To find the connection between the original key and the new key, you need to pay attention to enharmonically equivalent pitches.*

4. Valérie Boissier, *Trois Études*, no. 1 (1870)

EXERCISE 22-E   *Harmonizing Melodic Fragments that Modulate Chromatically*

Each melodic fragment implies a (quick!) chromatic pivot-chord modulation from one major key to another major key related by chromatic mediant. Harmonize each fragment in four voices: numbers 1 and 2 in chorale style, and numbers 3 and 4 in keyboard style. Analyze what you write.

1.

2.

3.

4.

ASSIGNMENT 22.3

EXERCISE 22–F   *Analyzing Chromatic Pivot-Chord and Common-Tone Modulations*

Each passage below includes a modulation to a chromatically related key. First, label the starting and ending keys and add a roman numeral showing the relationship of the new key to the original key. Next, label cadences. Then, determine whether the modulation uses a pivot chord or a common tone, and label it accordingly.

1. Franz Schubert, *Suleika II* ("Ach um deine feuchten Schwingen"), D. 717 (1824). *Hint: The key at the start of this passage does not match the key signature.*

Translation: Flowers, meadows, woods, and hills grow tearful at your breath.

2. Bob Cole (words by James Weldon Johnson), "Everybody Wants to See the Baby" (1903)

Now he has a lit-tle ba-by, So Tommy's quite a hap-py man you know.

Tommy's quite a hap-py man you know. Now the ba-by looks the same as an-y ba-by in a bed

3. Ludwig van Beethoven, Violin Sonata ("Spring"), op. 24 (1801), *Adagio molto espressivo*

EXERCISE 22-G *Harmonizing Longer Melodies that Modulate Chromatically*

Each melody implies a chromatic pivot-chord modulation from one major key to another major key related by chromatic mediant. Harmonize each melody in four voices: number 1 in chorale style, and number 2 in keyboard style. Analyze what you write.

1.

2.

ASSIGNMENT 22.4

EXERCISE 22-H   *Analyzing Chromatic Modulations in Texted Music*

1. Johannes Brahms, "Die Mainacht" ("May Night") from *Vier ernste Gesänge* (*Four Serious Songs*), op. 43, no. 2 (1857–1864). First, listen to the passage. Next, label all cadences and roman numerals, and mark when, how, and to where the modulation takes place. Then, choose three images, sentiments, or changes that occur in the text and, in one to two paragraphs total, discuss how details of Brahms's musical setting convey them.

mm. 3–5: When the silvery moon gleams through the bushes,
mm. 6–8: and spreads its slumbering light upon the grass,
mm. 9–10: and the nightingale is singing,
mm. 11–14: I wander sadly from one bush to another.
mm. 15–16: Covered by leaves[, two doves coo to me …]

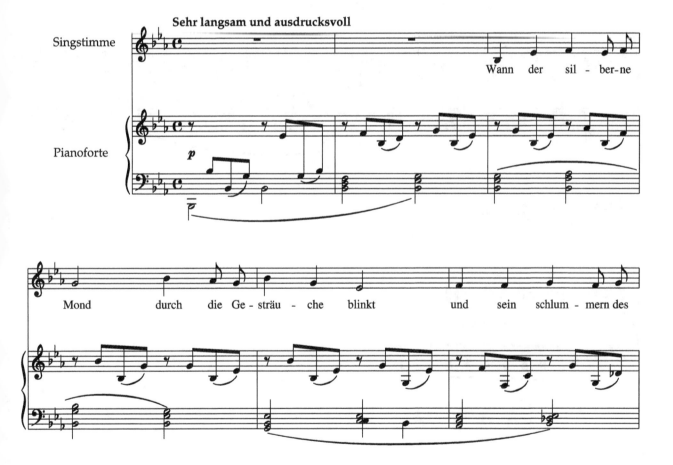

2. Maria Malibran, "Il Silfo" (1846). First, listen to the passage. Next, label all cadences and roman numerals, and mark when, how, and to where the modulation takes place. Then, in one to two paragraphs, discuss the change that takes place in the *text* beginning at m. 42 and how it is portrayed musically. Is there any musical evidence that the speaker might be experiencing feelings of coldness, rejection, or doubt even *before* the text makes them explicit?

mm. 27–41: You open me, ah you open me
mm. 42–49: The wind is already cold at night. What will happen if you reject me?

ven - to   che sa - rà,   se___ mi   ri - cu - si   E___ già

ASSIGNMENT 22.5

EXERCISE 22-1   *Writing Modulations*

Write each modulating phrase according to the instructions. Analyze and play what you write. Each phrase should contain between five and eight chords.

1. In keyboard style, modulate from C major to A♭ major by means of a common-tone modulation.

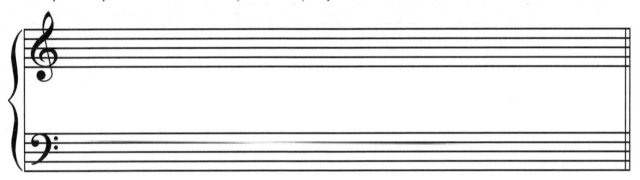

2. In chorale style, modulate from E major to ♭III using a modal mixture harmony as a pivot chord.

3. In chorale style, modulate from B♭ major to D major by means of a common-tone modulation.

4. In keyboard style, modulate from A major to F major using a modal mixture harmony as a pivot chord.

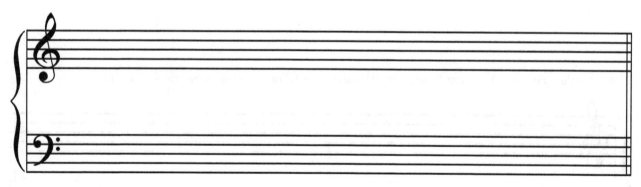

5. Use an F minor triad as the pivot chord in three different pivot-chord modulations in keyboard style:

   a. C major to A♭ major

   b. E♭ major to C minor

   c. A♭ major to F minor

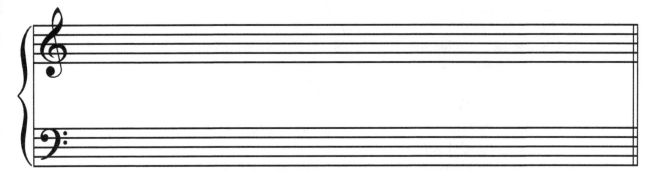

EXERCISE 22–J   *Analyzing Texted Music*

First, listen to Franz Schubert's song, "An Emma" ("To Emma"), D. 113 (1820), and study the text and its translation. Next, label all cadences and analyze the whole song using roman numerals, noting any passages that you find puzzling or interesting. Then, write two to three paragraphs analyzing how the music and text of this song interact, guided by the following prompt:

In this poem, a jilted lover reflecting on happier times is repeatedly jarred back to the reality of loss. The rhyme scheme of the text is *ababcc*. The last two lines of each strophe are distinguished both by rhyme scheme and by meaning, acting as a refrain. In the first two strophes, this refrain and the preceding verse are set in opposition to each other: The verse expresses the protagonist's longing for love, while the refrain redirects this thought toward the painful truth. The first verse emphasizes past happiness, and the distance between the speaker and the object of their gaze—the star—is symbolic of the time that separates the speaker from the beloved one, Emma.

1. Are particular words highlighted in the musical setting? How? Consider the use of accidentals, chromatic harmony, and dramatic pauses.
2. Locate all of the A major triads. Are certain words associated with this chord and with D minor (its chord of resolution)?
3. Are any harmonic progressions left incomplete? How might these interact with the text?
4. In the second verse (starting in m. 20), consider the analogy of death with night and slumber. Is the beloved dead, or only dead to the love of the speaker?
5. Is there a change in the speaker's perspective? Where is the climax? In the closing verse, the speaker poses a question to the beloved: If true love can never die, and that which we shared has died, then how could it have been love? Is there a poetic sentiment that helps to explain the curious musical sojourn into A♭ major?

Weit in nebelgrauer Ferne	*Far in the great misty distance*
Liegt mir das vergangne Glück,	*lies my past happiness.*
Nur an einem schönen Sterne	*My gaze still lingers fondly*
Weilt mit Liebe noch der Blick.	*on one lovely star alone;*
Aber, wie des Sternes Pracht,	*but the splendor of the star,*
Ist es nur ein Schein der Nacht.	*it is only an illusion of the night.*
Deckte dir der lange Schlummer,	*If the long sleep of night*
Dir der Tod die Augen zu,	*had closed your eyes*
Dich besässe doch mein Kummer,	*my grief might still possess you;*
Meinem Herzen lebtest du.	*you would live on in my heart.*
Aber ach! du lebst im Licht,	*But oh, you live in the light,*
Meiner Liebe lebst du nicht.	*but you do not live for my love.*
Kann der Liebe süss Verlangen,	*Emma, can love's sweetness*
Emma, kann's vergänglich sein?	*fade and die?*
Was dahin ist und vergangen,	*That which is past and gone,*
Emma, kann's die Liebe sein?	*Emma—can that be love?*
Ihrer Flamme Himmelsglut,	*Can the heavenly glow of its ardor die,*
Stirbt sie wie ein irdisch Gut?	*like some earthly possession?*

(trans. John Reed, *The Schubert Song Companion*)

Flam - me   Him - mels - glut,   stirbt sie   wie ein ir - disch Gut?

CHAPTER 23

Neapolitan Chords

ASSIGNMENT 23.1

EXERCISE 23–A   *Transposing Short Paradigms at the Keyboard*

Each paradigm illustrates a common usage of a Neapolitan sixth chord. Play as written and then transposed to the two other minor keys indicated. Transpose the two outer voices first, then the full chords.

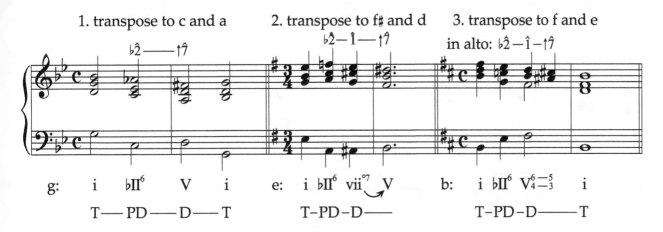

EXERCISE 23–B *Analyzing Neapolitan Chords*

After listening, analyze each passage on two levels, including labeling any cadences.

1. Giacomo Meyerbeer, "Scirocco" (1837). *Translation: Poor child, the wind is blowing south, poor child.*

2. Isabella Colbran, "Povero cor tu palpiti" (1805). What is the form of this passage? *Hint: Start by locating the three cadences. The form would have been more straightforward had the passage ended at m. 24. How do the last four measures relate to what has sounded previously?*

Translation: *[You have lost] your love forever, whose image Cupid's hand engraved upon you.*

3. Johannes Brahms, Clarinet Sonata in F minor, op. 120, no. 1 (1894). *Hint: The Clarinet in B♭ sounds a major second lower than it reads.*

ASSIGNMENT 23.2

EXERCISE 23-C *Contextualizing and Resolving ♭II⁶*

Each given triad is ♭II⁶ in a minor key. First, determine *which* key and add the appropriate key signature. Then, resolve each Neapolitan chord as specified by the given roman numeral and figured bass. Play your work on keyboard.

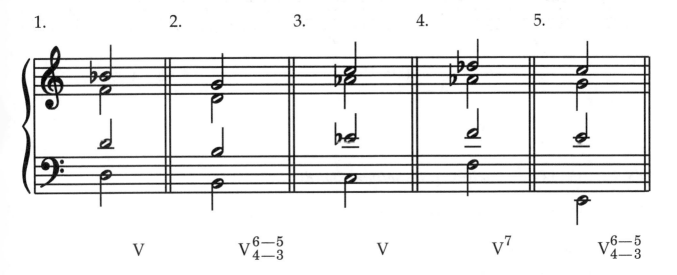

EXERCISE 23-D *Realizing Figured Basses That Include the Neapolitan Chord*

First, analyze each figured bass on two levels. Then, using the provided soprano pitches as head starts, realize each bass in keyboard style. Play your realizations.

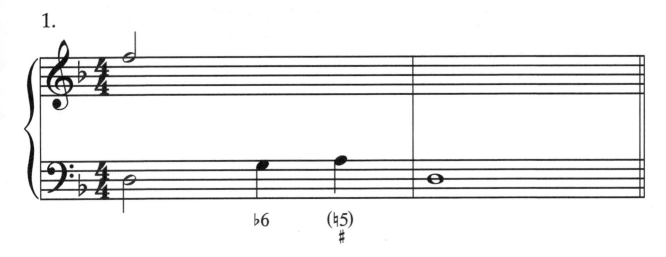

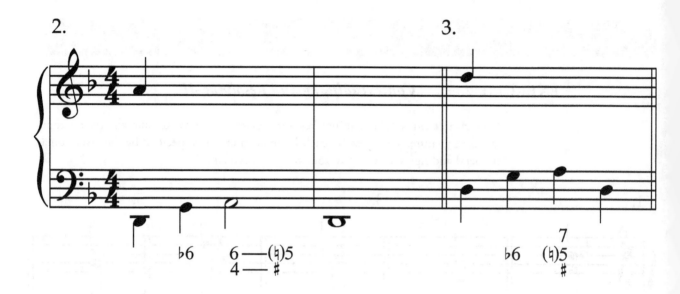

EXERCISE 23-E   *Analyzing Neapolitan Chords*

After listening, analyze each passage on two levels, including labeling any cadences.

1. Ludwig van Beethoven, "Sehnsucht," WoO 134 (1807)

Translation (first stanza only): Only those who know longing know my suffering.

2. Louise Reichardt (text by Pietro Metastasio), "Giusto Amor" (c. 1819)

Translation: True love, you who turn me on, advise me and defend me in my peril and fear.

3. Maria Szymanowska, *Six Minuets for Piano*, no. 1 (1819). What type of period defines the form of this passage? Szymanowska adds two compelling plot twists to the consequent phrase in order to prevent it from becoming a completely predictable repeat of the antecedent. First, although the *melody* in mm. 11–12 duplicates mm. 3–4, its harmonization does not: How does the harmonic arrival at m. 12 (marked by a *sforzando*) differ from the one at m. 4? The second plot twist is even bolder: How do the predominant chords of the two phrases differ?

ASSIGNMENT 23.3

EXERCISE 23-F   *Contextualizing ♭II⁶*

First, use the bass note of each ♭II⁶ chord to determine which minor key it is in, and add the appropriate key signature. Next, realize the given roman numerals in chorale style.

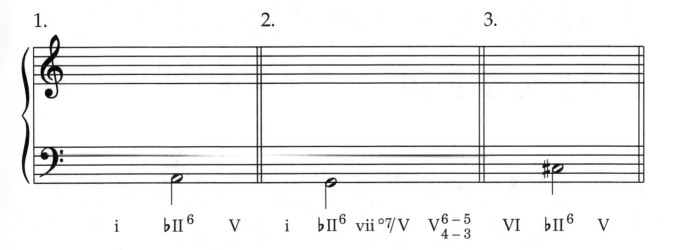

1.   i   ♭II⁶   V

2.   i   ♭II⁶   vii°7/V   V⁶⁻⁵₄₋₃   VI   ♭II⁶   V

EXERCISE 23-G   *Realizing a Figured Bass That Includes the Neapolitan Chord*

First, analyze the figured bass on two levels. Then, using the provided soprano pitches as head starts, realize the bass in keyboard style. Play your realization.

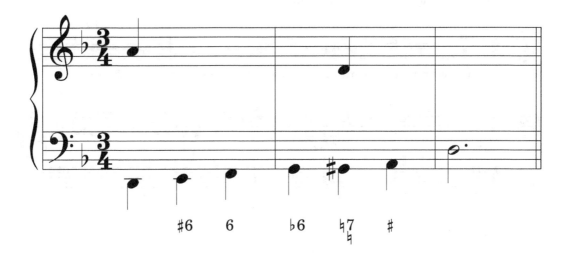

♯6   6   ♭6   ♮7♮   ♯

EXERCISE 23-H   *Analyzing Neapolitan Chords*

After listening, analyze each passage on two levels, including labeling any cadences. In addition, answer the questions.

1. Frédéric Chopin, Mazurka in C♯ minor, op. 30, no. 4, BI 105 (1836). How many times does the Neapolitan chord appear? Are they exact repeats, or does something change to provide interest?

2. Florence B. Price (text by Odessa P. Elder), "Sunset" (1938). This passage is saturated with accented dissonances such as appoggiaturas, suspensions, and retardations. Circle and label each of them. The sun's descent is narrated, paradoxically, by a rising melodic line. Is the idea of descent captured by any other features of the music?

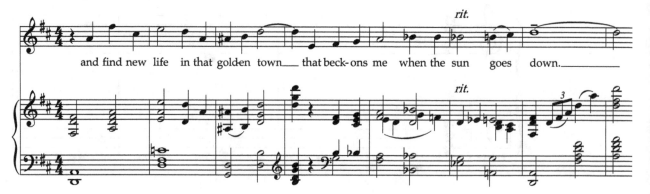

3. Pietro Antonio Locatelli, Sonata no. 3 in G minor from *Twelve Sonatas for Flute and Continuo* (1732), *Largo*. What is the form of this piece? Label any harmonic sequences. In a paragraph, describe the importance of Neapolitan chords to this short piece. In which keys, and in which contexts, do they appear? Is a Neapolitan chord ever used as the pivot chord in a modulation?

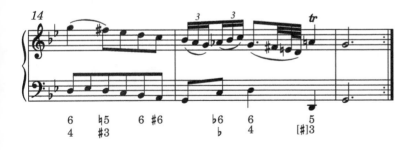

ASSIGNMENT 23.4

EXERCISE 23-1   *Harmonizing Short Melodies Using the Neapolitan Chord*

First, decide on a logical harmonic progression for each melody, making sure to include one Neapolitan chord in each harmonization. Add the appropriate bass notes and a two-level analysis. Then, add inner voices to create the specified texture. Finally, play your harmonization.

1. in keyboard style

g:

2. in chorale style

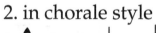

g:

EXERCISE 23-J   *Analyzing Passages that Feature the Neapolitan Chord*

1. Frédéric Chopin, Nocturne in C minor, op. 48, no. 1 (1842). Analyze the passage with roman numerals, including labeling any cadences. *Hint: Show the brief visits to nontonic keys as extended tonicizations rather than as modulations.*

2. Florence B. Price (text by Paul Laurence Dunbar), "Because" (1939). What is unusual about the Neapolitan chord in this passage? What is unusual about the material that *precedes* the Neapolitan chord? In a paragraph, answer these questions and speculate on how Price's particular usage of this harmony might relate to the passage's text.

EXERCISE 23-K   *Realizing Harmonic Progressions in Figurated Textures*

Realize each set of instructions in a meter of your choice. Add the necessary time signatures, key signatures, bar lines, and rhythmic values. Analyze on two levels and play your compositions.

1. In B minor, realize the progression i–vii°⁶–i⁶–♭II⁶–vii°⁷/V–V–I. Figurate the three upper voices with broken chords on the upper staff, and embellish the bass voice with octave leaps on the lower staff.

2. In C minor, realize the progression i–V⁶/III–III–♭II⁶–V$_{4-3}^{6-5}$–i. Figurate the three upper voices with repeated block chords on the upper staff, and embellish the bass voice with a mix of neighbors, passing tones, and chordal leaps/ skips on the lower staff.

ASSIGNMENT 23.5

EXERCISE 23-L   *Realizing a Figured Bass*

Analyze the figured bass on two levels. Then, realize it in chorale style, using the given soprano pitches as a head start. Play your realization.

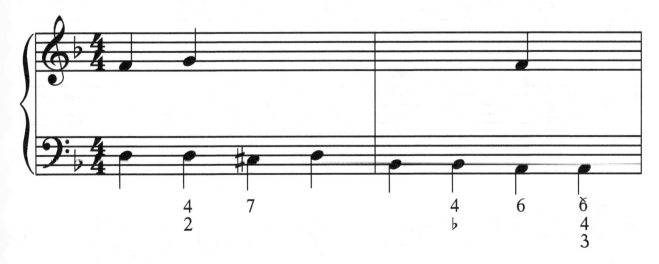

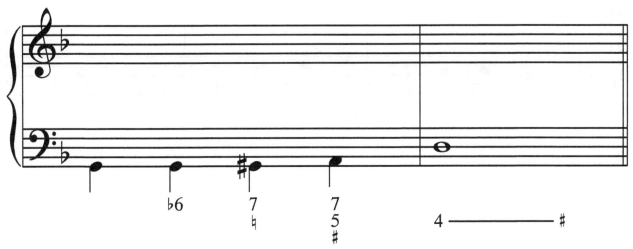

EXERCISE 23–M   *Filling in Outer Voices in Keyboard Style*

Use the given outer voices to determine the implied harmonies, which include multiple chromatic harmonies and a modulation. Analyze the passage. Then, add inner voices to create a keyboard-style realization. Play your realization.

EXERCISE 23-N   *Analyzing a Longer Passage*

Analyze the passage from Ludwig van Beethoven's String Quartet no. 8 in E minor, op. 59, no. 2 (1806), *Allegro*, on two levels.

EXERCISE 23-O   *Analyzing a Longer Passage*

The passage on the following page, from Ludwig van Beethoven's Rondo in C major, op. 51, no. 1 (1797), includes a lengthy tonicization. Analyze the entire passage with roman numerals.

Augmented-Sixth Chords

ASSIGNMENT 24.1

EXERCISE 24–A *Spelling Augmented-Sixth Chords*

First, add the key signature for each specified key, noting that uppercase letters indicate major keys and lowercase letters indicate minor keys. Next, notate each requested augmented-sixth chord *in chorale style*, making sure to include all necessary accidentals. Finally, resolve each augmented-sixth chord to the dominant (including a cadential six-four in the case of Ger_5^6).

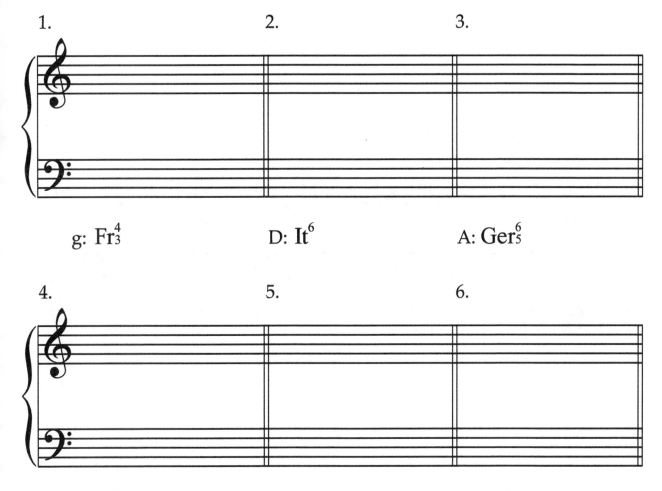

1.

g: Fr_3^4

2.

D: It^6

3.

A: Ger_5^6

4.

c♯: Fr_3^4

5.

b: Ger_5^6

6.

B♭: It^6

EXERCISE 24-B *Analyzing Augmented-Sixth Chords*

Analyze each passage on two levels.

1. Josephine Lang (1815–1880), *Arabeske* from *Drei Klavierstücke. Hint: This passage does not begin on a tonic chord. Listen to the whole excerpt and identify the cadence type at the end before deciding what the key is.*

2. Louise Reichardt (1779–1826), "Giusto Amor"

Translation: Defend me, true love.

3. J. S. Bach (1685–1750), "Ich hab' mein' Sach' Gott heimgestellt," BWV 351. The pitch that creates the characteristic interval of the augmented sixth appears just *after* the other chord tones. What type of embellishing tone postpones this pitch?

4. Scott Joplin, *Fig Leaf Rag* (1908). *Hint: Beware of modal mixture in addition to an augmented-sixth chord.*

EXERCISE 24-C   *Transposing Short Paradigms at the Keyboard*

Each paradigm illustrates a common usage of an augmented-sixth chord. Play each as written and then transposed to the two minor keys indicated. Transpose the two outer voices first, then the full chords.

1. French
transpose to f and b

2. German
transpose to c and e

3. Italian
transpose to g and d

ASSIGNMENT 24.2

EXERCISE 24-D   *Writing Phrygian Half Cadences and Augmented-Sixth Chords*

Label the *minor* key implied by each key signature. Next, write four short progressions in each key, following the sample: (1) a Phrygian half cadence (iv⁶–V), (2) It⁶–V, (3) Ger$_5^6$–V$_{4-3}^{6-5}$, and (4) Fr$_3^4$–V. Write in chorale style throughout.

Sample solution:

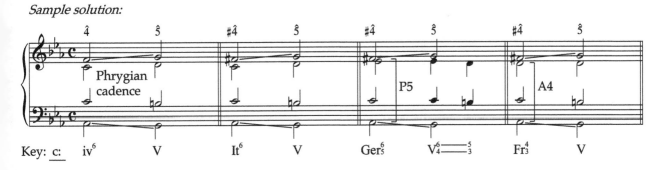

1.

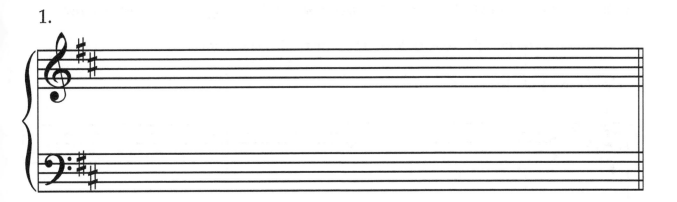

2.

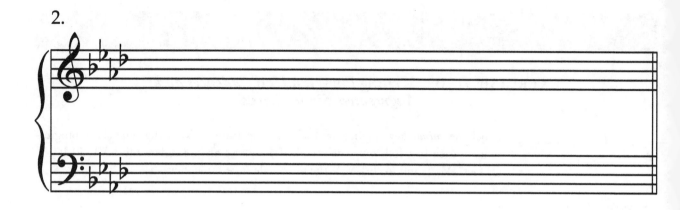

EXERCISE 24–E   *Realizing Figured Basses That Include Augmented-Sixth Chords*

Analyze each figured bass on two levels. Then, realize it in the specified texture.

1. Keyboard style

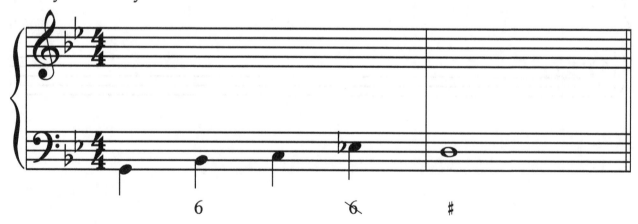

2. Chorale style

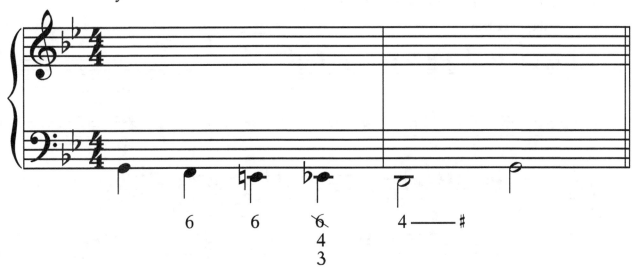

EXERCISE 24–F   *Analyzing Augmented-Sixth Chords*

Analyze each passage on two levels.

1. W. A. Mozart, Piano Trio no. 7 in E♭ major, K. 498 (1786), *Allegretto*

2. Elfrida Andrée, Piano Trio no. 2 in G minor (1884). *Hint: This passage does not begin on a tonic harmony. Listen all the way through before deciding on its key.*

ASSIGNMENT 24.3

EXERCISE 24-G   *Moving to and from Augmented-Sixth Chords*

First, label the *minor* key in which each given augmented-sixth chord would be found, and add the appropriate key signature. Next, *precede* each augmented-sixth chord with a root-position tonic chord. Finally, *resolve* each augmented-sixth chord to the dominant (including a cadential six-four in the case of Ger$^6_5$).

EXERCISE 24–H   *Analyzing Augmented-Sixth Chords*

1. Ludwig van Beethoven, Violin Sonata no. 7 in C minor, op. 30, no. 2 (1802), *Allegro.* One could argue that all three forms of augmented-sixth chords appear briefly in this passage, but which form is most prominent? Why?

2. Louise Farrenc, Trio for Flute, Cello, and Piano, op. 45 (1857), *Andante. Hint: Treat the chord in the seventh measure (with an asterisk) as a pivot chord from C major to G major. You'll have to listen carefully to determine what happens before and after it, as well as how and when the music eventually returns to C major.*

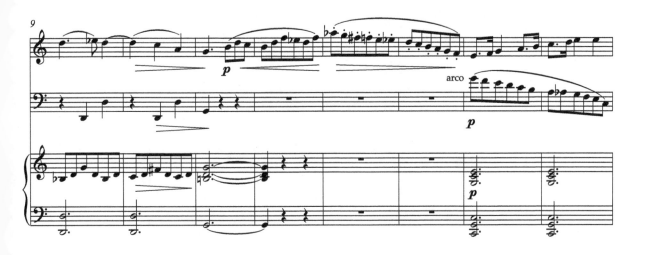

3. W. A. Mozart, Piano Concerto in E♭ major, K. 449 (1784), *Allegro*

ASSIGNMENT 24.4

EXERCISE 24–1   *Analyzing Longer Passages that Include Augmented-Sixth Chords*

Analyze on two levels and label all cadences on the score. In addition, diagram and label the form of each passage.

1. Franz Schubert, Waltz in F major, *36 Originaltänze*, no. 34, D. 365 (1815)

2. Franz Schubert, Waltz in A major, *Wiener-Damen Ländler*, no. 6, D. 734 (1822)

3. Hélène Tham, *Eight Piano Pieces*, no. 2 (1894)

EXERCISE 24-J   *Harmonizing Melodies in a Variety of Textures*

Harmonize each melodic fragment in a minor key according to the instructions. Analyze on two levels. Play your work.

1. *Three-Voice Texture (melody, bass, and one inner voice).* Include an It⁶ and a step-descent bass. Omit the chordal fifth when necessary.

2. *Keyboard Style.* Include an applied chord and a Ger$_5^6$.

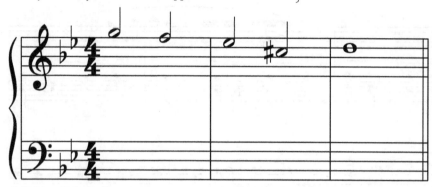

3. *Chorale Style.* Include a Fr$_3^4$ and end with a deceptive cadence.

ASSIGNMENT 24.5

EXERCISE 24–K   *Analyzing Texted Music*

Label cadences and roman numerals in both passages from Clara Schumann's "Was weinst du, Blümlein" from *Sechs Lieder*, op. 23 (1853). Then, in one to two paragraphs, describe the musical similarities and differences between the two passages and discuss how they relate to the sentiments expressed in the text.

Translation (first passage): Why do you weep in the morning light, little flower?

Translation (second passage): O, morning sky, you are blood red as if the sun lay dead in the sea.

EXERCISE 24–L *Analyzing Augmented-Sixth Chords that Signal Tonicizations*

The operatic excerpts below contain augmented-sixth chords that act not only in the tonic key, but also as part of tonicizations. First, locate the number of augmented-sixth chords indicated in parentheses. Next, bracket and label each tonicization with a roman numeral. Finally, within those brackets, analyze each augmented-sixth chord and the chord that follows it.

1. Giuseppe Verdi, "Qual voce! Come! Tu, donna?" from *Il Trovatore* (1853), part 4, no. 18 (two +6 chords)

2. Amilcare Ponchielli, "Ombre di mia prosapia" from *La Gioconda* (1876) (three +6 chords)

EXERCISE 24-M   *Realizing a Figured Bass That Includes Augmented-Sixth Chords*

Realize the figured bass in keyboard style. Analyze on two levels. Play your realization.

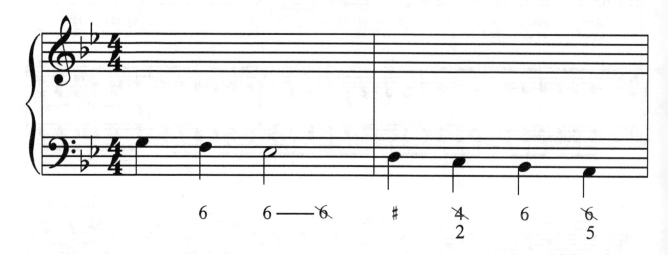

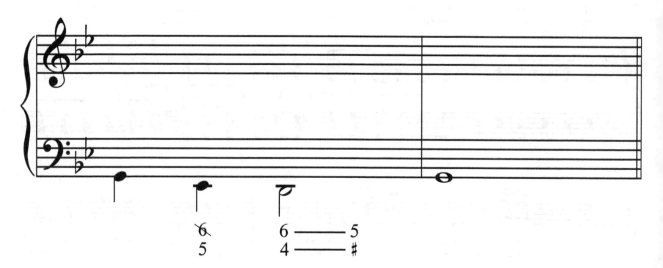

ASSIGNMENT 24.6

EXERCISE 24–N   *Transposing Short Paradigms at the Keyboard*

Each paradigm illustrates a voice exchange with one or more augmented-sixth chords. Play as written, then transposed to the two minor keys indicated. Transpose the two outer voices first, then the full chords.

1. with Ger^7 and Ger$^6_5$
transpose to e and g

2. with iv and Ger$^6_5$
transpose to d and a

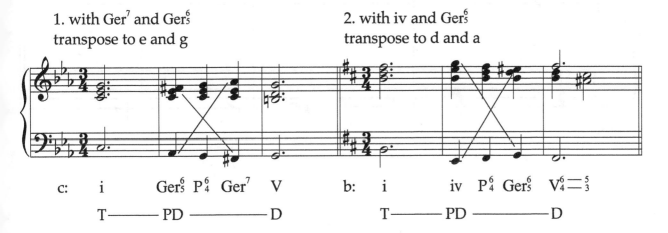

c: i   Ger$^6_5$ P$^6_4$ Ger^7 V   b: i   iv P$^6_4$ Ger$^6_5$ V$^6_4$—$^5_3$

   T———PD ————————D   T———PD ————————D

EXERCISE 24–O   *Writing Diminished-Third Chords*

Add the appropriate key signature for each minor key. Then, write the specified progression in chorale style.

1.   2.   3.   4.

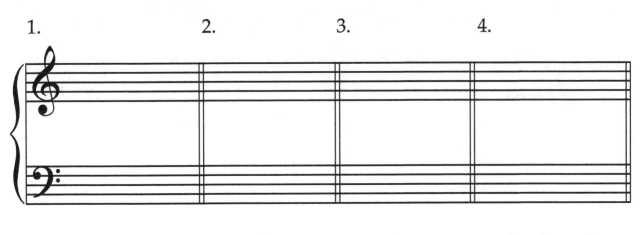

c: Ger^7 V   d: Ger$^6_5$ V   c♯: Ger^7 V   a: Ger$^6_5$ P$^6_4$ Ger^7 V

                                                    (use voice exchange)

EXERCISE 24-P *Realizing a Figured Bass in Keyboard Style*

Using the given first chord as a head start, realize the figured bass in keyboard style. In m. 2, write a voice exchange in the two outer voices. Analyze on two levels and play your realization.

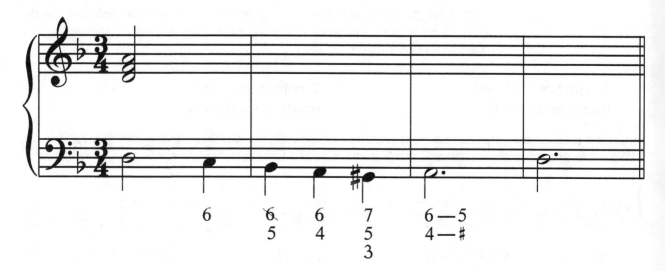

EXERCISE 24-Q *Analyzing Expanded Pre-Dominants*

Analyze each passage on two levels, including labeling any cadences.

1. Franz Joseph Haydn, Piano Sonata in E major, Hob. XVI:31 (c. 1775), *Allegretto*

2. Robert Nathaniel Dett, *Cave of the Winds* (1902). *Hint: This passage does not begin on a tonic harmony.*

(Emb.)

3. Ludwig van Beethoven, String Quartet no. 11 in F minor, "Serioso," op. 95 (1810), *Larghetto espressivo*

4. Elisa Delaye-Fuchs (b. 1872), *Ave Maria*, op. 21. The last measure of this passage begins with a chord that you have not encountered. However, you have studied a harmony that is very similar to it. What might you call this chord? Write a sentence explaining the chord as best you can.

ASSIGNMENT 24.7

EXERCISE 24-R   *Analyzing Enharmonic Reinterpretations*

Analyze each passage on two levels, guided by the hints. Label all cadences.

1. Mélanie Bonis (1858–1937), Menuet, op. 14. *Hint: Use your ears, rather than your eyes, to locate the chord that is enharmonically reinterpreted.*

2. Show two modulations (rather than tonicizations) in this passage, one *away* from the original key and the other *back to* the original key.

3. Samuel Coleridge-Taylor, Quintet in F♯ minor, op. 10 (1895), i. The analysis is done for you
   except in the third measure, which begins with an enharmonic pivot chord (at the arrow). *Hint:*
   The upper staff is a transposing instrument, Clarinet in A. However, it doubles the first violin (the
   second staff), which you can read more easily because it is a non-transposing instrument.

4. Ludwig van Beethoven, Piano Sonata no. 27 in E major, op. 90 (1814), *Nicht zu geschwind und sehr singbar vor-zutragen. Hint: In this passage, the respelling actually comes before you probably notice the modulation aurally.*

5. Franz Schubert, Piano Sonata in A minor, op. 42, D. 845 (1825), *Moderato. Hint: Two chords that look quite different actually sound alike, which will help you in your analysis.*

EXERCISE 24-S   *Filling in the Blanks*

Complete the following passage in keyboard style. Include one of each type of augmented-sixth chord. Analyze on two levels. Play what you write.

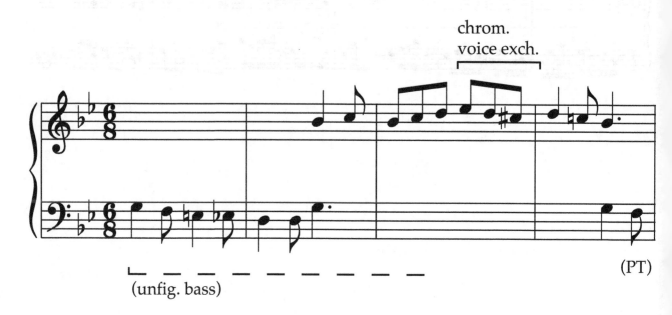

(unfig. bass)

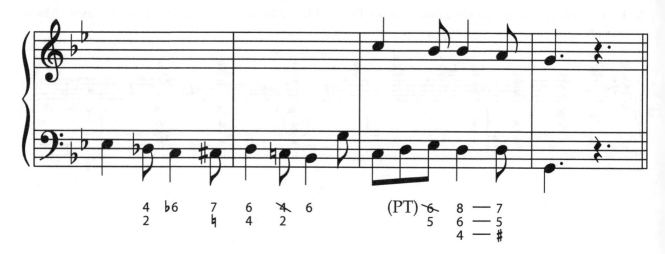

ASSIGNMENT 24.8

EXERCISE 24–T   *Analyzing Longer Passages*

Analyze each passage on two levels and answer the accompanying questions.

1. Franz Schubert, *Originaltänze*, op. 9, no. 14, D. 365 (1822). Label and diagram the form of this passage.

2. Will Marion Cook, "Cruel Papa" (1914). A tonicization bracket and a pivot-chord box are given as hints.

3. W. A. Mozart, Piano Trio in G major, K. 564 (1788), *Allegretto. Hint: Do not overlook the two uppermost staves!*

4. Frédéric Chopin, Mazurka in C♯ minor, op. 63, no. 3 (1846). What type of metrical disruption takes place in the fifth and sixth measures of this passage?

EXERCISE 24–U   *Composing the Consequent Phrase of a Period*

Write a consequent phrase to follow the given antecedent phrase in order to create a parallel progressive period. Incorporate a Neapolitan chord and an augmented-sixth chord into your consequent. Preserve the given texture and basic rhythms in your consequent phrase if you can. Analyze on two levels and play what you write.

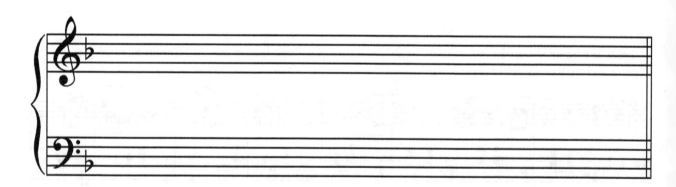

CHAPTER 25

Ternary Form

EXERCISE 25-A *Josephine Lang (1815–1880), Arabeske in F major from* **Drei Klavierstücke**

First, listen to the piece multiple times. Next, annotate the score with section labels, keys, cadences, and embedded smaller forms (such as periods, sentences, or binary forms). Finally, construct a detailed form diagram that shows this information. Include measure numbers in your diagram. Think especially carefully about the role that mm. 53–79 play in the piece as a whole. *Hint: What harmony do they prolong?*

ASSIGNMENT 25.2

EXERCISE 25–B   *Frédéric Chopin, Mazurka in E minor, op. 17, no. 2, BI 77 (1832)*

First, listen to the piece multiple times. Next, annotate the score with section labels, keys, cadences, and embedded smaller forms (such as periods, sentences, or binary forms). Finally, construct a detailed form diagram that shows this information. Include measure numbers in your diagram. Think carefully about whether you believe this piece has a retransition and, if so, when it begins.

ASSIGNMENT 25.3

EXERCISE 25–C   *Amancio Jacinto Alcorta (1805–1862), Minué "Los abrazos"*

First, listen to the piece multiple times. Next, annotate the score with section labels, keys, cadences, and embedded smaller forms (such as periods, sentences, or binary forms). Finally, construct a detailed form diagram that shows this information. Include measure numbers in your diagram. *Hint: The road map of this piece (i.e., its repeats) tells you something about its form.*

D.C. al Fine
sin repet.

ASSIGNMENT 25.4

EXERCISE 25-D   *Ludwig van Beethoven, Bagatelle no. 1 in G minor, op. 119, no. 1 (1823)*

First, listen to the piece multiple times. Next, annotate the score with section labels, keys, cadences, and embedded smaller forms (such as periods, sentences, or binary forms). Finally, construct a detailed form diagram that shows this information. Include measure numbers in your diagram. *Hint: Listen for the moment where the piece could have ended, and consider what happens between that point and the double bar.*

ASSIGNMENT 25.5

EXERCISE 25–E   *Reynaldo Hahn,* Pavane D'Angelo *(1909)*

First, listen to the piece multiple times. Next, annotate the score with section labels, keys, cadences, and embedded smaller forms (such as periods, sentences, or binary forms). Finally, construct a detailed form diagram that shows this information. Include measure numbers in your diagram. Think carefully about the form of the A section on its own. In addition, is there anything unusual about the proportions of mm. 2–11?

CHAPTER 26

Rondo Form

EXERCISE 26–A *Franz Joseph Haydn, Piano Sonata no. 50 in D major, Hob. XVI:37 (1780),* **Finale**

First, listen to the piece multiple times. Next, annotate the score with section labels, keys, cadences, and embedded smaller forms (such as periods, sentences, or binary forms). Finally, construct a detailed form diagram that shows this information. Include measure numbers in your diagram.

FINALE

ASSIGNMENT 26.2

EXERCISE 26-B   *Sophia Dussek,* **The New German Waltz** *(c. 1799)*

First, listen to the piece multiple times. Next, annotate the score with section labels, keys, cadences, and embedded smaller forms (such as periods, sentences, or binary forms). Finally, construct a detailed form diagram that shows this information. Include measure numbers in your diagram.

EXERCISE 26-C   *Sophia Dussek, Sonata in G major, op. 2, no. 2*
(c. 1800)

First, listen to the piece multiple times. Next, annotate the score with section labels, keys, cadences, and embedded smaller forms (such as periods, sentences, or binary forms). Finally, construct a detailed form diagram that shows this information. Include measure numbers in your diagram.

ASSIGNMENT 26.3

EXERCISE 26–D   *W. A. Mozart, Viennese Sonatina in C from* **Five Divertimenti for Two Clarinets and Bassoon, K. Anh. 229 (1785), Allegro**

First, listen to the piece multiple times. Next, annotate the score with section labels, keys, cadences, and embedded smaller forms (such as periods, sentences, or binary forms). Finally, construct a detailed form diagram that shows this information. Include measure numbers in your diagram.

ASSIGNMENT 26.4

EXERCISE 26-E   *Reynaldo Hahn,* **L'Inspiration** *(1896)*

First, listen to the piece multiple times. Next, annotate the score with section labels, keys, cadences, and embedded smaller forms (such as periods, sentences, or binary forms). Finally, construct a detailed form diagram that shows this information. Include measure numbers in your diagram.

CHAPTER 27

Sonata Form

ASSIGNMENT 27.1

EXERCISE 27–A *Marie-Elizabeth Cléry, Three Harp Sonatas, op. 1, no. 2 (1795), i*

First, listen to the piece multiple times. Next, annotate the score with large sonata-form sections (exposition, development, recapitulation), smaller sections (FTA, Tr, STA, Cl), cadences and their keys, themes, and any other distinctive features. Then, construct a detailed form diagram that shows this information. Include measure numbers in your diagram. Finally, in one to two paragraphs, point out any unusual features of this piece's form and discuss any sections that gave you trouble in your analysis.

ASSIGNMENT 27.2

EXERCISE 27–B   *Ludwig van Beethoven, Piano Sonata no. 1 in F minor, op. 2, no. 1 (1795), i*

First, listen to the piece multiple times. Next, annotate the score with large sonata-form sections (exposition, development, recapitulation), smaller sections (FTA, Tr, STA, Cl), cadences and their keys, themes, and any other distinctive features. Then, construct a detailed form diagram that shows this information. Include measure numbers in your diagram. Finally, in one to two paragraphs, point out any unusual features of this piece's form and discuss any sections that gave you trouble in your analysis.

ASSIGNMENT 27.3

EXERCISE 27-C *Hélène de Montgeroult (1764–1836), Piano Sonata in E♭ major, op. 1, no. 2*

First, listen to the piece multiple times. Next, annotate the score with large sonata-form sections (exposition, development, recapitulation), smaller sections (FTA, Tr, STA, Cl), cadences and their keys, themes, and any other distinctive features. Then, construct a detailed form diagram that shows this information. Include measure numbers in your diagram. Finally, in one to two paragraphs, point out any unusual features of this piece's form and discuss any sections that gave you trouble in your analysis.

ASSIGNMENT 27.4

EXERCISE 27-D   *Joseph Bologne, String Quartet, op. 1, no. 3 (1773), i*

First, listen to the piece multiple times. Next, annotate the score with large sonata-form sections (exposition, development, recapitulation), smaller sections (FTA, Tr, STA, Cl), cadences and their keys, themes, and any other distinctive features. Then, construct a detailed form diagram that shows this information. Include measure numbers in your diagram. Finally, in one to two paragraphs, point out any unusual features of this piece's form and discuss any sections that gave you trouble in your analysis.

CHAPTER 28

Tonal Ambiguity and Symmetrically Constructed Harmonies

ASSIGNMENT 28.1

EXERCISE 28–A   *Warming Up Enharmonically at the Keyboard*

1. As a warmup, play the four short progressions below. Notice that they all begin with the same diminished seventh chord spelled in four different ways. Study the key and roman numerals of each progression.

c: vii°⁷   i   a: vii°⁶₅   i⁶   f♯: vii°⁴₃   i⁶   e♭: vii°⁴₂   V⁷   i

2. Label the minor key that each of the four enharmonically equivalent diminished seventh chords suggests. *Hint: The root of the chord is the key's leading tone, and the four keys will be related by minor thirds.* Then, write the chord that follows (and resolves) each diminished seventh chord within its key. Finally, analyze with roman numerals.

3. Finally, reinterpret the initial diminished seventh chord enharmonically by respelling it according to how it would function in each of the minor keys listed. Resolve all four diminished seventh chords properly and analyze all four two-chord progressions with roman numerals.

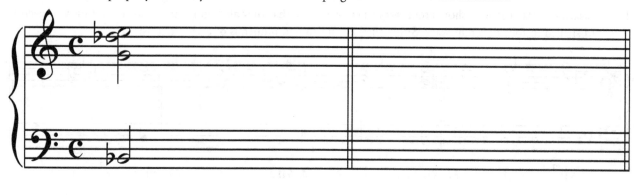

f: g#:

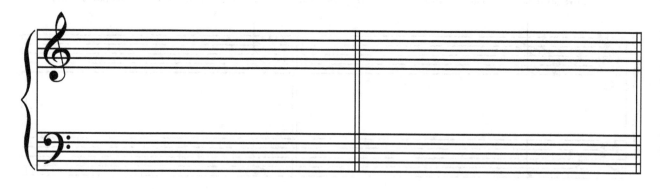

b: d:

EXERCISE 28–B   *Analyzing Enharmonic Modulations*

Analyze each modulating passage with roman numerals, including a clearly marked enharmonic pivot chord.

1.

2.

3. Hugo Wolf, "Verschling' der Abgrund meines liebsten Hütte" ("May the Abyss Swallow Up My Beloved's Cottage"), *Italienisches Liederbuch*, no. 45 (1896)

Leidenschaftlich bewegt

Ver - schling' ___ der Ab - grund mei - nes lieb -sten

4. Judith Ribas, *Fleur D'Avril* (1886). What is the logic of the bass voice across the first four measures?

ASSIGNMENT 28.2

EXERCISE 28-C   *Realizing a Figured Bass That Modulates Enharmonically*

Realize the figured bass in keyboard style. Be on the lookout for an enharmonic pivot chord. Analyze the whole passage, and play your realization.

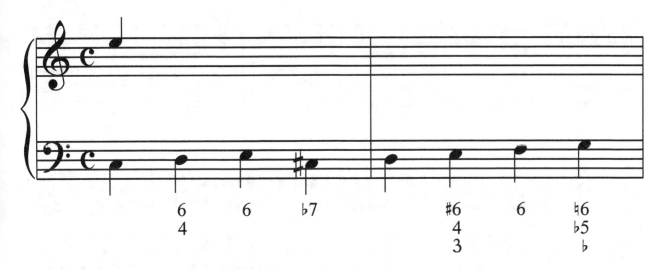

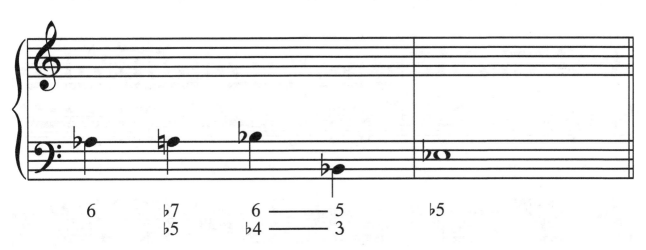

EXERCISE 28-D *Locating Enharmonic Reinterpretations*

First, listen to each passage and circle every diminished seventh chord. Then, locate the enharmonic pivot chord(s) in each passage and label each clearly in both keys. You do not need to analyze every chord.

1. Ludwig van Beethoven, Symphony no. 2 in D major, op. 36 (1802), *Larghetto*

2. Richard Wagner, Overture from *Der fliegende Holländer* (*The Flying Dutchman*) (1843)

EXERCISE 28-E   *Composing the Consequent Phrase of a Period*

The antecedent phrase of a period is already written. Preserving the same broken-chord figuration, compose the consequent phrase of a parallel progressive period, which will modulate by enharmonically reinterpreting the diminished seventh chord from m. 3 in m. 7. Analyze the entire period with roman numerals and a clearly marked pivot chord, and play your composition at the keyboard.

ASSIGNMENT 28.3

EXERCISE 28–F   *Analyzing Common-Tone Diminished Seventh Chords*

Each passage below contains one or more common-tone diminished seventh chords. Analyze each entire passage, including labeling any cadences. Draw an asterisk (*) above each common-tone diminished seventh chord in addition to labeling it in your analysis.

1. Eugène Dédé, *Buenas Noches*, op. 243 (1893)

2. (same piece)

3. Teresa Carreño, *Reminiscences de Norma*, op. 14 (1867)

Allegro con brio

EXERCISE 28-G   *Writing Common-Tone Diminished Seventh Chords*

Fill in each prompt to end with a chorale-style progression.

1. Insert a CT°7 chord.   2.

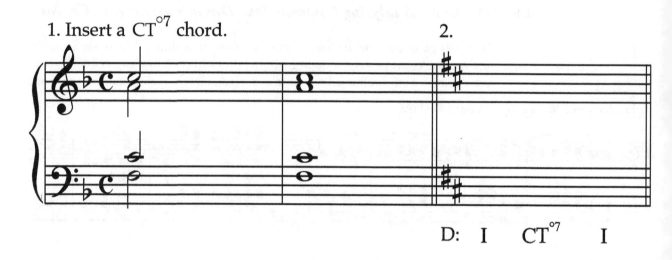

D: I   CT°7   I

3.

CT°7 $\frac{4}{3}$ vii°7/ii $\frac{4}{3}$

EXERCISE 28–H   *Analyzing Common-Tone Chords*

Analyze each passage on two levels.

1. Frédéric Chopin, Nocturne in A♭ major, op. 32, no. 2, BI 106 (1837)

2. Johannes Brahms, "Salamander," op. 107, no. 2 (1889)

Translation: Just as hot love suits a cool devil such as me.

3. Francisca Edwiges Neves Gonzaga, *Chi* (1883)

ASSIGNMENT 28.4

EXERCISE 28–1   *Analyzing Common-Tone Chords*

Analyze each passage with roman numerals.

1. Elisa Delaye-Fuchs (b. 1872), *Pièce* in A♭ Major, op. 25

2. This passage modulates. Show the pivot chord clearly.

3. Teresa Carreño, *Le Ruisseau*, op. 29 (1869)

4. Franz Schubert, "Am Meer" from *Schwanengesang* (1828)

Translation: The sea shone far out in the last light of evening.

5. Johannes Brahms, Symphony no. 3 in F major, op. 90 (1884), *Allegro con brio*

EXERCISE 28-J   *Writing Common-Tone Chords*

Fill in each prompt to end with a chorale-style progression.

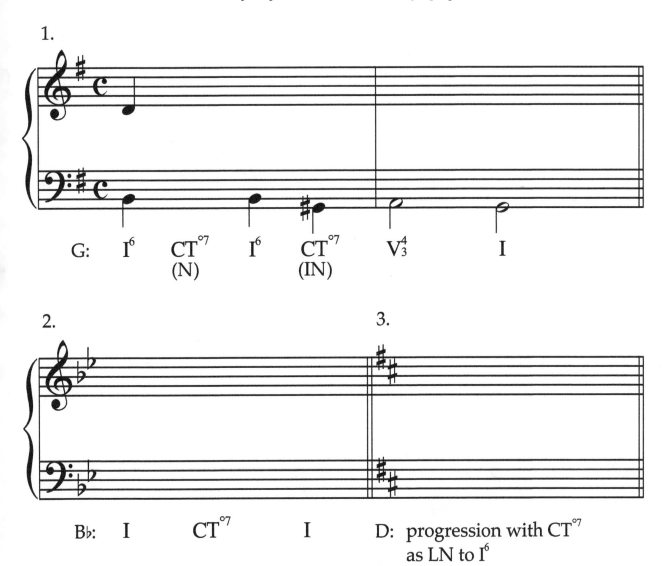

ASSIGNMENT 28.5

EXERCISE 28-K *Analyzing Augmented Triads and Altered Dominant Chords*

Each example below contains one or more augmented triads and/or altered dominant seventh chords. Analyze each entire passage. When possible, show the chromatic alterations as melodic motions in the figured bass (e.g., "5–♯5").

1.

2.

3. Ludwig van Beethoven, Theme and Variations in G major, WoO 77 (1801), *Thema: Andante, quasi Allegretto*

4. Scott Joplin, *Pleasant Moments* (1909)

EXERCISE 28-L *Writing Augmented Triads and Altered Dominant Chords*

Realize each progression in keyboard style.

1.

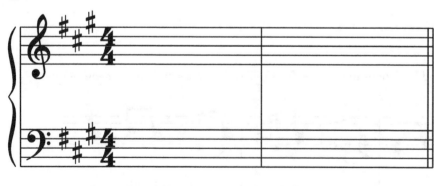

2.

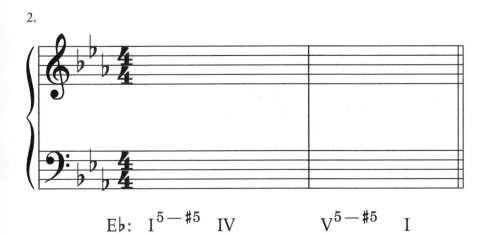

$E\flat\colon\ I^{5-\sharp5}\quad IV\qquad\quad V^{5-\sharp5}\quad\ I$

EXERCISE 28-M   *Analyzing Common-Tone and Altered Dominant Chords*

Analyze each passage on two levels.

1.

2.

3.

ASSIGNMENT 28.6

EXERCISE 28–N *Analyzing and Filling In the Blanks*

First, play through the given outer voices at the keyboard. Next, use their harmonic implications to analyze the passage with roman numerals. Finally, realize your analysis in keyboard style by adding two inner voices to the upper staff. Be sure to play your realization.

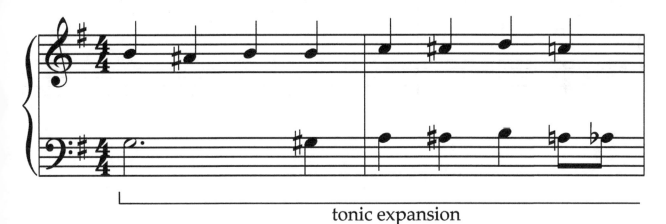

tonic expansion

EXERCISE 28-O *Harmonizing Short Melodies*

Harmonize each given melody in keyboard style, following the instructions for what to include. Analyze your harmonization and be sure to play it at the keyboard.

1. Begin in D major and modulate to E minor. *Hint: Think about how you will create an authentic cadence with ♭2̂–1̂ in the soprano.*

2. Begin in F major and modulate to D minor.

EXERCISE 28-P *Analyzing Augmented Triads and Altered Dominant Chords*

Each example below contains one or more augmented triads and/or altered dominant seventh chords. Analyze each entire passage. When possible, show the chromatic alterations as melodic motions in the figured bass (e.g., "5–♯5").

1. Ludwig van Beethoven, *Diabelli Variations*, op. 120 (1823), Variation 14. *Hint: Multiple suspensions create the dissonant sound that appears on the downbeat of m. 3. Label them using figured bass.*

2. Giacomo Puccini, *Madama Butterfly* (1904), Act I. Label the harmonic sequence.

ASSIGNMENT 28.7

EXERCISE 28-Q   *Analyzing Off-Tonic Beginnings*

The following examples do not begin on tonic harmony. First, label the key of each passage, which will require careful listening and study of cadences and other contextual clues. Then, analyze the first chord with a roman numeral.

1. Irving Caesar and Vincent Youmans, "Tea for Two," as performed in 1933 by Art Tatum

2. Pyotr Ilyich Tchaikovsky, *Sleeping Beauty* (1889), Act 1: *La Fée des Lilas*

3. Franz Schubert, Waltz from *12 Ländler*, op. 171, no. 4, D. 790 (1823)

4. Robert Lamm, "Saturday in the Park" (1972)

5. Felix Mendelssohn, "Wedding March" from *Midsummer's Night Dream*, op. 61 (1826). Analyze the entire passage with roman numerals. *Hint: You will need to show extended tonicizations.*

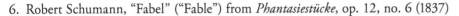

6. Robert Schumann, "Fabel" ("Fable") from *Phantasiestücke*, op. 12, no. 6 (1837)

7. Johannes Brahms, "Mein Herz ist schwer" ("My Heart Is Heavy"), op. 94, no. 3 (1884). Write two to three sentences about the ending of this passage. Is it an authentic cadence or a half cadence? Why? How might this ambiguity express the meaning of the song's text?

CHAPTER 29

Symmetry Stretches Tonality: Chromatic Sequences and Equal Divisions of the Octave

EXERCISE 29–A *Continuing Chromatic Sequences*

First, play or listen to the provided opening of each chromatic sequence. Then, write the next six chords in the sequence.

1. DM2 (↓P4,↑m3)

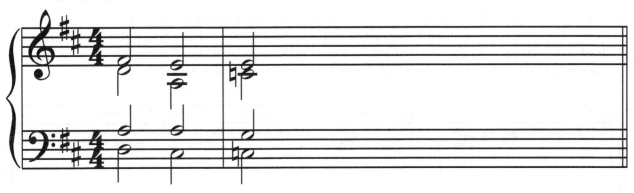

2. Am2 (↓M3,↑P4)

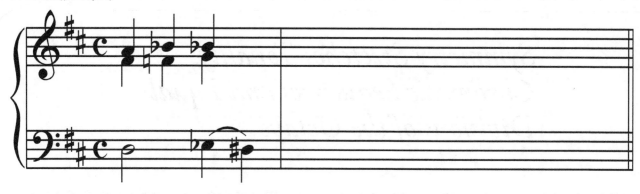

3. DM2. The model of this sequence includes the *second and third* chords shown, not the first and second chords. No roots are shown because the sequence alternates between an augmented-sixth chord (German, then French, since the alto voice moves midway through) and a dominant seventh chord. *Hint: Both outer voices will descend chromatically throughout the sequence.*

4. DM2 (↓P5,↑P4) with dominant sevenths in each chord except the very first D major triad.

EXERCISE 29–B *Analyzing Chromatic Sequences*

Bracket and label each sequence, and circle each bass note involved in the sequence.

1. Samuel Coleridge-Taylor, Ballade in C minor, op. 73 (1909). *Hint: There are two sequences.*

2. Franz Schubert, String Quartet in G major, D. 887 (1826), *Allegro molto moderato*. In addition
to analyzing the sequence, analyze the entire phrase on two levels, including the cadence.

ASSIGNMENT 29.2

EXERCISE 29–C   *Analyzing Chromatic Sequences*

Bracket and label each sequence, and circle each bass note involved in the sequence.

1. Vicente Lusitano, *Heu me Domine* (1553). *Translation: When the heavens will be moved.*

2. Richard Wagner, Overture from *Rienzi* (1840)

3. Robert Schumann, Symphony no. 1 in B♭ major ("Spring"), op. 38 (1841)

4. Franz Schubert, Symphony no. 4 in C minor ("Tragic"), D. 417 (1816), *Allegro*

ASSIGNMENT 29.3

EXERCISE 29-D   *Analyzing Chromatic Sequences*

Bracket and label each sequence, and circle each bass note involved in the sequence.

1. Felix Mendelssohn, Prelude in B minor, op. 104, no. 2 (1836)

2. Gaetano Donizetti, "Esci, fuggi" from *Lucia di Lammermoor* (1835), Act 2, Scene 5

3. Ludwig van Beethoven, Symphony no. 1 in C major, op. 21 (1800), *Menuetto*

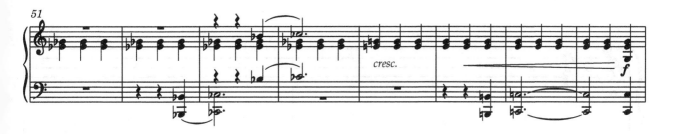

EXERCISE 29-E *Realizing Figured Basses That Include Chromatic Sequences*

Analyze each figured bass, including bracketing and labeling each sequence. Be on the lookout for modulations. Then, realize each figured bass in keyboard style. Play your realizations.

1.

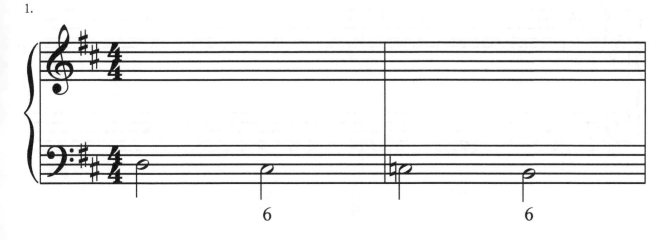

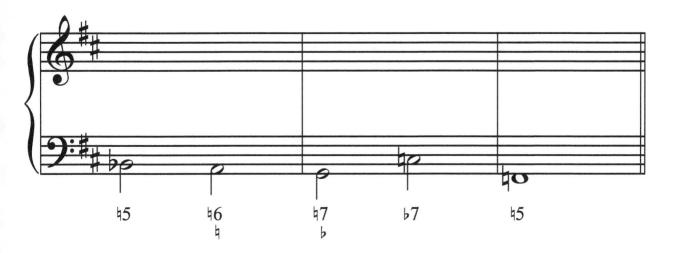

2.

ASSIGNMENT 29.4

EXERCISE 29-F   *Filling in the Rest of a Four-Voice Texture*

Analyze the passage. Then, realize it in chorale style by adding inner voices.

EXERCISE 29-G   *Analyzing Chromatic Sequences*

Bracket and label each sequence, and circle each bass note involved in the sequence. There may be multiple sequences in a passage.

1. Ludwig van Beethoven, Piano Concerto no. 1 in C major, op. 15 (1800), *Allegro*

2. Frédéric Chopin, Piano Sonata in C minor, op. 4, BI 23 (1828), *Allegro maestoso*

ASSIGNMENT 29.5

EXERCISE 29–H *Analyzing Contrary-Motion Chromaticism*

In the passage below, from Franz Schubert's Violin Sonata in D major, D. 384 (1816), circle the outer-voice pitches that participate in contrary-motion chromaticism. The first pair is circled for you as a head start. Then, label the root, quality, and inversion of each chord that participates in the contrary-motion progression.

EXERCISE 29–I *Realizing a Figured Bass*

Analyze the passage. Then, realize it in keyboard style. Play your realization.

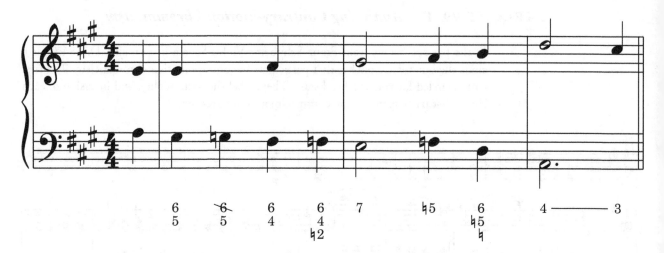

EXERCISE 29–J *Writing Extended Illustrations*

1. In three voices, write a progression in F♯ minor as follows: begin on tonic, move through a chromatic Dm2 sequence of descending six-three chords with 7–6 suspensions, reach a dominant decorated by a cadential six-four chord, resolve deceptively to ♭VI, use the ♭VI chord as a pivot chord in a chromatic modulation, and conclude with a PAC. Play and analyze what you write.

2. In three voices, write a progression in E♭ major as follows: begin with a chromatic AM2 (↓m3,↑P4) sequence using applied V⁶ chords that resolve to major triads, exit the sequence after reaching III, expand III with an extended tonicization, and conclude with an authentic cadence in the original key of E♭ major. Play and analyze what you write.

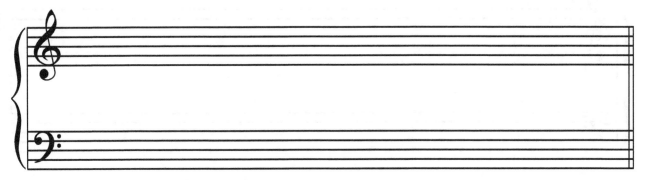

3. In three voices, write a progression in G major as follows: begin with a chromatic Am2 sequence that moves from I to ♭III (e.g., I … ♭II … ♮II …), use at least one more modal mixture harmony after breaking the sequence, and conclude with an authentic cadence in G major. Play and analyze what you write.

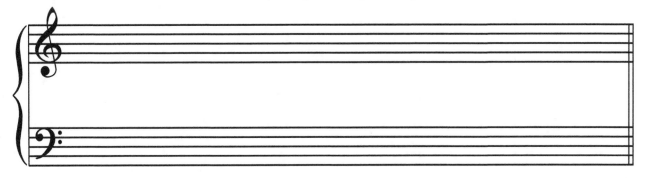

4. In keyboard style, write a progression in D major as follows: move from I to ♭VI via a chromatic DM2 (↓P4,↑m3) sequence, expand the pre-dominant with a voice exchange that includes an augmented-sixth chord, and close with a PAC in D major. Play and analyze what you write.

ASSIGNMENT 29.6

EXERCISE 29-K *Analyzing Chromatic Sequences and Contrary-Motion Chromaticism*

Using brackets and text in the score, as well as a few sentences of prose, show how the sequential progression works in the passage from Franz Schubert's "Sanctus" from Mass no. 6 in E♭ major, D. 950 (1828).

Translation: Holy, Holy, Holy, Lord God of Hosts.

EXERCISE 29-L *Realizing a Figured Bass*

Analyze the figured bass. Then, realize it in keyboard style. Play your realization.

EXERCISE 29–M *Harmonizing Melodies with Guidance*

Following the detailed guidance, harmonize each melody in keyboard style. Analyze and play what you write.

1.

2.

chromatic sequence   chromatic pivot

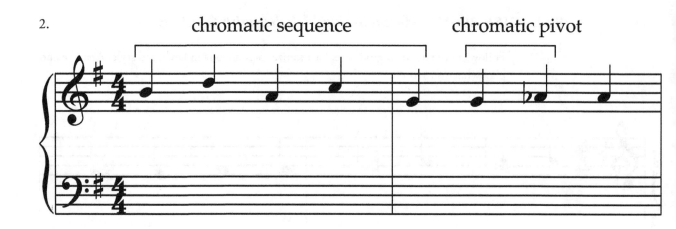

cadential progression in new key

3.

chromatic   deceptive   cadential progression
sequence   motion   in new key

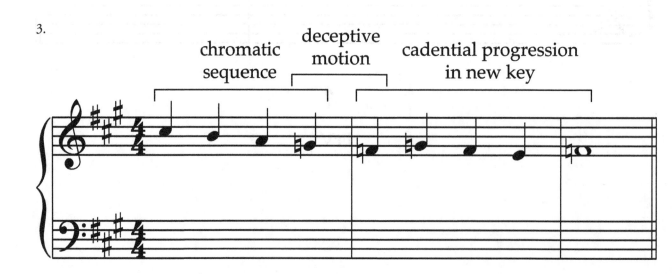

ASSIGNMENT 29.7

EXERCISE 29–N   *Analyzing Progressions that Divide the Octave Evenly*

Use brackets and labels to indicate the keys that are tonicized in each passage. Then, specify how the octave is divided equally, and state whether this is done sequentially or nonsequentially.

1. Hugo Wolf, "Und steht Ihr früh am Morgen auf" ("And When You Rise Early") from *Italienisches Liederbuch*, no. 34 (1896)

> *And when you rise from your bed at dawn,*
>
> *You chase all clouds from the sky,*
>
> *You lure the sun onto those hills*
>
> *And angels compete to appear*
>
> *And bring at once your shoes and clothes.*
>
> *Then, when you go out [to Holy Mass]*
>
> *(Translation by Richard Stokes)*

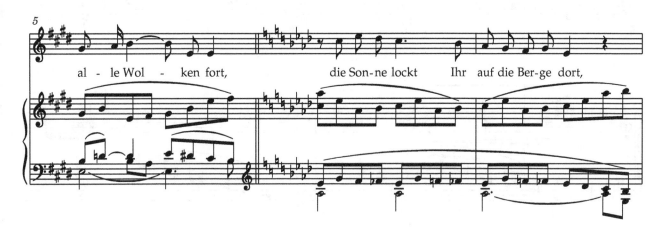

und En - gel-ein er - schei - nen um die Wet-te, und brin-gen Schuh __ und Klei -

- der Euch so-fort.

Dann, wenn Ihr aus-geht in die

2. Richard Wagner, *Lohengrin* (1850), Act 1, Scene 2

Allmählich noch etwas langsamer

3. Giacomo Puccini, *Tosca* (1900), Act 2

ASSIGNMENT 29.8

EXERCISE 29-O   *Realizing a Figured Bass*

Analyze the figured bass with roman numerals, marking all sequences and tonicizations. Then, realize it in chorale style. Play your realization.

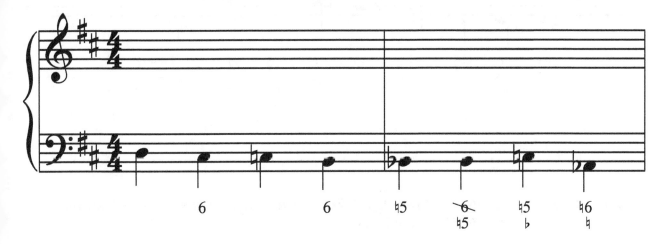

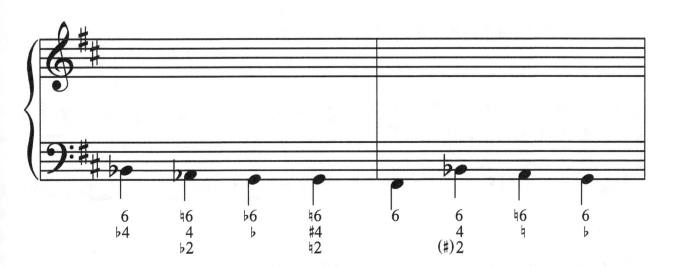

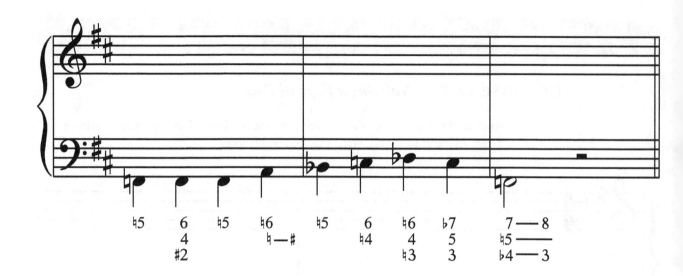

EXERCISE 29-P *Analyzing Pyotr Ilyich Tchaikovsky, Symphony no. 4 in F minor, op. 36 (1878),* **Scherzo**

The passages below provide snapshots of several themes and tonal areas of this movement, as well as transitions between them. On the score, show when and how each new tonal area is secured. Then, in a paragraph, interpret the large-scale tonal structure of the movement.

1.

3.

ASSIGNMENT 29.9

EXERCISE 29-Q   *Analyzing Frédéric Chopin, Mazurka, op. 56, no. 1 (1844)*

The passages below show the beginning of each section in this Mazurka. On the score, mark each key as well as how and when it is tonicized or secured. Focus on tricky harmonic areas, such as the sequential passage that opens the piece and the transitional and retransitional passages that link larger sections. Then, in a paragraph, summarize the large-scale tonal structure of the entire piece and speculate on what you think the form might be.

CHAPTER 30

Centricity, Extended and Non-Tertian Sonorities, and Collections

EXERCISE 30-A *Building Modes and Collections*

Notate each mode or collection, ascending from the given pitch to the pitch one octave higher. Use accidentals rather than key signatures.

1. F Aeolian

2. B♭ Lydian

3. G Phrygian

4. E Mixolydian

5. A Dorian

6. C Locrian

7. WT_odd

8. WT_even

9. OCT$_{0,1}$ 10. OCT$_{1,2}$

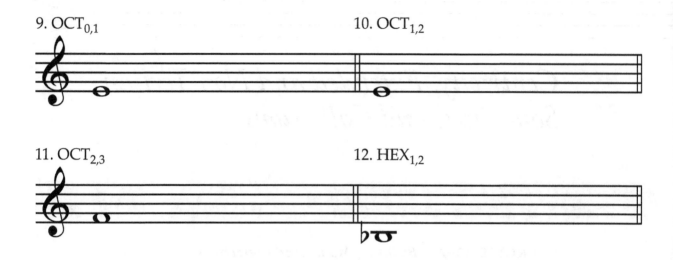

11. OCT$_{2,3}$ 12. HEX$_{1,2}$

EXERCISE 30–B   *Composing with Sonorities and Collections*

First, sing or play this melody:

Next, listen to or play on keyboard the following harmonization for piano, which features tonal harmony:

Now, create your own harmonizations of the same melody using some of the post-tonal techniques that you have studied:

1. Use extended tertian chords and added-sixth chords. Feel free to use pitches that are not diatonic in the key of F major.

2. Use quartal and quintal sonorities. Avoid the monotony of simply repeating the same chord structure underneath every melody note.

3. Use subsets of the whole-tone collection. Feel free to move back and forth between the two whole-tone collections. Don't feel obligated to stick to the same whole-tone collection as the given melody note.

4. While preserving the rhythm and basic contour of the melody, alter some of its pitches so that it remains entirely within the $OCT_{0,1}$ collection. Then, harmonize it with subsets of that same octatonic collection.

ASSIGNMENT 30.2

EXERCISE 30–C *Identifying Collections and Their Subsets*

First, identify each collection. Then, use stems and beams to extract the specified subsets. A sample is provided. Keep in mind that you will need to spell some triads enharmonically in order to find them.

Sample. Collection: _____WT_{even}_____. Extract two different augmented triads.

1. Collection: _____. Extract two different fully diminished 7th chords.

2. Collection: _____. Extract four different major triads.

3. Collection: _____. Extract four different minor triads.

4. Collection: _____. Extract three different major triads (stems up) and three different minor triads (stems down).

5. Collection: _____. Extract three additional tritones.

6. Collection: _____. Extract three different tritones.

EXERCISE 30-D   *Identifying Collections*

First, listen to each passage. Next, circle the centric pitch class (just one of the times that it occurs) if you believe that there is one, and write two sentences explaining the musical features that led you to your conclusion. Finally, write the name of the mode(s) or collection(s) that the passage uses.

1.

2.

3. Dorothy Rudd Moore, "Willow Bend and Weep" from *From the Dark Tower* (1970). What types of harmonies are present in the piano part?

4. Dorothy Rudd Moore, "Southern Mansions" from *From the Dark Tower* (1970). A few pitches in this passage do not belong to the underlying collection. Draw a box around them and name the other collection that they hint at.

5. Dorothy Rudd Moore, "From the Dark Tower" from *From the Dark Tower* (1970). Draw a box around the one pitch that does not belong to the underlying collection.

ASSIGNMENT 30.3

EXERCISE 30–E   *Composing a Whole-Tone Invention*

Continuing the imitation that is featured in the given opening, compose the rest of a short invention that features whole-tone collections. Label the moments when you switch from one whole-tone collection to the other one.

Moderato

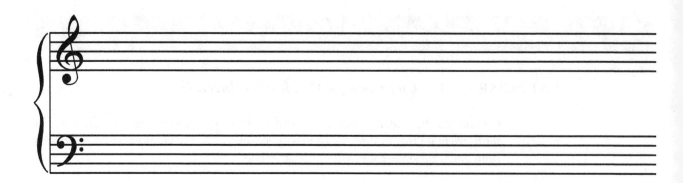

EXERCISE 30-F   *Identifying Collections*

First, listen to each passage. Next, circle the centric pitch class (just one of the times that it occurs) if you believe that there is one, and write two sentences explaining the musical features that led you to your conclusion. Finally, write the name of the mode(s) or collection(s) that the passage uses.

1. Igor Stravinsky, Finale from *Firebird Suite* (1910)

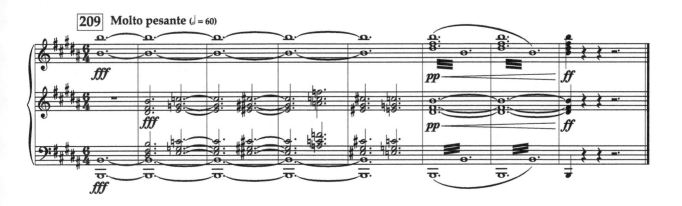

2. Maurice Ravel, Trio for Violin, Cello, and Piano (1914), iii

ASSIGNMENT 30.4

EXERCISE 30-G   *Composing with the Octatonic Collection*

Compose with octatonic collections as follows: First, compose the rest of the ostinato on the lower staff. Change to a different octatonic collection at least once in order to create form. Next, compose a melody on the upper staff. Build your melody from the same octatonic collection as the ostinato that accompanies it.

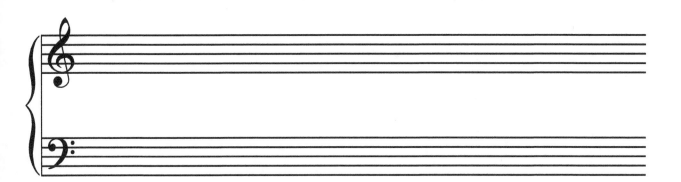

EXERCISE 30-H *Identifying Collections*

First, listen to each passage. Next, circle the centric pitch class (just one of the times that it occurs) if you believe that there is one, and write two sentences explaining the musical features that led you to your conclusion. Finally, write the name of the mode(s) or collection(s) that the passage uses.

1. Dorothy Rudd Moore (text by Langston Hughes), "Dream Variation" from *From the Dark Tower* (1970)

2. Charles Ives, "Mists" (1910). Discuss how the voice's collection differs from the collections in the piano part (which change from measure to measure). What contrapuntal feature do we hear in the lowest register?

3. Alfredo Casella, *11 Pezzi Infantili*, op. 35 (1920), *Preludio*. Treat the two staves as separate. Does the upper part maintain the same collection throughout or switch from one to another?

ASSIGNMENT 30.5

EXERCISE 30-I   *Identifying Collections*

First, listen to each passage. Next, circle the centric pitch class (just one of the times that it occurs) if you believe that there is one, and write two sentences explaining the musical features that led you to your conclusion. Finally, write the name of the mode(s) or collection(s) that the passage uses.

1. Béla Bartók, Violin Duos, no. 33 (1931)

2. Zenobia Powell Perry, Sonatine for Clarinet (1963)

Moderato, quasi aria

3. Dorothy Rudd Moore, "For a Poet" from *From the Dark Tower* (1970). Do you hear a pitch center in the opening cello solo? Does that change once the piano enters? Why or why not?

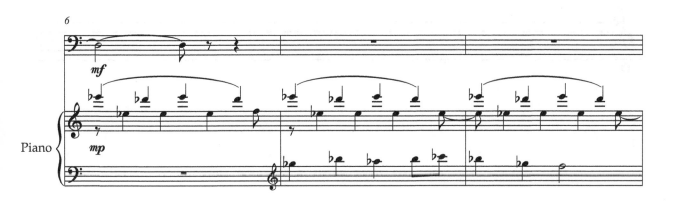

EXERCISE 30-J   *Composing with a Diatonic Mode*

Label the mode of the melodic fragment. Then, compose the rest of the melody, preserving the same center and mode as at the opening.

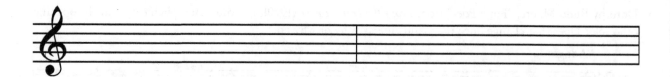

Analysis with Sets

EXERCISE 31–A *Identifying Intervals in Pitch Space and in Pitch-Class Space*

First, label each pitch with its pitch-class integer. Next, play the given dyad at the keyboard. Then, label the ordered pitch interval (OPI), unordered pitch interval (UPI), ordered pitch-class interval (OPCI), and unordered pitch-class interval (UPCI, or interval class) of the given dyad. A sample is provided.

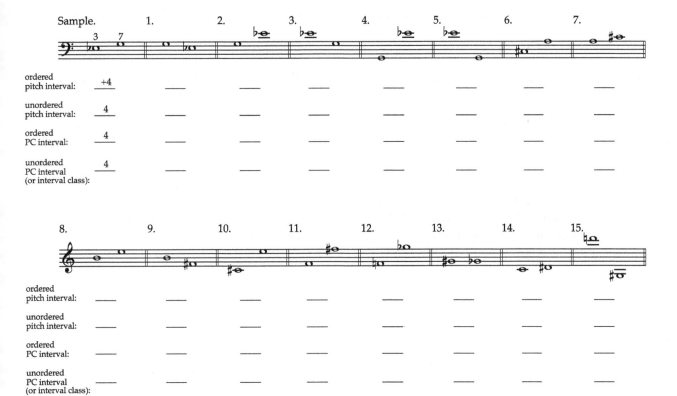

EXERCISE 31–B *Analyzing with OPIs and UPCIs*

First, listen to the two passages from the first movement of Zenobia Powell Perry's *Sonatine for Clarinet and Piano* (1963). Next, on the score, label the pitch-class integers, which are the same on both staves because they double each other at the double octave. Finally, label the ordered pitch intervals (OPIs) and unordered pitch-class intervals (UPCIs, or interval classes) of both excerpts on the blanks beneath the score. The blanks' numbers correspond to the bracket annotations immediately under the score.

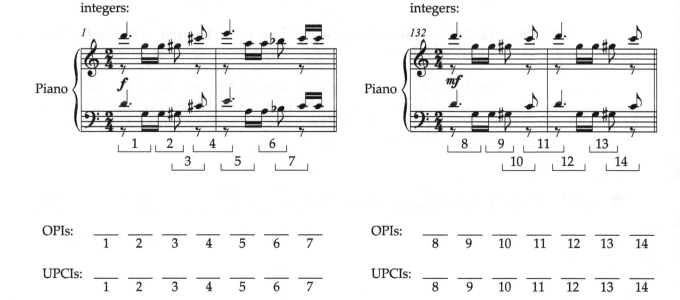

Now, in a paragraph, compare these two excerpts. What is similar between them, and what is different? Which of these similarities and differences are revealed more clearly by the OPIs, and which by the UPCIs? Do we lose anything by "zooming in" all the way to OPIs? Do we lose anything by "zooming out" all the way to UPCIs?

EXERCISE 31-C   *Analyzing with OPIs and UPCIs*

First, listen to the passage from the third movement of Julius Eastman's *Piano 2* (1986). Next, label the pitch-class integers (just once for each group of four sixteenth notes) and both the ordered pitch interval (OPI) and ordered pitch-class interval (OPCI) of each boxed dyad. This is begun for you.

Then, identify patterns from your analysis. Write a paragraph summarizing your findings. Are there any patterns in the contour of the passage? Which features of the music can be identified more easily by OPIs than by OPCIs? What do the OPCIs help you to notice about this passage?

ASSIGNMENT 31.2

EXERCISE 31–D   *Transposing in Pitch Space*

First, label the pitch-class integers of the given melodic fragment. Then, transpose it in pitch space by the specified number of semitones upward or downward, and label the pitch-class integers of the transposed version. Finally, play the original and transposed versions to proofread your work aurally. A sample is provided.

Sample.

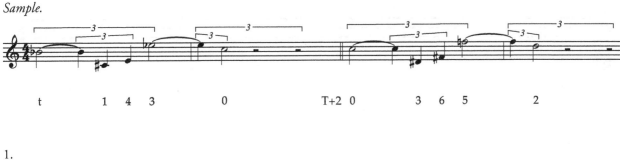

1.

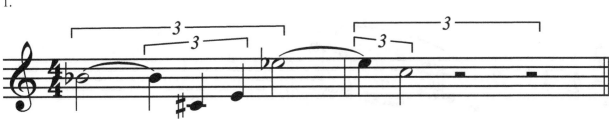

T+5

2.

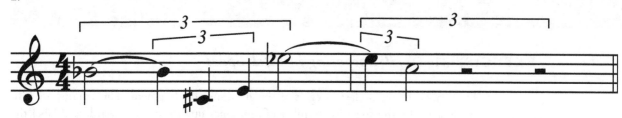

T-3

3.

T-7

4.

T+8

5. Transpose the original, and then transpose the transposed version.

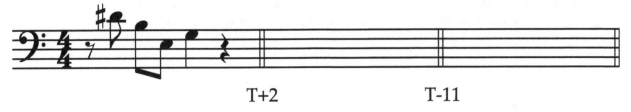

T+2   T-11

6.

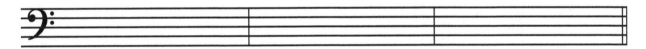

T-10

EXERCISE 31–E   *Inverting in Pitch Space*

1. In each example, the melodic fragments on the two staves are related by inversion in pitch space. First, play the short duet. Next, label the pitch-class integer of each pitch. Finally, between the staves, label two things: (1) the sum (or index) that each pair of pitch classes adds to, and (2) the pitch or pair of adjacent pitches that serves as the axis (or mirror) of symmetry. A sample is provided.

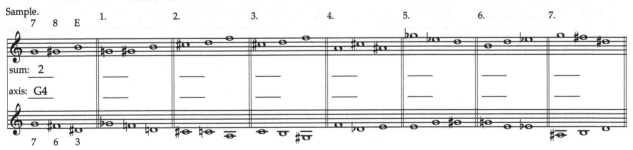

2. First, label the pitch-class integers of the given pitches on the upper staff. Next, use the given axis of symmetry to write on the lower staff the pitches that are the *same distance* away from that axis as the given pitches are, but in the *opposite direction*. Label the pitch-class integers of the pitches that you write on the lower staff. Finally, to check your work, calculate the sum of each pair of pitch classes to ensure that it is the same for all pairs. A sample is provided.

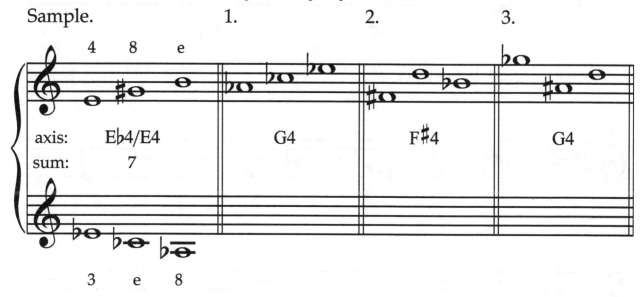

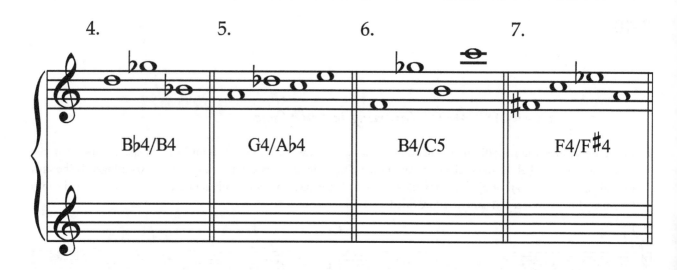

EXERCISE 31–F   *Transposing and Inverting Sets in Pitch-Class Space*

Transform each given pitch-class set by transposition and/or inversion as requested. Write each resultant pitch-class set in normal order.

1. Transform [137]
   - by T_2:

   - by T_6:

   - by I_5:

2. Transform [te25]
   - by T_1:

   - by I_8:

   - by I_e:

3. Transform [37e]
   - by T_4:

   - by T_8:

   - by I_2:

4. Transform [0369]
   - by T_3:

   - by I_2:

   - by I_9:

5. Transform [4568t]
   - by T_7:

   - by T_e:

   - by I_0:

6. Transform [0134679t]
   - by T_9:

   - by I_4:

   - by I_t:

ASSIGNMENT 31.3

EXERCISE 31-G   *Working with Sets and Set Classes*

First, label the pitch-class integer of each pitch. Then, write the [normal order] and the (prime form) of each group of pitch classes.

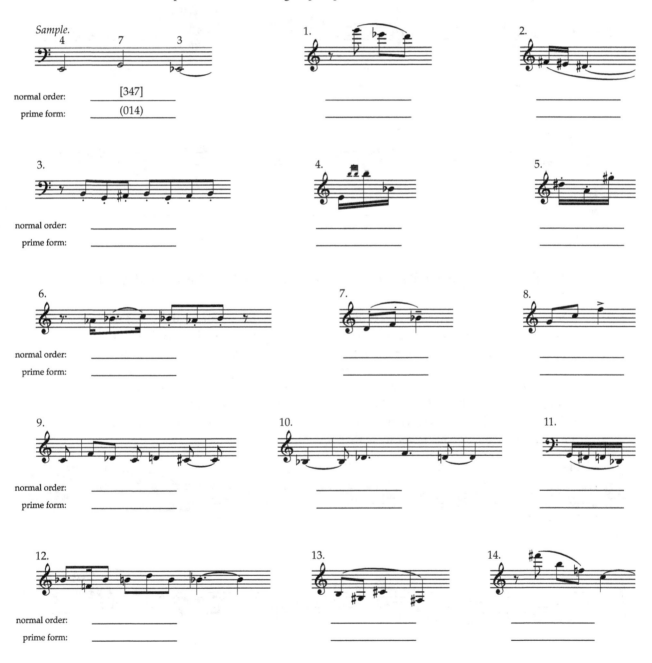

Sample.

normal order: [347]

prime form: (014)

normal order: _____   _____   _____

prime form: _____   _____   _____

normal order: _____   _____   _____

prime form: _____   _____   _____

normal order: _____   _____   _____

prime form: _____   _____   _____

EXERCISE 31-H   *Analyzing Ruth Crawford's Diaphonic Suite 1 (1930), mvt. 2*

The opening of this passage highlights the semitone: D–E♭ in measure 1 and C–C♯ in
measure 2. First, mark with an asterisk each additional appearance of interval-class 1
between consecutive pitches, remembering that IC 1 can be represented by several different UPIs (1, 11, 13, etc.). Then, locate and mark on the score at least one instance of
each of the following set classes that include IC 1, limiting yourself to pitches that sound
consecutively: (012), (013), (014), (015), (016). Finally, use Crawford's phrase markings
to locate and mark three larger set classes (tetrachords, pentachords, or hexachords). Can
you find any larger sets that occur more than once?

EXERCISE 31–I   *Analyzing Ruth Crawford's Piano Prelude no. 9 (1927–1928)*

Interval-class 1 plays an important role in this passage. After you listen, mark as many instances of it as you can on the score, taking care to include both melodic and harmonic appearances in multiple registers and contours. Then, write a paragraph summarizing the role that IC 1 plays in how you hear this passage.

ASSIGNMENT 31.4

EXERCISE 31-J   *Composing with Pitch-Class Sets*

The upper part of a duet for treble and bass instruments is provided. Compose the lower part such that the two voices exchange ideas as if in dialogue. This dialogue will be rhythmic (one part "speaking" while the other is "listening"), but it will also involve pitch. Before you write, label the normal order and prime form of each individual gesture of the given upper part. Then, as you write the lower part, use the same set classes. See if you can use melodic contour to enhance the sense of relatedness (or empathy) between the parts.

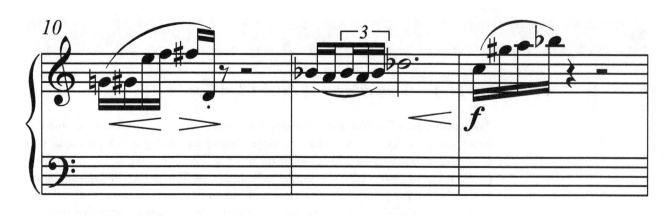

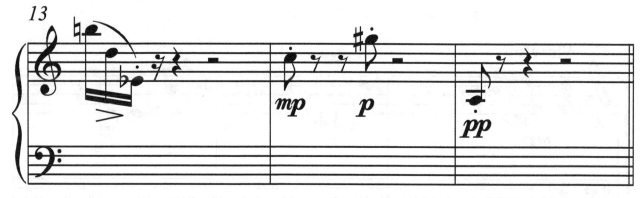

EXERCISE 31-K   *Analyzing Anton Webern's Movement for String Quartet, op. 5, no. 2 (1909)*

First, listen to the passage below. Then, complete the subsequent tasks in order.

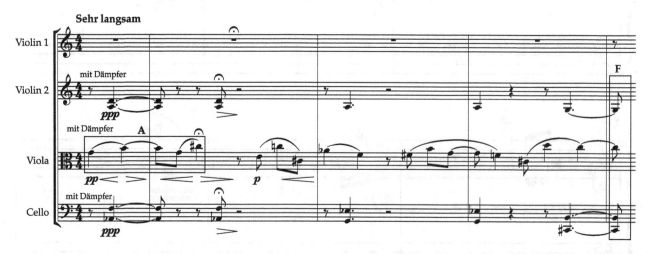

1. Identify the normal order and prime form of the viola's trichord at the opening, which is boxed and labeled "A":

   normal order of "A": _____   prime form of "A": _____

2. Locate four other instances of the same set class among pitches that are meaningfully associated (e.g., melodically or harmonically). Circle these trichords on the score and label them "B" through "E." Write the normal order of each of these trichords below, along with the transposition (such as T_4) or inversion (such as I_4) that would transform trichord "A" into each of them.

   normal order of "B": _____   T or I that transforms set "A" into set "B":
   normal order of "C": _____   T or I that transforms set "A" into set "C":
   normal order of "D": _____   T or I that transforms set "A" into set "D":
   normal order of "E": _____   T or I that transforms set "A" into set "E":

3. Label the normal order and prime form of the tetrachord that sounds among Violin 2, Viola, and Cello at the very end of the excerpt, which is boxed and labeled "F."

   normal order of "F": _____   prime form of "F": _____

4. Locate one other instance of this same set class within the same passage among pitches that are meaningfully associated (e.g., melodically or harmonically). Circle this tetrachord on the score and label it "G." Write its normal order below along with the transposition (such as T_4) or inversion (such as I_4) that would transform trichord "F" into it.

   normal order of "G": _____   T or I that transforms set "F" into set "G":

5. Label the normal order and prime form of the tetrachord played harmonically by the Violin 2 and Cello at the very beginning of the same excerpt. Then, through a combination of score annotations and two or three sentences of analytical prose, show how this initial trichord relates to the very end of the piece (shown on the next page).

   normal order: _____   prime form: _____

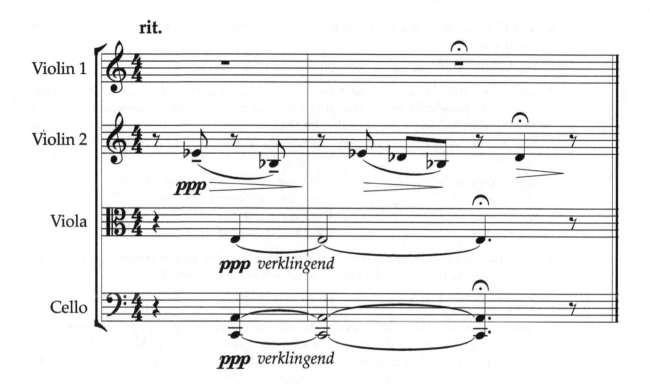

ASSIGNMENT 31.5

EXERCISE 31-L   *Analyzing Arnold Schoenberg's* **Das Buch der hängende Gärten,** *op. 15 (1908–1909), no. 11*

First, listen to the passage below. Then, complete the subsequent tasks in order.

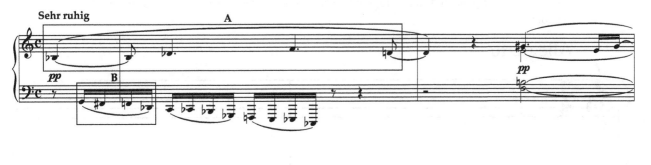

1. Identify the normal order and prime form of the tetrachords formed by the first four notes on each staff:

    right hand ("A"):   normal order: _____   prime form: _____

    left hand ("B"):   normal order: _____   prime form: _____

2. Locate as many other instances of these same two tetrachordal set classes as you can, limiting yourself to pitches that are meaningfully associated (e.g., melodically or harmonically). On the score, circle each of these and label its normal order and prime form. Then, in the space below, write the transpositions (such as T_4) and/or inversions (such as I_4) of tetrachords "A" and "B" that you found in the passage. Include measure numbers.

3. Through a combination of score annotations and a paragraph of prose, identify other musically important pitch groupings in the excerpt. Which intervals, sets, and relationships stand out to you?

EXERCISE 31–M   *Composing with Pitch-Class Sets*

Complete the eight-measure etude for piano that is partially written below. However, before you write, analyze what is already there. Which intervals (or interval classes) stand out as a result of being grouped either harmonically or melodically? When a pattern repeats, how does the repetition relate to the original statement (e.g., by some transposition)? Summarize your analytical findings in the space on the next page. Then, compose an upper-voice melody that is based upon these same sets and relationships. Analyze your work both on the score and in a paragraph, accounting for the decisions that you made as a composer.

Allegretto

Analysis:

Description of compositional decisions:

CHAPTER 32

Metrical and Serial Techniques

ASSIGNMENT 32.1

EXERCISE 32–A *Analyzing Metrical Techniques*

Each passage below employs one or more of the following metrical techniques: changing meters, asymmetric meters, polymeter, ameter (absence of meter), and/or a difference between perceived and notated meter. Through a combination of score annotations and two to three sentences of prose, identify and describe the metrical techniques at play in each excerpt.

1. Pierre Boulez (1925–2016)

2. Aleksandr Scriabin, Prelude for Piano, op. 15, no. 1 (1897)

3. Julius Eastman, *Piano 2* (1986), mvt. 3

4. Béla Bartók (1881–1945), Scherzo from *Mikrokosmos*, Sz. 107, Vol. 3, no. 82

5. Tania León, "Oh Yemanja" from *Scourge of Hyacinths* (1994)

6. Dorothy Rudd Moore, "From the Dark Tower" from *From the Dark Tower* (1970)

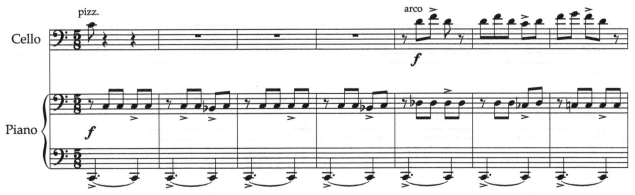

EXERCISE 32–B   *Composing with Metrical Techniques*

Compose a phrase of music that features the specified rhythmic technique.

1. Asymmetric Meter: Write for a trio of three different instruments of your choice.

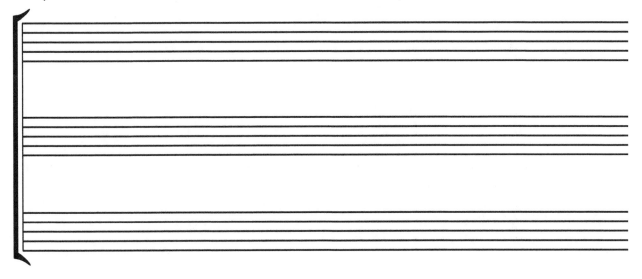

2. Polymeter: Write for piano.

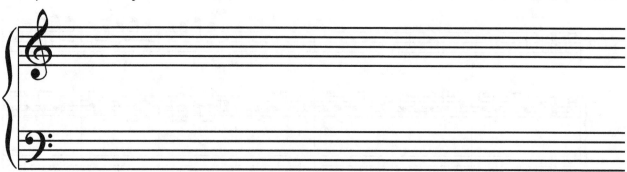

ASSIGNMENT 32.2

EXERCISE 32–C *Composing with Metrical Techniques*

Compose a melody where the perceived meter would be different from the notated one. Write for any pitched instrument of your choice. Under the staff, use a dot diagram to show your interpretation of the perceived meter.

EXERCISE 32–D *Analyzing Metrical Techniques*

Each passage below employs one or more of the following metrical techniques: changing meters, asymmetric meters, polymeter, ameter (absence of meter), and/or a difference between perceived and notated meter. Through a combination of score annotations and two to three sentences of prose, identify and describe the metrical techniques at play in each excerpt.

1. György Ligeti, "Fém" from *Etudes for Piano*, Book II, no. 8 (1988)

2. Igor Stravinsky, "Marche du soldat" from *L'Histoire du soldat* (1918), piano arrangement

3. Henry Cowell, *Exultation* for Piano (1922). *Note:* The notation in the left hand indicates black-key tone clusters spanning the entire range between the upper and lower notes.

ASSIGNMENT 32.3

EXERCISE 32–E *Analyzing Twelve-Tone Rows*

The row in each repertoire passage is a prime form. First, label each pitch with a pitch-class integer. Next, label the ordered pitch-class intervals (OPCIs) between adjacent tones in the row. Finally, write the pitch classes of each of the four requested row forms in order. *Hint: Remember how the OPCIs change when a row is transposed, inverted, retrograded, and retrograde-inverted.*

1. Arnold Schoenberg, Variations for Orchestra, op. 31 (1926–1928). Notice the tenor clef!

PCs: __ __   __ __   __   __ __ __   __ __   __

OPCIs: __   __   __   __   __   __   __   __   __   __   __

P_1: __ __ __ __ __ __ __ __ __ __ __ __

I_7: __ __ __ __ __ __ __ __ __ __ __ __

R_{10}: __ __ __ __ __ __ __ __ __ __ __ __

RI_7: __ __ __ __ __ __ __ __ __ __ __ __

2. Anton Webern, String Quartet, op. 28 (1936–1938)

PCs: __   __   __   __   __   __   __   __   __   __   __   __

OPCIs: __   __   __   __   __   __   __   __   __   __   __

P₁: ___ ___ ___ ___ ___ ___ ___ ___ ___ ___ ___ ___

I₁: ___ ___ ___ ___ ___ ___ ___ ___ ___ ___ ___ ___

R₄: ___ ___ ___ ___ ___ ___ ___ ___ ___ ___ ___ ___

RI₇: ___ ___ ___ ___ ___ ___ ___ ___ ___ ___ ___ ___

3. Alban Berg, *Der Wein* (1929)

PCs: __   __   __ __ __   __ __ __ __ __ __ __

OPCIs: __   __   __ __   __   __ __ __ __ __ __

P₁: ___ ___ ___ ___ ___ ___ ___ ___ ___ ___ ___

I₇: ___ ___ ___ ___ ___ ___ ___ ___ ___ ___ ___

R₃: ___ ___ ___ ___ ___ ___ ___ ___ ___ ___ ___

RI₁₁: ___ ___ ___ ___ ___ ___ ___ ___ ___ ___ ___

4. Luigi Nono, *Il canto sospeso* (1955–1956)

PCs: __   __   __ __ __ __ __ __ __ __ __ __   __

OPCIs: __   __   __ __ __ __ __ __ __ __ __   __

P₉: ___ ___ ___ ___ ___ ___ ___ ___ ___ ___ ___ ___

P_9:   ___ ___ ___ ___ ___ ___ ___ ___ ___ ___ ___ ___

I_6:   ___ ___ ___ ___ ___ ___ ___ ___ ___ ___ ___ ___

R_7:   ___ ___ ___ ___ ___ ___ ___ ___ ___ ___ ___ ___

R_{13}:   ___ ___ ___ ___ ___ ___ ___ ___ ___ ___ ___ ___

EXERCISE 32–F   *Recognizing Row Forms*

Each of the following rows is a form of one of the rows in Exercise 32E. Identify the composer (either Schoenberg, Webern, Berg, or Nono) and label the row form of each row. A sample is provided. *Hint: You may find it helpful to determine the OPCIs for each row below, for ease of comparison to the work that you did in Exercise 32E.*

	Row	**Composer**	**Row Form**
Sample.	1 7 9 6 8 0 5 4 t e 2 3	Schoenberg	P_1
A.	e 5 7 4 6 t 3 2 8 9 0 1		
B.	5 6 3 4 0 e 2 1 9 t 7 8		
C.	t 4 2 5 3 e 6 7 1 0 9 8		
D.	t e 9 0 8 1 7 2 6 3 5 4		
E.	9 5 6 2 0 7 4 3 1 e t 8		
F.	0 t 9 7 5 4 1 8 6 2 3 e		
G.	9 8 e t 2 3 0 1 5 4 7 6		
H.	t 9 e 8 0 7 1 6 2 5 3 4		
I.	8 7 4 3 9 t 5 1 e 2 0 6		

ASSIGNMENT 32.4

EXERCISE 32–G   *Analyzing Arnold Schoenberg's Piece for Piano, op. 33a (1929)*

First, on an instrument of your choice, play this prime (P) form of the row that is used in this piece.

Next, construct a twelve-tone matrix for this row.

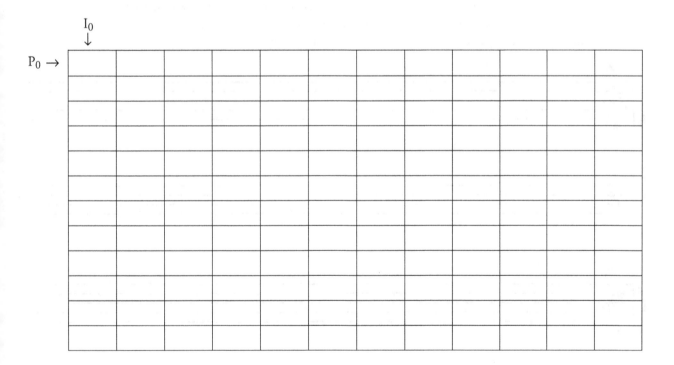

Now, listen to the following passage. On the score, label each row form and mark each individual pitch with an order number. *Hint: Treat the two staves separately, and beware that Schoenberg sometimes "backtracks" slightly by restating pitch classes that have already been introduced.*

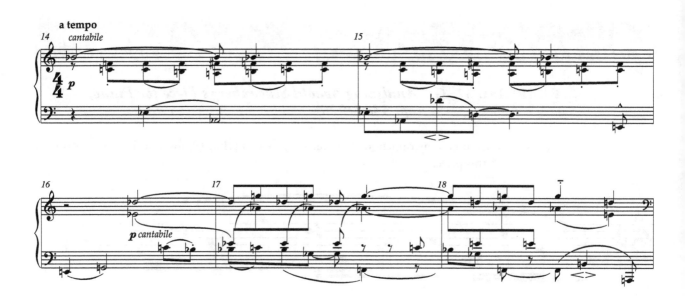

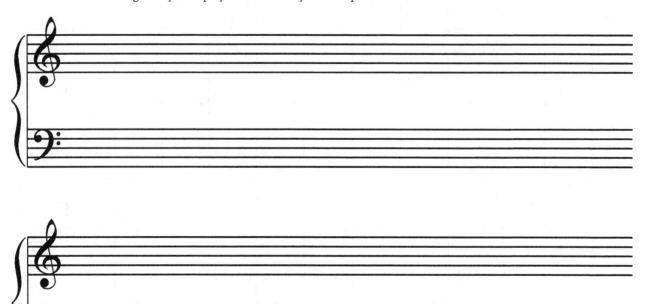

Using the same row, compose your own short piece for piano. The texture, meter, and relationship between the two staves (or hands) are all up to you. Label each row form that you use, and label each pitch with an order number. Once you finish, write a paragraph summarizing how you deployed the row in your composition.

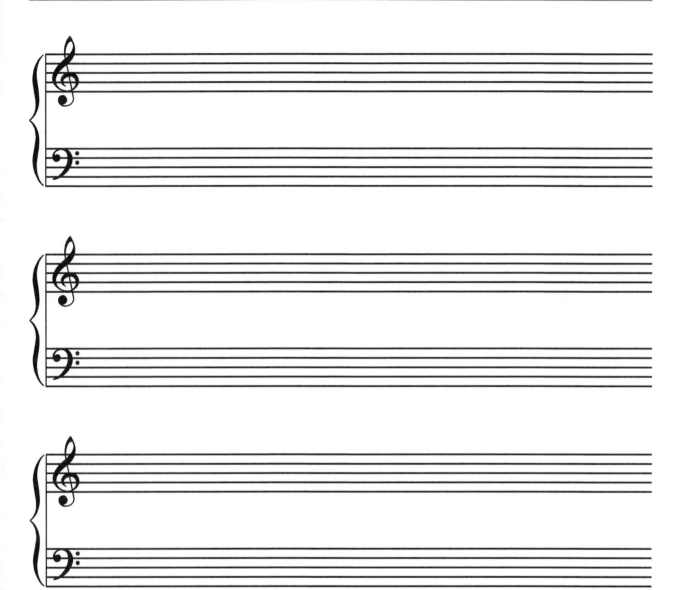

ASSIGNMENT 32.5

EXERCISE 32–H   *Analyzing Anton Webern's Symphony, op. 21 (1928)*

First, on an instrument of your choice, play this prime (P) form of the row that is used in this piece.

Next, construct a twelve-tone matrix for this row.

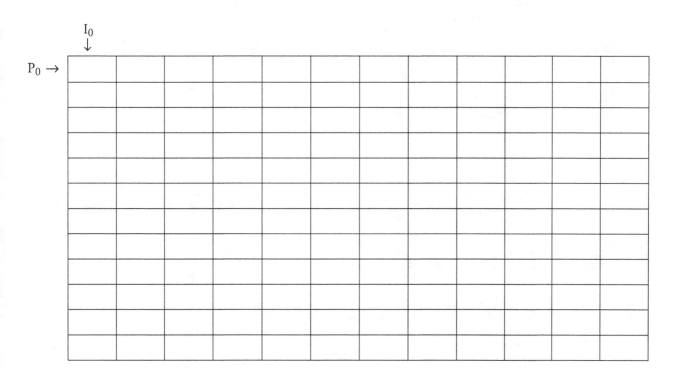

Now, using any prime form of the row as a reference, segment the row into two hexachords, into three tetrachords, and into four trichords, and determine the [normal order] and (prime form) of each pitch-class set.

hexachords: [_____] [_____]
               (_____) (_____)

tetrachords: [_____] [_____] [_____]
               (_____) (_____) (_____)

trichords: [_____] [_____] [_____] [_____]
               (_____) (_____) (_____) (_____)

The second movement of Webern's symphony is a theme and variations. On the scores of the first and seventh variations, label each row form and the order number of each pitch.

Variation 1:

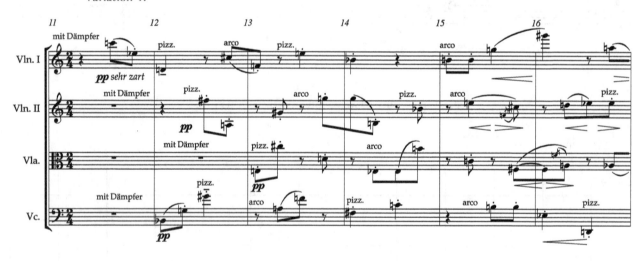

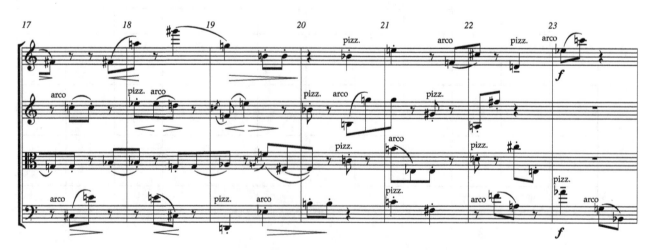

Variation 7:

Write a paragraph comparing the treatment of the row in variations 1 and 7. In the sense of a theme and variations, what is held constant between the variations, and what is varied?

Using the row from Webern's Symphony, op. 21, compose your own short piece for two different pitched instruments. The texture, meter, and relationship between the two staves are all up to you. Label each row form that you use, and label each pitch with an order number. Once you finish, write a paragraph summarizing how you deployed the row in your composition.

ASSIGNMENT 32.6

EXERCISE 32–I *Analyzing Luigi Dallapiccola's "Fregi" from* Quaderno Musicale Di Annalibera *(1952)*

First, on an instrument of your choice, play the prime (P) form of the row that is used in this piece. It is first presented on the upper staff from the beginning through the E^4 in m. 4.

Molto lento; con espressione parlante

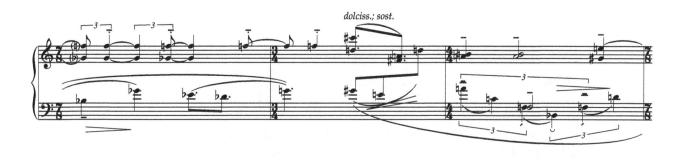

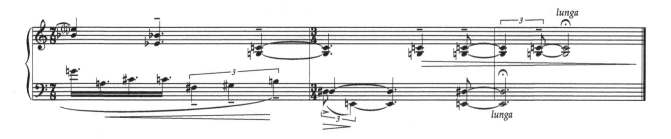

Construct a twelve-tone matrix for this row. Then, on the score, label each row form and the order number of each pitch.

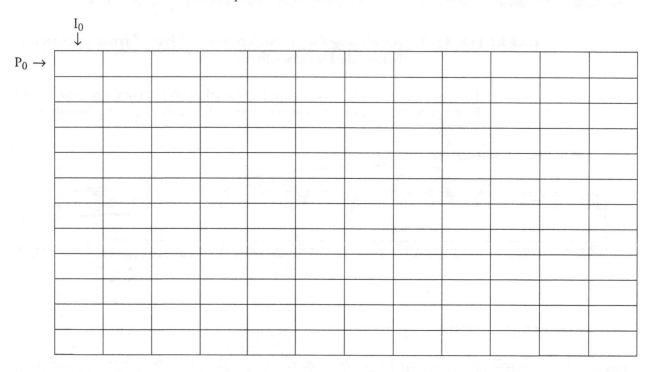

I_0
↓

$P_0 \rightarrow$

Now, using any prime form of the row as a reference, segment the row into two hexachords, into three tetrachords, and into four trichords, and determine the [normal order] and (prime form) of each pitch-class set.

hexachords: [_____] [_____]
               (_____) (_____)

tetrachords: [_____] [_____] [_____]
               (_____) (_____) (_____)

trichords: [_____] [_____] [_____] [_____]
               (_____) (_____) (_____) (_____)

Finally, in the space below, answer these questions in a paragraph: Where is there a varied return of the opening melody? What is different about it, and what is the same? How is the opening melody transformed in order to create the variation, and how does Dallapiccola draw attention to the relationship between them?

Credits